AND EUROPE

{ → ever auss of finitude
{ → desire/creation for the eternal

Democritus and the cases of the world → 81
                                          family

Ecstasy of self   → 95
                       → 107
agalzism

transformation of myth into religion –122
                                         –121
Socrates does not need to die
        Jew | Greek →/149/128

Cultural Memory
in
the
Present

Mieke Bal and Hent de Vries, Editors

PLATO AND EUROPE

Jan Patočka

Translated by Petr Lom

STANFORD UNIVERSITY PRESS

STANFORD, CALIFORNIA

2002

Stanford University Press
Stanford, California

© 2002 by the Board of Trustees of the
Leland Stanford Junior University

Printed in the United States of America
On acid-free, archival-quality paper
Library of Congress Cataloging-in-Publication Data

Patocka, Jan, 1907–1977.
 [Platón a Evropa. English]
 Plato and Europe / Jan Patocka ; translated by Petr Lom.
  p. cm. — (Cultural memory in the present)
 Includes bibliographical references (p.) and index.
 ISBN 0-8047-3800-9 (alk. paper) — ISBN 0-8047-3801-7
 1. Plato. 2. Philosophy, Ancient. 3. Europe—Civilization. I. Title. II. Series.
B395 .P3213 2002
141′.2—dc21

                                                    2001040029

Original Printing 2002

Last figure below indicates year of this printing:
11   10   09   08   07   06   05   04   03   02

Typeset by Keystone Typesetting, Inc. in 11/13½ Adobe Garamond

Acknowledgments

I thank the executor of the Jan Patočka estate, Ivan Chvatík, for his assistance in releasing the copyright for translation and in providing me with copies of the original Czech manuscript. I also thank Erazim Kohák for several of his translation suggestions.

I am grateful to my editor, Helen Tartar, for all of her assistance.

I also thank Jean Bethke Elsthain for initially pointing me toward prospective publishers and for reading my own thoughts on Patočka. I also thank Richard Rorty for similarly helpful suggestions.

I began studying Patočka at the European University Institute in Florence, first as a postdoctoral fellow and then as visiting professor. I owe tremendous gratitude to all those who made my stay there beautiful. I thank all my friends at the Badia: Patrick Masterson, Yves Meny, Arpad Szakolczai, Gianfranco Poggi, Jan Zielonka, Stefano Bartolini, Steven Lukes, Virginie Guiraudon, Miguel Vatter, and John Glenn. I am also grateful for the wonderful support from Marie-Ange Catotti, Eva Breivik, Maureen Lechleitner, and Liz Webb. I thank my former students, especially Nathalie Karagiannis, Alana Lentin, Jorg Forbrig, Armin Rabitsch, Zoe Bray, Mariagela Veikou, Kate Taylor, Johanna Polvi-Lohikoski, and Rory Domm, with whom I had the privilege of studying Patočka in my European Identity seminar. I wish them all the best.

Last of all, I thank Maria Kovacs, Yehuda Elkana, and György Geréby at my new home, the Central European University in Budapest.

For Josef Koudelka

Contents

Foreword

PETR LOM

This book is a rare gift. It asks how philosophy may help human beings live. This is an unusual question, both for how it is answered and that it is asked at all. Not only did the question arise in communist Czechoslovakia at the height of the cold war, where such questions could not be asked publicly, but also it arose amidst a global intellectual climate of radical doubt about the usefulness of philosophy, a doubt that extended beyond the Iron Curtain then and that bedevils us still today.

This book's author is Jan Patočka (1907–1977).[1] Today he is widely recognized as the most important Czech thinker since Comenius (1592–1670) and Thomas Masaryk (1850–1937) and as a preeminent thinker in postwar Eastern Europe. But his reputation is still largely restricted to the Continent, where most of his works have been translated into German, French, and Italian since the 1970s. In English, few of Patočka's writings—especially those on ethics and politics—are available; therefore, it is likely that the reader encounters him for the first time here.[2] Nonetheless, the

---

1. The Czech letter *c* is pronounced like the "ch" in cherry. Thus, the correct pronunciation of Patočka is Patochka.

2. The following works are available in English, all translated by Erazim Kohák: *Heretical Essays in the History of Philosophy* (New York: Open Court, 1996); *An Introduction to Husserl's Phenomenology* (New York: Open Court, 1996); *Body, Language, Community* (New York: Open Court, 1997); *Jan Patočka: Philosophy and Selected Writings* (Chicago: University of Chicago Press, 1989). In addition to selected essays, this last volume contains a valuable biographical introduction to the philosopher as well as references to works—both primary and secondary—available in other languages. Finally, for a new bibliography of all works of Patočka available in both original and translation, as well as secondary sources, see L. Hagedorn and H. Sepp, *Jan Patočka: Texte, Dokumente, Bibliographie* (Alber, 1999).

themes that Patočka raises should be familiar to the reader from another source, Václav Havel, president of the Czech Republic, whose insistence on living in truth, openness to transcendence, the precariousness of the current world, and the political and ecological responsibility indispensable as a consequence, all take their inspiration from Patočka. Indeed, Havel, like a whole generation of post-1968 Czech intellectuals, claimed Patočka as their "most important philosopher," their Socrates of Prague, their role model.[3]

Jan Patočka was one of the last students and disciples of Husserl, studying with him first in Paris and then at Freiburg—where he also attended Heidegger's lectures—before returning to Prague prior to World War II. After the war, upon refusing to join the Communist Party, he was banned from academia for twenty years. Working in marginal clerical and archival employment, he continued his research and writing in his tiny basement apartment, only able to return to the university with the liberalizations of the Prague spring of 1968. In 1972, after arguing that academic promotion should be based upon merit rather than on political allegiance, he was again forced out of the university, this time into retirement. Subsequently, he became one of the founding signers and spokesmen of the Charter 77 movement, which demanded recognition of the Helsinki agreements on human rights. He was harassed by authorities, eventually arrested, and during prolonged interrogation died of a heart attack.

Plato and Europe is a series of lectures Patočka delivered in the homes of friends after his last banishment from the academy just three years before his death. Thus what follows are transcribed, unedited conversations—left unedited and as literal as possible in this translation. The material is striking not only because it represents the high point of lifelong meditation, but also because of the urgency and unpretentious honesty it contains. In the obituary Havel wrote for the philosopher, he observed:

The strength of his exposition was not only in the breadth of his knowledge and unswerving manner in which he was able to penetrate beneath the surface of

---

3. Václav Havel, *Open Letters* (New York: Alfred A. Knopf, 1991), 276. On Havel's relation to Patočka, see E. Findlay, "Classical Ethics and Postmodern Critique: Václav Havel and Jan Patočka," *Review of Politics* 61, no. 3 (summer 1999); also A. Tucker, *The Philosophy and Politics of Czech Dissidents from Patočka to Havel* (Pittsburgh, Pa.: University of Pittsburgh Press, 2000).

phenomena and relationships, but also his entire personality, its openness, its modesty, its humor. These unofficial seminars pulled us into the world of philosophizing in its true original sense of the word: no classroom boredom, but rather the inspired, vital search for the significance of things and the illumination of understanding one's own situation in the world.[4]

This search was one conducted without hope of reaching a wider audience, for Patočka was forbidden to publish in Czechoslovakia for most of his life. Here the reader will find words not motivated by vanity, the peacock that often usurps the philosopher's place, but rather care.

Indeed, care is the guiding theme of *Plato and Europe*: care for the soul. Patočka claims this notion forms the fundamental axis of ancient philosophy. Such a reading of Greek philosophy will surprise many readers. Unlike contemporaries—like Hans Gadamer, Hannah Arendt, or Leo Strauss—Patočka concentrates on different aspects of the classics; he does not take up Gadamer's emphasis upon the scientific and mathematical achievements of the ancients, nor Arendt's focus on agonistic republicanism, nor Strauss's purported conflict between the philosopher and the nonphilosopher. And unlike those who have recently emphasized the care of the self in Plato—whether Foucault or Hadot—Patočka gives care of the soul even greater importance, insisting it is the fulcrum for all the great thinkers of antiquity. He argues that it rests at the root of not only Plato's reflections but also Democritus's atomism and Aristotle's concern for virtue.[5]

Plato and Europe should equally surprise those who now emphasize the fundamental importance of care in understandings of ethics.[6] While such recent approaches generally take their inspiration from Humean sentiment, Patočka raises the possibility of deriving similar concerns—not only care but also its culmination in sacrifice—from Socratic rationalism.

However, Patočka's most important claim is that this ancient concep-

---

4. From Havel's obituary for Patočka, in *Charter 77 and Human Rights in Czechoslovakia*, ed. H. G. Skilling (London: George Allen, 1981), 242.

5. The work of Pierre Hadot, which is also little read in the Anglo-American world, especially *Philosophy as a Way of Life* (Oxford: Blackwell, 1995), is particularly instructive as a comparison to Patočka.

6. For example, see Annette Baier, *Moral Prejudices* (Cambridge, Mass.: Harvard University Press, 1994).

tion of the care of the soul is crucial to contemporary self-understanding. He argues that European history must be understood as the fundamental inheritance of this conception of care of the soul. Although this inheritance is now precarious, the question guiding *Plato and Europe* is whether it can "still speak to us today."

But what is the soul, and what does its care entail? A caveat is in order. Patočka is neither mystic nor theologian. Although he recognizes the faith grounding all philosophical reflection, and although he claims we have responsibility to a higher authority, for Patočka philosophy is neither myth nor consolation. Instead, it is born from the destruction and remnants of myth, signifying the courageous transition from an unquestioned, passive acceptance of the given to the ability and willingness to seek the truth. That which enables human beings to carry out this task is the soul: it is "just that which is capable of truth within man," and its essential care is "living in truth."

Patočka explains there are three fundamental modes of care of the soul formulated in antiquity: care as ontocosmology, as a plan for political life, and as the relation of the individual to mortality. The first is an understanding of the relation of the human being to the rest of the universe. Man is the only creature who is able to philosophize, to whom the world is revealed or uncovered [*odhalený*], to use Patočka's phenomenological terminology. The human being, or the soul, is thus the intermediary between existence and its particular manifestations in the world. This gives man a special place in the universe—indeed, for Patočka it is the source of human dignity as well as of human freedom.

Reminding us of Plato and Aristotle's remarks that philosophy is born from wonder that we are able to ask questions about existence, Patočka emphasizes this wonder is also bewilderment. For the discovery of questioning, seeking the truth is accompanied by the discovery that the world reveals itself in an equivocal or two-sided [*dvouznačnou*] way: it always oscillates between the comprehensible and the incomprehensible, identity and difference, truth and error, good and evil. Yet such equivocity or problematicity is a testament to human freedom: because of it, both philosophy and independence of action are possible at all.

With the birth of philosophy, human beings are called to a special responsibility. Although philosophy is the discovery of freedom, paradoxically it brings with it a universal, binding obligation—one that concerns all human beings, not merely a philosophical elite—to judge oneself against the bar of truth. This activity leads to individual internal transformation. To philosophize means to allow oneself to be problematized, to carry out a constant conversation both with others and with oneself about how one lives. This is care of the soul; it means "to want to be in unity with one's own self," to transcend the vagaries of changing opinion and the never-satisfied chaos of desire, to find inner stability and solidity. This responsibility cannot be refused without consequence once it has been discovered. To live passively, unphilosophically, leads to an internal transformation as well. It means to live according to what is always shifting and changing and, thus, to become perpetually inconstant. According to Patočka, philosophy confronts all of us—not just philosophers—with the choice: to be or not to be. This means that one must actively shape one's inner self in a lifelong process of constant questioning, or resign to the flux of opinion and thus passive internal dissolution.

Yet care of the soul is not only a call to truth but also equally a call to justice. That is how Patočka explains the Platonic and Democritan dictum that it is better to suffer injustice than to commit it. The soul that strives to live according to truth must also be one that lives according to justice, because its dedication to the truth binds it to the "morality of truth," and so to justice.

Two paths lead from this understanding. The first is Democritus's, culminating in a radical withdrawal from any involvement in practical affairs, whether of family, social, or political life. The second is Plato's, leading to a reflection on politics, to ask how it might be organized in order to allow for care of the soul. But here again Patočka emphasizes that Plato's political reflections take their point of departure from it: Plato undertakes his exploration of the just city in *The Republic* in order to see the care of the soul writ large, to see what is invisible—the soul—in the realm of the visible, in political life, and to make not only the soul but also the political world one of truth and justice, a world where the philosopher need not perish. Thus, for Patočka *The Republic* stands for neither a despotic nor a utopian regime nor one that is to reveal the limits of political transformation; instead, it serves as the historical impetus to judge all political claims against criteria of truth and justice. From here on, the political is forced into dialogue with philosophy, because its legitimacy depends upon its justification before it.

The third conception of care of the soul is human reflection upon mortality, or, more generally, on the relationship between the finite and the infinite. Care for the soul necessarily leads to a confrontation with death, because philosophy constantly reveals to the human being both the possibility of the divine—through the perpetual presence of wonder and mystery at the possibility of philosophical reflection—as well as the accompanying awareness of the chasm separating us from the divine; the realization that man does not have unproblematic access to the truth and that he alone of all creatures is aware of his own transience.

Patočka undertakes this three-fold exposition of the soul as a response to a crisis. This crisis is not merely, or even primarily, the distress of living under a communist regime. Rather, following Nietzsche, and more particularly Husserl and Heidegger, Patočka diagnoses it as common to both the East and the West. On the one hand, this crisis is the triumph of technical instrumental reason, which understands nature as a tool for domination and exploitation rather than for respect and contemplation. In this way, nature is unable to provide any noninstrumental standards or any guidance for how human beings ought to live. On the other hand, the crisis is the attempt to derive understanding purely from subjectivity, an attempt that historically has culminated in radical skepticism and so a temptation to gauge only will to power as the standard for all human conduct. Thus, Patočka's diagnosis: the crisis amounts to a total rationality of means that is paradoxically accompanied by an utter irrationality of ends.

Yet Patočka does not accept defeat. Unlike Heidegger, he neither counsels despair nor the belief that salvation can come only from a god. Instead, he insists that philosophy still is possible, that these three elements of care for the soul still speak to us today. However, this does not mean that he is advocating a return to classical antiquity. To the contrary, he remains within the phenomenological tradition of Husserl, with whose work he spent a lifetime grappling, and whose efforts to ground philosophy in the evidence of the experiential he recognizes as an unprecedented advance in philosophical thought. Moreover, he acknowledges Heidegger's critique of reason and of all metaphysical certainties of an ordered cosmos, admitting that the metaphysical era of philosophy has come to an end.

But how then is one to live according to the truth, to care for the soul if one admits the basic historicity of man and of the relativity of his orientation in the world? And why should this not lead either to despair or to the abandonment of philosophy if one acknowledges that two thousand years of philosophy have not yielded incontrovertible certainties? Patočka's answer is that contingency still does not foreclose the possibility of philosophy. For philosophy is rendered possible precisely by the phenomenological fact that we are able to *distance* ourselves from all that is given despite our contingency, a distancing that is always possible because we never experience the world in an incontrovertible, unequivocal manner. Yet this distancing does not mean that we are able to escape to some absolute precisely because of the way the world reveals itself to us. Thus, for Patočka, philosophy always occurs within the cave; however, it is still an exercise that constantly leads to overcoming, to a transcending of the given, pointing away—both outward as well as upward—out of the cave. Nevertheless, it would be the height of folly to pretend for the vantage point of the gods. The gift of philosophy is not the discovery of final solutions, but rather the discovery of the *problematicity* of human existence: we are not entirely slaves to the givens of language, society, politics, or history. Yet neither are we beings who may perch as gods upon the epicycle of mercury. Therefore one may characterize Patočka's thought as an attempt to reenchant the world, to remind us that to philosophize is always to step outside and above oneself and that this act of self-transcendence, itself testament to freedom and dignity, both begins and ends in wonder.

   Plato and Europe may thus be considered an invitation to reconsider transcendence. Should the invitation be accepted? In some cases it already has. Patočka has had a marked influence upon French postmodern thought, particularly in the recent shift from deconstruction and playful *jouissance* to the ethical and spiritual, especially in the later works of Foucault and Derrida, both of whom cite Patočka as a cardinal influence upon this transformation.[7] Elsewhere in Europe, in more practical political debates about collective self-understandings, or European identity, Patočka's ideas, particularly his claim that the heritage of Europe is fundamentally rooted in the philosophical idea of the care of the soul, have not been seriously considered, for the dominant positions here emphasize not cultural but purely political or juridical arrangements, or constitutional patriotism, as essential to contemporary collective identity for fear that any

   7. See Foucault, *Ethics, Subjectivity and Truth* (New York: New Press, 1991); Derrida, *The Gift of Death* (Chicago: University of Chicago Press, 1995). For a comparison between Foucault and Patočka, see A. Szakolczai, "Thinking Beyond the East-West Divide: Foucault, Patočka and the Care of the Self," *Social Research* 61, no. 2 (summer 1994).

cultural or spiritual appeals, however conceived, will neither reflect the transformations in an ever more diverse Europe nor be free from potentially exclusionary implications.[8]

On the other side of the Atlantic, there is evidence of an increasing scholarly interest in the spiritual,[9] but here positions usually depend upon the way the question is framed: whether the spiritual is to concern only ethics or politics as well. The former is not often perceived as threatening because it is insulated by the separation of church and state. But even here, there are those, for example, like Richard Rorty, who would rather that human beings forget about spirituality or transcendence of any kind, not just in public affairs, but entirely—to accept themselves as thoroughly and inescapably contingent.[10] Such positions are motivated by the fear of mixing spirituality with political or social life, because historically such combinations have been generally disastrous. We may agree that given the historical vicissitudes of the religious wars of modern Europe, effort to banish the spiritual in all its guises was both prudent and wise. Still, the question remains—and it is one increasingly discussed today whether in debates about religion,[11] globalization,[12] or political theory[13]—whether

8. See, for example, G. Delanty, *Inventing Europe* (New York: St. Martin's, 1995).

9. For example, D. Meyers, *The American Paradox: Spiritual Hunger in an Age of Plenty* (New Haven, Conn.: Yale University Press, 2000); R. W. Fogel, *The Fourth Great Awakening and the Future of Egalitarianism* (Chicago: University of Chicago Press, 2000).

10. For a comparison between Patočka and Rorty, see P. Lom, "East Meets West," *Political Theory* 27, no. 4 (August 1999). Rorty also must be acknowledged as one of few American academics recognizing Patočka's importance. See his "The Seer of Prague: The Influence of Czechoslovakian Philosopher Jan Patočka," *New Republic* 205, no. 1 (July 1991).

11. See, for example, Nancy Rosenblum, ed., *Obligations of Citizenship and Demands of Faith* (Princeton, N.J.: Princeton University Press, 2000); and P. J. Weithman, *Religion and Contemporary Liberalism* (Notre Dame, Ind.: University of Notre Dame Press, 1997).

12. See, for example, Benjamin Barber, *Jihad vs. McWorld* (New York: Ballantines, 1996); and P. Berger, ed., *The Desecularization of the World: Resurgent Religion and World Politics* (Grand Rapids, Mich.: Wm. B. Eerdmans, 1999).

13. See the debate between Quentin Skinner and Charles Taylor in *Philosophy in an Age of Pluralism*, ed. J. Tully (Cambridge: Cambridge University Press,

modern secularism and its efforts to banish transcendence does not emasculate the possibilities of the human spirit.

While this question itself is valuable, there is still another. For Patočka and Havel following him contend that without philosophical openness to transcendence, and the responsibility that accompanies it, we will not be able to avert the technological, environmental, and demographic pressures on our planet today. The question for contemporary democratic conceptions—be they liberal, communitarian, deliberative, or postmodernist—is whether they have a better way to respond to these challenges without giving central place to Patočka's understanding of transcendence: the humble awareness that humankind is neither the master nor perhaps even sole custodian of the universe.

1994); William Connolly, *Why I am not a Secularist* (Minneapolis: University of Minnesota Press, 1999); and P. Manent, *The City of Man* (Princeton, N.J.: Princeton University Press, 1998).

PLATO AND EUROPE

1

Introduction—The Situation of Mankind—The State of Europe

What I want to tell you today is not really a lecture. It is an introduction to general questions about the state of our contemporary world. We may continue with another lecture after this, if you are interested. I would like it if we could work together in a mutually supportive way by questioning and raising objections. And so, I should ask, please, that you do not take what I say as something definite or final, but rather as a conversation among friends. Today people often get together to talk about abstract and eventually lofty things to escape for a moment the distress in which we all find ourselves, so that they may lift both their spirits and their minds. While I think that this is all very well, it is more like entertainment for old ladies. Philosophical reflection ought to have a different purpose, it should somehow help us in the distress in which we are; precisely in the situation in which we are placed, philosophy is to be a matter of *inner conduct.*

The human situation is, you see, something that changes once we become self-conscious about it. A naive and a self-conscious situation are already different. Our reality is always situational, so that if it is reflected upon, it is already different by the fact that we have reflected. Of course, the question is whether by reflection reality is improved. This is not stated in the least. But, in any case, a reflected-upon situation—in contrast to a naive situation—is to a certain extent a clarified one, or at least on the way to clarification.

I am not saying that reflection always gets ahold of the heart of the matter, but we will not get to the heart of the matter without reflecting. But what is the truth of the matter? Of course we know well enough that every truth starts from error or half-error, that truth is always the conquest of progressive criticism of that which we originally thought, criticism of our opinions. Reflection moves along the path of opinion and its critique. If we reflect, then, upon our situation, we can change it, and change it into an enlightened, self-conscious one. This enlightening is on the way to truth about the situation.

But how exactly to reflect? Let us have a look at what the situation is. The concept of the situation is a peculiar one. Individuals are in a favorable or an unfavorable situation regarding the goal they are seeking. And a situation is, after all, characterized by that; that it is at the same time the reality in which I am, in which others are, and in which things are. At the same time, it regards material things and human beings. It is something, in which there are given elements, but the most interesting and most characteristic thing about situations is precisely that we have not given them to ourselves, that we are placed into them and have to reconcile ourselves with them. It is not something we create at will or according to our needs. It might seem that a situation is something regarding material things—for example, a ship that is sinking means a particular situation for people. Those people are there in a particular situation that they have, to a certain extent, brought upon themselves, but what they have brought upon themselves is certainly not the result of their efforts, does not follow the direction of their will. A situation is something extremely urgent so that it might seem that a situation is something that can be characterized first of all materially, objectively, what can be materially, objectively captured; except that these material elements are only one particular component of the situation.

A situation is entirely different, depending on whether people who are in a situation of distress give up or do not give up. In a hopeless situation it is still possible to behave in very different ways.

Of course, an important matter is that man always is essentially in a hopeless situation. Man is a being committed to an adventure, which, in a certain sense, cannot end well. We are a ship that necessarily will be shipwrecked. In this form our life is, in a certain sense, something that is not solely human. We are part of a process that is one of decline whether so deemed by ordinary human sentiment, or by modern science, which in a certain sense builds upon and underlies it. We are part of a universe that is in decline; we are part of a universe that is in an energetic *descensus*. All our reactions against it draw their possibilities and strengths from this universe, which is in a downfall. This is, we might say, one of the general components of each and every human situation—as long as we are incorporated into nature and are a part of it. We are also in this "hopeless adventure" in the peculiar form: every individual is mortal; and all our attempts in life are, from a certain perspective, only the holding back of decline, the slowing down of decay, a certain stationary form of an advancing march we can never reverse.

Please do not think that I have come here to scare you or to go on in morose talk. It is important to understand this thing in the contexts I will indicate.

We have already laid out several features of the situation and situatedness of man. These are its material and its nonmaterial components. These nonmaterial components are characterized, for example, by the fact that the situation changes once it becomes self-conscious. This means that it is not materially determined entirely, that it depends in large measure upon us.

Now another thing: When we talk about how I, you, she is in this or that particular situation, it is an abstraction. The situation of every human being is a part of the situation of the whole, which contains not only him alone but others as well. When someone is in a situation of crisis, it is probably because someone else is in a different situation. The situation of my crisis certainly is connected to other situations through which I am brought into relation with the situations of others. Where does this have its limits? In the end, the situation of all individuals is incorporated into some kind of general situation or, better said, into the entire human situation. And so to reflect upon what we are in—about our situation—ultimately means to reflect how mankind's situation appears today. To philosophize, I think, means to meditate within the entire situation, and to be its reflection. Of course, to philosophy belongs truth, being, the world, knowing, good and evil, beauty or art and other creations of the human spirit in their spirituality. But we have to tell ourselves clearly that all of these problems come from reflection upon our human situation, which can be concretely shown in the beginning of philosophy and from its development and the course of its evolution. Philosophy, you see, is not established in the way that scientific truths and scientific systems are; philosophy is not established objectively. Where philosophy is asked to establish and prove itself just like some mathematical or natural scientific theory, there it has already capitulated. This always tends to lead to skepticism about the possibilities, the purpose, and meaning of philosophy. All unsituated truths are in the end abstractions from our human situation. They grow out of our encounter with something in our situation that we then consider for itself. We do not measure it according to ourselves, our problems and our needs, our faith and our despair; we measure it, as it were, one thing with another. First, we must have encountered things in some way. We must have come upon them. And we come to them, after all, only because they come into our path, that they have meaning for us, that we have to turn to them. In other words, we are placed into them, among them; placed-ness and situated-ness are one and the same.

Now here is the problem that could keep us busy for a long time: What methodological approach should be employed to get a hold of something like the complete situation of contemporary mankind?

Of course, the social sciences all occupy themselves in some way with the human condition, but understandably in such a way that they try to abstract from the situation. Only indirectly, in a roundabout way, do they return to the situation. The sciences as such are after all bound by certain methodological assumptions. Science is at bottom objective, and the social sciences want to be just as purely objective as the natural sciences—which means that the sciences can glean something from the situation, but not the situation as such. Why? Because the situation is not totally an objective reality. The situation is something in which lies not only what can be stated—what is present and what has been described, the past—but also what cannot be described—the future. A situation is a situation precisely because it has not yet been decided. A decided situation is no longer a genuine situation.

We do not have any way to reflect upon a situation other than through certain objectivity. We do not have any other means, we cannot even think otherwise. If we want, then, to get some kind of methodological means to orient ourselves in our reality, we have to think of some way to objectify the occurrences of which we ourselves are a part. Here, offering itself above all, is the fact that currently there is, I think, something like a complete sense of the situation, something like a complete sense of the times. But a complete sense of the times, which is the times' self-understanding, is not yet knowledge. It is not yet something that would mean a definite reflection. Rather it is, like I say, a feeling, meaning a certain kind of reality, a certain kind of actuality, though of course a human one. I think that this complete sense of the times is expressed urgently by the element of the age regarding expressiveness—art. Expressing the sense of life, that is art. Something like that is expressed in the art of a period, or the art an age produces that is unlike that of the times preceding it.

Of course, artistic production is something extremely expansive and varied, and here it is necessary to choose the characteristic. Obviously, then the difficult question is: How shall we choose it? One of the guides, as I have just said, is to indicate what an age brings that is new in contrast to what used to be, something that is not just repetitive, that expresses something that is its very own. And if we were really to move forward methodically, then we would have to insert something like that here. Unfortunately, I cannot do that. In that respect, I find myself in a quandary. Then there are also the questions of how to specify from what period and so on. If that kind of analysis is not possible, then I think we can also rely on the fact that the artist, who expresses the temper of his period, is also to a certain degree able to reflect upon it. So we can use his own reflections themselves, which have an element of objectivity and generality within them, to tie our own reflections onto something. I am thinking here of Ionesco's inaugural speech at last year's Salzburg festival, which many of you have heard about, and many of you certainly know, in which he tried to put into words this entire spirit of the times.[1]

Before we get into the speech's content, I would like to say briefly that when we get a common expression of an age's temper, then we will have to formulate a hypothesis about how the situation so expressed arose and what its structure is. That is to a significant degree an objective hypothesis, one made up of historical, sociological, economic, and other elements, and, above all, of ideas. The hypothesis then has to be somehow confronted with practice.

What does Ionesco say then? Essentially, he says—and this is characteristic of him—that his analysis is not intended to be deeply sociological or something of that sort. He wants his analysis to be an expression of the

---

1. E. Ionesco, "Discoue d'ouverture du Festival de Salzburg 1972," in *Un homme en question* (Paris: Gallimard, 1979).

entire mood. And this mood is: a deep helplessness and inability to stand upon anything in any way solid. In the nineteenth century people still had, says Ionesco, the sense that they could somehow direct their fate, that humanity could control its affairs. This sentiment has completely abandoned us. Now we live with the opposite sentiment: something is carrying us away; and what is carrying us away is contradictory, it prevents us from taking a univocal position. We do not know what we want; no one knows.

We are the victims of contradictory prophets, some proclaim the unleashing of instincts, others absolute discipline and obedience; both seem to be two sides of the same thing. Thus a deep helplessness and distress. There does not exist any joyful work of art; nothing exists except an enormous tangle of human activities. Every human initiative or deed is socialized, controlled, and integrated into current affairs and carried off alone into the unknown. This is the sentiment of alienation. What grows from it is surprisingly something like a will to power, but power that has no subject. It is not that someone should want this power; it is just accumulated and does what it wants with us. Here is an awareness of a horrible trend toward the abyss. That we cannot get off the ship carrying us is in a certain sense the sad recognition of this worldly fall, this decline of nature and man, as if it were an irreversible and inescapable fall. In this situation something like metaphysics (only to say that word) is laughable! For us, recalling something like metaphysics or Mozart's art, or the art of the Chartres cathedral, makes it seem absolutely unreal. We no longer are able to find and experience any joy in it, or to raise ourselves up to something like it. That is the entire *sentiment* of our time.

What is *reality* then? Or let us say: here is a certain hypothesis. Here, I would insert a remark about what has been a trendy, but terribly shlocky, socioeconomic tune of the last several years: the well-known paper about the limits of growth, the paper drafted by the "club of Rome"—a group of economists, sociologists, and industrialists who gave themselves this name because they first met in Rome in 1969, and who through objective economic methods, and with the help of computers, posed the question: What is the overall economic trend of the world in which we live today?[2]

Fundamental thoughts are simple, evident, and not new. Take, for

2. D. H. Meadows et al., *The Limits of Growth* (New York: Universe Books, 1972).

example, an old book, accessible to us here, Lévi-Strauss's *Sad Tropics*: you will find there that the oriental cities of India are predecessors of what humanity calls the future: a demographically overpopulated complex— terminal and exhausted.[3] Excessive demographic growth in a closed system has exhausted all of its supplies. The analysis of the club of Rome carries this out for the entire planet. Here, there is a calculation of the supplies of raw materials, availability of arable land, demographic growth, environ- mental pollution, capital growth, and it is shown that with current means of exponential growth, within the not so distant future, that is, within the next century, an economic collapse must take place, one of enormous proportions that hitherto had not and could not have occurred, the result of which cannot be other than, so to speak, a planet without human society, without any society that might be deemed human, a return some- where into the cave, because it would mean an entirely desolate planet, without food, without possibility of development, without energy sources, in a state of overpopulation—initially in a state of overpopulation and then, of course, in a state of famine, war, revolution, poverty, scarcity, and so on.

Where did this all come from? For Europe lived, for example, in complete contrast to Near-Eastern civilizations, for a long period, for thou- sands of years, in a state of equilibrium with the human environment. The problem that contemporary mankind is in a state of disequilibrium, that the wars and revolutions of our century have their origin in this disequilib- rium, is the sentiment of various analysts, including philosophical ones, of long ago.

In the nineteenth century, Auguste Comte spoke of alternating or- ganic and critical periods in the evolution of mankind, and he character- ized his contemporary society as a critical one, as one that looks for an organic state of equilibrium. He saw just this state before him and devel- oped it in his positive philosophy.

Comte's philosophy is extremely interesting from a certain perspec- tive, although it has banal sides to it as well. Yet it has such extraordinarily sensitive and profound parts to it that we should not forget that he was one of the greatest philosophers of the modern age. Under the influence of his youthful Comtism, Masaryk also conceptualized his philosophy of the

3. C. Lévi-Strauss, *Tristes Tropiques* (Paris: Plon, 1955).

xxxx First World War. This was also a philosophy of disequilibrium. War was understood as a world revolution, one that seeks a certain equilibrium. This equilibrium, according to Masaryk, was achieved by the antithesis of obsolete theocratic regimes with democracy, settled in the favor of democracy (which is modern, subjective, rational, and so forth and yet still not only extremely subjective but also, as things should be and as is reasonable): Masaryk's work ends with the popular conviction, in 1925, that the peak of the crisis was behind us. You can read all this in that book.[4]

In 1927 Max Scheler published his *Philosophische Weltanschauung*, in which he considered *Die Welt im Stadium des Ausgleichs*—a world in a state of equilibrium. There you see, equilibrium is already in the title, and it was also ideologically conceptualized there. Scheler went through a conversion—the First World War was a deciding point in his life. He began as a zealot against the decadent tendencies of the modern leveling of social distinctions, of modern thinking. Just what Masaryk called democratic was for Scheler the summit of decline. Then came the war, and what Scheler took for strength, what Scheler understood as strength, was swept aside with this decline (that means central powers, where that hierarchical principle—what Masaryk called "a theocratic principle"—was so completely at home). Scheler was a very alert thinker and was not a dishonest one, nor the manufacturer of any ad hoc ideologies. For him this was an opportunity for reflection, to withdraw into himself, and then to formulate this
xxxx conception of equilibrium: in reality, leveling and democratizing tendencies have their important function, and it is possible to bring them into a certain harmony with the other—the tendency to a higher life, with its metaphysical intentions and traditions. The effort to find this equilibrium, in which his philosophy developed, was the reason for his ethico-sociological studies.

These philosophical attempts are evidence that equilibrium was sought perhaps even through war and revolution. A kind of equilibrium was sought, but it was conceptualized by all from the perspectives of European history and European ideology of history. But the question is, when we go to the roots of our contemporary disequilibrium, whether we do not need to go to the very origins of Europe and through these beginnings to the very relation between mankind and his place in the world; or rather,

---

4. T. G. Masaryk, *Světová Revoluce* (Prague: Orbis, 1925).

whether the disequilibrium we are positing today is not something that concerns solely European man in a particular historical period, but rather regards man *sui generi* today in his relation with the planet. I think this question really must be answered in the affirmative: it regards man in his relationship with the planet. It is clear today, when Europe has come to an end. Europe, that two-thousand-year-old construction, which managed to lift up mankind to an altogether new degree of self-reflection and consciousness, and strength and power as well, when this historical reality, which for a long time supposed that it encompassed all of mankind, that it is mankind and that all else is worthy of neglect, is definitely at an end. Europe truly was the master of the world. It was the master of the world economically: she after all was the one who developed capitalism, the network of world economy and markets into which was pulled the entire planet. She controlled the world politically, on the basis of the monopoly of her power, and that power was of scientific-technological origin. All this was Europe. Naturally, this was further connected to its activity of reflection, to that, that she had science, the sole rational civilization, a monopoly over it, and so on. And this reality, this enormous power, definitely wrecked itself in the span of thirty years, in two wars, after which nothing remained, nothing of her power that had ruled the world. She destroyed herself, through her own powers. Naturally, she harnessed the entire world into this, just as she made the whole world hers before that, in a very crude material way. She forced it to completely engage itself in those horrendous enterprises. The result is, of course, that here are its inheritors, and these inheritors will never allow Europe to be what it once was.

What led us into this state? What brought Europe here? The answer is simple: her disunited and enormous power. Disunity after all lies in the fact that there was a row of sovereign states at various levels here. What does a sovereign state mean? It is what does not recognize any higher authority above it, so that it is impossible to decide conflicts between these states. These states had various degrees of internal organization, wealth, and economic development, and they (or those most important) were, above all, simultaneously engaged in an enterprise to take possession of the world. In these circumstances conflict was inevitable. These were circumstances of disunity, when nothing common existed that would unite them, either external—that is organizational, of the state, and so forth—or even spiritual. In addition, an immense power, power of the entire world. In such a conflict all of the power these societies have at their disposal is used up for mutual destruction—and this also occurred. These very enormous powers of science and technology and all that was gained by them were yoked to the enterprise of mutual destruction. Not from without, rather it was an internal fate, or, how might we put it, the internal logic of the European situation. Do not forget that *this* is the modern situation. Its components are science and technology as the knowledge of the great powers, sovereign states—sovereign states in disunity—as the concrete organization of human society. This disunity was not solely a negative thing, but it meant that these states did not have anything above them which might unite them. In that lies the difference with earlier Europe.

Naturally, Europe was not always unified. Nineteenth-century Europe was fractured and disunited. This is no longer any organism, but there were periods when Europe was something like a unity. In the writings of his youth, Hegel says something about the German constitution: Germany is not a state and cannot be, but it once was.

From Hegel's point of view, a state is every world organization capable of united defensive or aggressive action. Above all it has to be able to defend itself. Historical inquiry has somehow unanimously and tacitly accepted that European expansion from the eleventh to the thirteenth century was an expansion of Europe as a unity. The Crusades made Europe a closed whole in regard to the Islamic world. This whole has its own boundaries; it is a whole that moves all the way to eastern Europe toward the boundaries of Slavic tribes, Baltic and so forth, this whole colonizing trend—all of this is European history, Europe as a whole.

How did this Europe come into existence? Since when is Europe spoken of? In antiquity, Europe was a mere geographical concept. Europe became a historical-political concept that we can use as a name for a certain united singular reality, only in the Middle Ages. The Roman Empire is not any kind of Europe—of course Africa and a large part of Asia belonged to the Roman Empire—but this whole development had its own stamp. European history or the birth of Europe as a political reality took place in two waves. These waves are characterized by a sort of creative destroying. How is this to be understood? I will say it in definite terms right now. Europe came into existence upon the wreckage, first of the Greek polis, and then of the Roman Empire. And like the Greek polis, so the Roman Empire became extinct, because within them took place a development that alien-

ated their own inhabitants, their own public, from the life form in which
they lived. The Greek polis killed itself with the decline of the Greek world.
The Greek world was a world of city communities, city-states that first
showed their vitality through amazingly successful resistance to the monarchies of the Near East, but then destroyed themselves amongst themselves.
Except they left behind an inheritance.

This inheritance is of such a character that on its basis, the subsequent social whole, which took the place of the Greek polis, was able to
become the genuine heir of life of the polis. In a certain sense we can say
that the Hellenistic states are naturally also loss and discontinuity—something in the Greek polis was lost there, freedom of political life was lost
there, its initiative, and just this peculiar sense for a *vita activa*—which
Hannah Arendt beautifully analyses in her well-known writings.[5] Yet, the
Hellenistic period is extremely important, because there is the genesis of
something like a conception of mankind, mankind as something universal,
where everyone has a share in the common. All the problems that have not
left humanity since originated there: the problem of the universal state,
universal religion, social reconciliation, reconciliation among different nations. All these are problems of Hellenism, which found their crystallization in the Roman Empire. And the Roman Empire lived spiritually off the
inheritance of the Greek polis, because she wanted to be the juridical state
where *ius civile* (civil law) was based upon *ius gentium* (law of the people);
and *ius gentium* depended on what the Greek philosophers, namely, Plato
and Aristotle, who reflected upon the state of justice, elaborated. But the
Roman Empire likewise estranged itself from its own public. I did not
concretely illustrate this process in the Greek polis, but in the Roman
Empire, this process is very evident. The Roman citizenry was estranged
from the state because the program, about which I have spoken, filled this
state only provisionally and imperfectly, so that it became unreliable and
unsatisfactory. External clashes were only a symptom of the moral situation
into which this complex got itself. Just as in history in general, here is also
the moral element, which is much, much more important than any other.
But in that time, there was also an inheritance there, and this inheritance
goes back to the Greek polis. What was in common, what could still allow

5. H. Arendt, *The Human Condition* (Chicago: University of Chicago Press,
1958).

– the universalism of Hellenism
combined with the particularity ? ??
of elective monotheism → EUROPE

for the possibility of joining together and living, and what could even be generalized such that entire new tribes, or nations, were all harnessed into this new complex—all of this was formed by the spirit of Greece. Thus was later born medieval Europe. Whoever joined this project, whoever agreed with the project of the kingdom of God—which naturally had its own projection on earth and its own perspective that it would come to earth—he belonged to Europe.

Of course, to a certain extent, this project also belongs to Islam as well, although with certain nuances. The struggle between Europe and Islam, which occurred approximately until the thirteenth century, was a kind of crystallization of these two related and yet very different conceptions.

Now there is the question, from whence did all this arise? What was this inheritance that could have such an effect and that was needed so that historical realities could arise which would for such a long time maintain equilibrium, keeping humanity at the same time in a state of spiritual elevation and in balance with the natural ecological situation on this planet?

Another question is whether within this, which we could designate as the European inheritance, there exists something that could to some extent be believable even for us, that could affect us in a way so that we could again find hope in a specific perspective, in a specific future, without giving in to illusory dreams and without undervaluing the toughness and gravity of our current situation.

So you see, I have spoken for such a long time, just to indicate what I really want to talk about. I cannot lay out in detail this particular thesis for you now, but I should just like to round it off a little more.

First of all, mankind has always known, in a certain sense, this general trend—the world is one of decline. I have already spoken about the fact that this is a universal experience. The Greek philosophers sometimes seem naive to us, when in some pre-Socratic fragments we read that they argue against claims that in existence and being something might be disappearing, that existence could age—as Parmenides and Melissos assert. When Anaximander talks about being as never-aging (ἀγήρως), behind this stands this experience: the world is in decline. But philosophy says: no, the world is not in decline, because the core of the world is being, and being has no beginning and will not perish, being can neither begin nor end—it is eternal.

The philosophical discovery of eternity is a peculiar thing. Naturally, from the perspective of modern natural science it is incomprehensible. But what is encompassed by it? It is after all a resistance, a battle against that **xxxx** fall, against time, against the entire declining tendency of the world and of life. In a certain sense, this battle is understandably futile, but in another sense it is not, because the situation in which man finds himself varies accordingly to how he confronts it. And the freedom of mankind lies— perhaps—exactly in this! The Greeks, the Greek philosophers in whom the Greek spirit is expressed most sharply, expressed human freedom by the term: care of the soul. Modern science made even the concept of the soul problematic. The Greek philosophers all know the concept of the soul— whether they are, as we now say, materialists or idealists.

In what consists the care of the soul? In what does the soul consist? The Greek philosophers conceptualized an idea of an *immortal* soul—but not all of the philosophers do so. But all of them, including those who affirmed an immortal soul and those who affirmed a mortal, perishable soul, believed that it is necessary to care for the soul; and the care of the soul can get man—without considering his short life, its finitude—into a state similar to that of the gods. Why? Because man, or the human soul—that which knows about the whole of the world and of life, that which is able to present this whole before its eyes, that which lives from this position, that which knows about the whole and in that sense is wholly and in the whole within this explicit relation to something certainly immortal, that which is certainly eternal, that which does not pass away, beyond which there is nothing—in this itself has its own eternity.

There is great strength and depth in what Epicurus, one of the most lax Greek philosophers (I do not mean to say regarding morals—to the contrary), tells us through nonetheless immensely profound soundings, even though they appear so superficial: it is not necessary to fear death. Death is after all our own boundary, our own finitude, it is that shipwreck, that frontier where we are heading. When death is present, we are no longer, and as long as we are, death is not. While to this, of course, can be objected that death exists just then, when we are, and with this death within us, with this we have to reconcile ourselves; but it is only possible to reconcile ourselves with death with the thought that in man lives an essential relation, which cannot be forfeited either from man or from the world, and that it is the same whether we realize it for a short time or whether it is realized by the gods for a long time—in this it is the same thing. Just for this reason Epicurus says: philosophy is what brings man close to the gods. And that is why Epicurus needs gods.

You know what I perhaps want to say: <u>Can the care of the soul, which is the fundamental heritage of Europe, still speak to us today?</u> Speak to us, who need to find something to lean on in this common agreement about decline, in this weakness, in this consent to the fall?

So then, this is just to start. If you are interested, then next time I should try to explain to you something about what the care of the soul meant in Greek philosophy.

2

What Is the Phenomenon?—Phenomenology and
Phenomenological Philosophy—Phenomenon and Truth

Last time I ended by telling you that care of the soul is the central
theme around which, I think, the life plan of Europe crystallized. Now our
task is to determine what the soul means, and what is meant by the care of
the soul; why it is necessary to care for the soul, and what is its significance.
But before we go into this historical account, I would like to—so that I
might clarify the entire gravity of the question—take my point of departure
from something more recent, from certain themes of new, contemporary
philosophy. At first glance, this is going to seem like a digression. But, I
hope that we will soon see that it has not led us astray, but rather has helped
us more precisely determine the problem of the soul and the care of the soul
as the central European thematic.

The philosophical thematic I would now like to develop relies on
certain texts. The main text that we are concerned with is in Husserl's *Ideas
for a Pure Phenomenology*, volume I §31, and I will largely comment on it
here. Of course, we will not just translate, but we will try to get from his
own words to the problem in which we are interested. In §31, Husserl
explains the so often discussed, so often criticized, so often dismissed
and then again defended idea of the so-called phenomenological reduction. Phenomenological reduction literally translated means conversion
into phenomenon. Now the important thing is: The conversion of what
into phenomenon? And what does phenomenon mean? Why is some kind
of conversion necessary? From whence to where are we to be converted?

What does phenomenon mean? We could start with this. The standard translation is "apparition/appearance." What do we usually associate with the word appearance? Something not only is here but also shows itself. Not every thing also shows itself. On the one hand, things are in themselves and are what they are; on the other hand, they *show themselves*. It seems that this is about the problem of knowing, as if our consideration regarded a specialized philosophical discipline, called the theory of cognizance. But things also show themselves even where the purpose is not directly cognizing. Everywhere concerning human activity, as we are used to defining it as the human, everywhere where precisely the human comes into consideration, there before us, we have not only things that are but also things that show themselves. Just when man wants to know, when he at the same time wants to act, when he orients himself with respect to good and evil, everywhere there something—and this is obvious—has to show itself. Just that which he marks as good and evil has to show itself to him. And naturally, because good and evil are something that regards us, at the same time we show ourselves to ourselves. Phenomenon then, in this sense means the *showing of existence*: things not only are but also they are manifest. An appearance/apparition naturally in a certain sense is, in its own way, also a specific thing. Then it is easy to pose the question of how these two are related: thing and apparition/appearance; or the existing apparition and the manifesting-itself thing. How are they distinguished and how do they overlap, how do they meet?

It looks like a secondary problem, like something of second rank. After all, it is obvious that if something is to manifest itself, then in the first place there has to be that which manifests itself. Manifesting just because it is the manifesting of something existing and itself is, after all, to be specified as some kind of feature, some kind of characteristic, a relation in the existent manifesting itself, or eventually in some kind of other existents, which are necessary so that something manifests itself. For certainly there are actual structures of existents where it is obvious to think, straight away, when we think about it, that something manifests itself: a reflection in water, in a mirror. An image appears in a mirror. And we know well enough that behind something like this image lies a certain physical process, that there exists a reflection of light and that the reflection of light has certain structures that are reproduced, that is, certain geometrical features of objects are reproduced by geometrical features of optical formations that arise from the reflection of rays of light. This is after all something that already shows us how the image in a mirror appeared. Except that the image appeared in the mirror. Certain structural coincidences took place, but these structural coincidences are not more or less phenomena than the mirror itself and the light that reflects it. The coincidence of structure is after all just as objective a fact as the mirror, light, and so on. Each is also a thing as well. Where then do we have something like appearing, manifesting itself?

Perhaps the thing will be different if we say that it is still necessary to add something. In order that something manifests itself, it is necessary that it manifests, appears *to someone.* Something like mind or experience is needed. Mind is something that is always occupied—or at least under normal circumstances—with something other than itself. It also occupies itself with itself, but above all it occupies itself with something else. Already it is possible to say here: for mind something shows itself, something different shows itself than that which it is itself. In the case of objects reflecting in a mirror, we still only have material objects, and only when mind comes and posits the coincidence between the object of reflection and the reflecting do we have a discovered coincidence, a coincidence that not only is but also really has shown itself. But has this thought really helped us to say what is a phenomenon? Have we really helped ourselves distinguish the difference between manifesting and mere existence, between the fact that something is and the fact that something shows itself? After all, mind is also something that just is, mind is also an existing thing. How can we get a grasp on phenomenon, on manifesting as such?

As you see, the problem is starting to become more difficult and more entangled. We brought mind into this because it concerns itself with something other than what it is itself, and because for it, it seems fundamental that there is something like a relation to something else, something that can appear. But as soon as we start to look at mind like something existent, then surprisingly right away the phenomenon as such begins to decay. We start to think that what manifests itself has to belong to the being, the existence of mind, that it is as if it were its moment or part. Thus, that which we need so that something will show itself starts to break down, and we begin to have before us the structure of mind, which also of course has various aspects, moments, and so on. But these moments and aspects belong to it merely as its aspects, and that means that mind shows itself to us as a thing and nothing else shows itself within it other than it itself. But this, after all, is true of every kind of existent: it is and has its own aspects and moments. But where then is the phenomenon?

We do not want to answer this question right away. As far as possible, we want to let it ripen in the form of a problem. But in any case, it is clear that we are still working within our experience that something appears to us, something shows itself, that basically for us—as is said—something is here. In fact, in a certain sense, we have to say that *everything* shows itself to us. And that in general, as long as in our relation to things and to those near us there is something like clarity, that we somehow know about them, that we orient ourselves within them, that we are always working with that, that things appear to us. We work with the concept of appearing; yet at the same time this concept itself is not clear to us. On the one hand, it is the most common, the most regular; on the other hand, to get to the phenomenon as such, to get to the appearing is not, as you see, so obvious: it is a difficult thing.

I said that, in a certain sense, everything is constantly appearing to us—naturally, everything not in the same way. That which manifests itself to us has a certain center of gravity. To each of us, this core appears slightly differently, each of us would move around in this core a little differently. The crux of that which manifests itself to us, is our immediate perceptual environment. It shows itself. But then there is the very strange reality, that this core is just merely a center of gravity; it is not the combination of some specified things: within this core is *simultaneously manifested* that which is not so entirely manifestable. What is present here, what shows itself as present, also shows me something further, something that is not directly present, but that undoubtedly is here and somehow indicated in my presence. This means that *the nonpresent also shows* itself here. When we ask where are the boundaries of this *indirect* showing, this showing through our center of gravity, we are unable to answer. It sends us from our immediate surroundings to more distant ones, and these more distant surroundings, which perhaps might be unfamiliar to us, still bring with them the certainty that they are and that their style is in a certain sense familiar. And this entire style leads further and further away and in the end encompasses everything that is—with certain alterations and modifications. Everything that is in some way shows itself to us—of course not in the sense of something explicitly and in the original showing itself. But is showing—appearing—just showing in its original?

Of course, there are substantial differences here. What we have directly before our eyes, this book, your persons—these are here in the original. There are other things that are not here so originally. For example, what is out there in the hallway is not accessible to me in the same way. I could express let us say some kind of conjecture about that and characterize it. Then it might be shown, if I would step outside, that it was not like that. There are ways of dubious showing, there are ways of probable showing, and so on—and there are methods for convincing oneself about what is showing itself, and how to change this uncertainty and probability into certainty, or else to transform what seemed to be an apparent certainty into doubt, into probability, and so on. At the same time it is also important to realize that—and this is an extremely consequential thought—that all our conjectures, *all our opinions* are a *showing itself* of its own kind and that every original showing that somehow convinces me, when that thing itself is here, nonetheless still is within the framework of this universal showing. Every individual thesis is a part of the universal thesis. What is a thesis? Thesis, that is showing itself, which convinced me so far that I say about that thing: it is.

We have now described in a long-about and boring way a kind of large triviality. All our life takes place within the very showing of things and ✗✗✗ in our orientation among them. Our life is constantly profoundly determined by the fact that things show themselves and that they show themselves in their totality. How did we really get to this totality? We got to it by that; every singular thing in our center of gravity appeared to us as part of its surroundings and this surrounding led us step by step further and further. Here, a certain structure of what shows itself as indispensable, not-freely chosen, as something that must be within this manifesting, showed itself. Does this belong to the part of manifesting, or does it belong to the part of things themselves, to the aspect of things that manifest themselves?

After all, it is the character of existence itself, that it extends through space and that this space forms something like the whole. So again we did not get to the phenomenon as such. The general features of what shows itself, the common structure of space, time—these again are just common features of existence, of what shows itself, but not of showing itself. Nonetheless, there is something peculiar here: during the showing of individual things I also know about their connection with the whole. This also equally regards showing itself alone. It looks as if the existence of the whole of the world—or rather what causes the world to not be merely a connection of individual images, that they are not *membra disjecta* (scattered parts), but rather that they somehow form a unity—naturally belongs to existence as such. Yet showing itself is also determined by it. This is then shown in that what shows itself to us from the world is constantly forming a whole. Not only the world itself but also that which we already have somehow before us, as that which shows itself to us, is constantly forming a whole, in such a way that no individuality is independent from other individualities. What shows itself to us also forms the whole of showing, the whole that wants to be in agreement. We cannot freely just dispose of what shows itself in the original, nor of what shows itself not-originally, what shows itself only in a derivative form. In a certain sense, we know how the reality that is not actually before us would appear to us, and as a result we know that solely experience of a certain kind could be in agreement with what actually is showing itself to us.

So then we have two theses before us: on the one hand, in what manifests itself we always have, in some way, the whole, and manifesting itself equally constantly points to some kind of whole. We are, so to speak, embedded within this manifesting. In regard to what shows itself, we are not free. The manifesting world in its whole has always already engaged us and has always already imposed its law upon us. To the character of what manifests itself belongs just that *things* show themselves, that existence shows itself, something that is not our creation, a matter of our free will.

Let us also try to characterize this showing again from that perspective: this entire whole shows itself precisely *to us*. We are somehow not free within this showing; just what shows itself binds us, expresses itself by the fact that *we believe* in what presents itself to us in just this way, that which is here, which is present. We believe—this is our specific act, our own deed. This deed is conditional, but it is ours. We have to believe in every object that presents itself to us, which manifests itself to us. That is to say, every individuality is the subject of our thesis—whether faith or thesis. But because every individual thesis is simultaneously a part of the thesis of the whole, it must be said that individual theses, individual acts of faith, are within the framework of the general thesis, the thesis of the all-encompassing, general whole. When we extract from our entire active orientation within things just what we call knowing or judging—that is, if we look away from practical activity and concern ourselves only with recognizing or rejecting things, that we judge them, that they are or are not, that they are probable or doubtful and so on—then we can say that every activity of this kind, every judgment of this kind takes place within the framework of the general thesis, the thesis of the whole, which itself is not any kind of form of judgment in the common understanding of the word. At least it is not a form of judgment from the start. We do not explicitly realize that we pose our individual judgments and findings within the framework of the general thesis, in the framework of the universe in its whole. This thesis is not originally a judgment, but it may become one.

But how do we acquire new theses? How do we get to them from those that are clear and urgent for us, which lie within that center of gravity, in that center? Such that we somehow shift this center—that, this center—means that which manifests itself directly gets into motion.

Do excuse me that I am boring you with trivialities, but it is good to realize explicitly some of these absolute banalities, because precisely within them is hidden the secret of appearing [*objevování*]. When I now spoke about the shifting of the center of gravity it means: I just move and come into different surroundings and so naturally I have different things which surround and show themselves to me. At the same time, my past experiences remain preserved for me, or better said, what previously showed itself to me, while it is no longer in its original form, but in the form of something that I merely somehow have in memory—in immediate memory of course. But this means that it has disappeared from the present, from actual original showing of the form "here I am," and yet still it has remained the same. Of course, not such that the manner of givenness would be identical, but *the same thing* has remained here.

You can say: but I can forget, I can make a mistake! Understandably, unoriginal givenness can present things to me somewhat differently than they are in reality. But what convinces me of how they are? That after all I simply know: I go back and have another look. Banalities, so utterly terribly common banalities—this goes without saying, does it not? But how is it possible that what is here, what shows itself in its original can also be just like what is not here? It shows itself, but not in the original. That it is not in the original understandably presents itself apart from other things, also by the fact that it begins, we might say, to wobble, that it starts to be doubtful. Nonetheless, even within this doubtful I still somehow have the one and the same. What do I see now?

I have a peculiar structure before me here: the original initial surroundings where things are what they are, where they show themselves to me as what they are and how they are; they show themselves such that they could not be shown any better. When I have things at the tip of my fingertips, here, in their sentient actuality, there is no way to see them better and become more familiar with them. But when I leave, they remain what they are. I do not see them; perhaps my imagination renders this table entirely differently than it actually is. But I know that I am thinking about the same object when I go outside and want to return to that glass that has just refreshed me. How is this possible? Where does this unity come from throughout the different ways of showing, through different ways of how things show themselves to us?

The same shows itself to me in different ways. And this *"through various ways the same"*—this is that terribly important thing.

Showing is not then, as it may seem, only just an objective structure, because the objective, material structure is that *which shows itself.* Showing is also not mind and is not the structure of mind, because that is also just a thing, it is also only something that is and that eventually can also manifest itself. It is likely—no, certain—that it is showed to someone always pertains to showing; someone, who, as it were, accepts it, and who as a result expresses or formulates his own theses. But showing itself is not any of these things *that* show themselves, whether it is a psychic or physical object somewhere out there in space and so on—and yet it is still showing of *those* things, it is showing of things within space as much at it is showing of realities such as myself and my mind.

Now allow me still a few other trivialities. I spoke about the center of gravity of our sentient reality, of our optical reality. All this seems extremely contingent. After all, there are people who do not know this kind of showing, and it seems that when we consider showing in an optical example, we are considering only its own particular and contingent structure. But perhaps optics is suitable to show very succinctly something about manifesting itself. The core, the center of gravity of objective things around me can be at once narrow, wide, limited by these four walls; at other times I am under the wide open sky and I have the impression of infinite space and so on. It can widen and it can narrow. Can it expand to infinity? Never. It is also not conceivable that our experience, that how things show themselves to us could be reduced only to that core, to that center of gravity—that is out of the question. This means that to showing there always belongs the duality of what manifests itself here as existing here in its original and as its not-original, as together-present. As we have already said, in this, after all, everything is encompassed.

We said that somehow within showing there is everything; within showing there is a tendency toward unity, to unity of our theses, and that showing unavoidably has this character: the core, which itself is present, and what is together-given with it.

When we think about what can be directly given to me in this way, in a certain sense, it is everything as long as I get to it, as long as I get there, as long as it is at all physically possible for me. But at the same time a kind of fluctuation always takes place. There is always a core and always a periphery; this core changes, transforms into other cores. What was core becomes periphery; from periphery to the contrary we also choose new parts of the core—and so it goes, on and on. In this fluctuation always is maintained something like a unity; in this fluctuation is maintained unity of all those things that are capable of showing themselves to us. From all this, at the same time is evident, that in our judgments we are never free to posit whatsoever at all, that it is not a matter of free will. Only in certain circumstances am I able to consider something as doubtful, as probable, and so on. When I see, when before my eyes I have what I see as visible—it cannot be other than present. Only that which is not present can also eventually be doubtful, and so on.

And this means another deepening of the thought about the general thesis: no individual thesis is, so to speak, free. Every individual judgment can only be modified under certain circumstances, and it can always only be modified by advancing another thesis. This means that every judgment is somehow justified and that experience is the connection of this justification. Our manifesting is justified manifesting. It somehow has its own inner "logic," "structure." That it has logic I say in quotation marks. You know that structure, logic, these are exceptionally uncertain words. In the end it seems that manifesting forms a certain solid interconnected system. So, to say with Kant, there is something here like a unity of our experience that has its own solid framework. Experience—what is present here in this kind of perceptual presentation—has its own structure. It is what is present here that is in unity with what is not present, both are indispensable, and we simultaneously know about both, about this unity. This *unity* cannot come from experience; rather, it is the "structure" that precedes it. We have here something like a solid and *prior to experience* "structure" of showing.

So I might say: showing, that is really our experience. Except that when we say, it is our experience, we again run the risk that we will always place emphasis precisely on this "our," that we will say that it is something that takes place with us, and so we again run the risk of losing sight of manifesting as such, that it will again disappear.

For the moment we only know that much, that we have some kind of solid not-freely chosen structure, that we are determined by something, that every individual thesis we express occurs within the framework of the universal thesis. So it seems that the manifesting of the world is the last fact that we simply have to take into mind. We are forever moving within its framework, we cognize within its framework, we act within its framework. But do we already know what manifesting is when we realize in this way that it has its own precise laws and its own precise structure? We were a little on the right track after this manifesting—I mean back when we said: the same appears to us in various ways of givenness. But are not these various manners of givenness also our own, let us say, states?

Look, when I go out into the hall and perceive different things, my previous perceptions are changed by my recollections. In the first instance I have perceptions; in the second I have memories. From these perceptions and memories together, when I ascertain some of their agreements and differences, from this then follows just what I am calling manifesting. Is this the phenomenon of manifesting? Has this taken us to the heart of the matter? On the one hand, I have perceptions; on the other, memories. Then I can imagine, then I can daydream, and these I can compare, and on the basis of their accord say: a thing showed itself to me. Is manifesting this connection of my states? In a certain sense, my states are important here, fundamental. But are these states manifesting? Or is manifesting their characteristic, is it their aspect? What is the accord or what can even be found in common between two states like the mere awareness that outside there are some coats, hangers, and so on, and the present perception of these things themselves? From the outside, where is there any agreement? Is there something within one of my states and another mutually similar, in agreement, that we could abstractly extract?

What I am constantly explaining here has one sole purpose, that we realize that manifesting in itself, in that which makes it manifesting, is not reducible, cannot be converted into anything *that* manifests itself in manifesting. Manifesting is, in itself, something completely original.

In what then consists manifesting as such? Do not think that I will now pull it out of a hat, I should only want that in these trivialities I have put before you, we encounter a certain core of the phenomenon as such. We were on the way after the phenomenon there where the same thing was manifested to us in various manners: *that is in various ways of givenness.* A chair as present here in one case, in its original, in its full perceptual givenness, in the other, a something merely together-given.

There are other, no less urgent phenomena. When we speak, by speaking we constantly mean some things. When we speak, we know what we are talking about, without graphically imagining these things, and also without actually having these things before us. Nonetheless we know that we are speaking about these particular things. Speaking is showing of its own kind; it is a showing-at [*poukazování*] but within showing-at there—obviously—is showing. Speaking is connected fundamentally with perceptual manifesting, for speech after all points to things, and mere opinion about things is in a certain way their inadequate and not-independent *givenness.*

Now this is important: in our daily life showing is the ground upon   × ✶ which life constantly moves, but at the same time *showing as such* does not in the least bit *interest us.* We are interested in things after all. They interest us in what, which, and how they are. We are interested in *what* shows itself—in our practical orientation and in our cognizing. Neither knowledge nor practice—we have already spoken of this—are possible any other way except when something shows itself, but at the same time we are not aware of this showing either in practice or in cognizance. For this reason, whether we learn of things outside us, or whether we learn about ourselves, *we never know about showing.* Showing, phenomenon, that on the basis of which things are for us what they are, is itself constantly hidden from us. For this reason, in knowledge about things, in science, whether it is science about nature, about the structure of things or science about physics, psychology, or science about human behavior in society, sociology—there is nothing about showing as such there.

In what way can we get a grasp on manifesting? How to get to the nub of this most important thing—that thing on the basis of which only then can we have something like truth and error—because manifesting is the ground, without which truth and falsehood do not make sense. If man is most deeply determined by the fact that he is the creature capable of—in contrast to all else in the world—truth and falsehood, good and evil, from what we have just talked about it follows that neither objective nor subjective science, neither science about objects, about the subjects of nature, neither science about ourselves as beings, will tell us anything about manifesting. Nonetheless, I have to say that from the most distant past to our present day, nothing has been such a cause and axis of human questioning about the nature of things as manifesting.

From what I have just said, does it follow that manifesting cannot be the object of any actual knowledge, that it cannot be the object of a strictly conceptual analysis, or that there does not exist anything like a science of manifesting?

It has not yet been settled by what I have just told you—that it is not from science about existents as such neither those objective nor those that regard human existents. Naturally, it is also not in any way proven, it is *in suspenso* for the moment. But should this problem be solved in some kind of way, then manifesting as such must be researched somehow systematically. In these last sentences I have indicated why this is so terribly important: the entire essence of man, the whole question of his distinctiveness and his possibilities is connected to the problem of manifesting.

What is truth? And is man capable of truth? You know that people died for truth, that they gave themselves the task of living in truth, to judge an entire life against truth. If truth is the manner in which things manifest themselves, of how they are, *how is manifested the very nature of things*— then naturally these human peaks, this fundamental possibility of man coincides with the problem of manifesting.

I said that from the very beginning of explicit reflection about the whole of the world and about human life within it this problem has really been the center of attention. And I would like to point to one contemporary effort to bring this problem to the stage where it might be ripe for solution: Husserl's attempt at phenomenology, the science of phenomena as phenomena, of manifesting in its essence. And now the most important thing, be careful, why do I want to take my point of departure from this modern attempt? Because you will see much more expressly in it rather than in those ancient and historical attempts, the specificity of looking for the nature of existence as such. Historically this problem was always begun in some way, in some way perceived, but never was it distinguished with this kind of energy from that other, the problem of what and how are things that manifest themselves, that appear to us.

I said that we want to find an approach to the problem of the care of the soul. Now I can say it more precisely: the conceptualization of the soul in philosophy from its Greek origins consists in just *what is capable of truth within man*, and what, precisely because it is concerned about truth, poses the question: how, why does existence in its entirety, manifest itself, how, why does it show itself? Is showing only a contingent occurrence in the world, just as it is contingent that there are red and white roses, or is there something like human destiny and human task here, that it is possible to encounter or miss? Is not manifesting, light in the world, something that distinguishes man from all else, and is not the consequence of this manifesting, which is after all in a certain sense the human privilege, something that also places duties before man? Care of the soul is fundamentally care that follows from the proximity of man to manifesting, to the phenomenon as such, to the manifesting of the world in its whole, that occurs within man, with man.

But if we now turn to the contemporary attempt to grasp the phenomenon as such, then first of all I would like to point out this particular important element: this attempt to grasp the phenomenon as such, the attempt to grasp the appearance in its phenomenality begins with Husserl saying that if we wish to grasp the phenomenon as such, then we cannot persist in our ordinary dealing with phenomena; rather, we have to entirely and radically change our whole stance.

How do we commonly deal with phenomena? We said that the phenomenon is everything for us. In the domain of cognizance, our dealing with phenomena seems as if we use them to get from one to another and so that on the basis of this approaching from one to another we get, as it were, to the nub of things. Like when I want to go and get my hat or my coat, I use how my immediate surroundings orient me to get to the entranceway, there I then see what is there, take my hat and so on. In this way, we essentially operate in our reality all the time. We use one experience to get to the other. But we are not interested in *how* we get from one to the other. We are not interested in *how* is it possible that, in various manners of the given, unity is maintained. How is it possible that from one concrete surrounding I move to another and there I carry out what must be ascertained and so on. All this does not interest us. We are interested in what is, for example, over there in the entrance way, what is in the test-tube, what is the result of such and such an act, and so on.

In what way is developed the revealing of things, that is the same in various guises and that cannot manifest itself other than by these various guises—in this consists the phenomenon of phenomena. A thing never is, so to speak, just there before us as a block, like some kind of given—this does not exist. Givenness in the sense of an opinion that lights up before us—it is not like this. *Existence* is given precisely *through phenomenon,* but *through phenomenon* is given *existence.*

This is an important thing. Husserl expresses it when he says: we use our phenomena, and that means our judgments, our beliefs about things as a premise. By this he does not mean the premises of syllogism, but rather thinking conceptualizations or thoughts that we use to acquire other thoughts, experiences, and so on. But we are not interested in the fact that at the same time we still presuppose the manifesting of things in various forms as the same. How do we get to this?

The first condition is that we exclude and are not interested in the attitude toward thoughts as only of instrumental use, as ready-made tools to acquire more and more experiences. It is not that we stop trusting these thoughts. Everything we have believed and experienced to that point—this room around me, its surroundings, the city, and eventually the universe— all this remains. All of my conceptual instruments remain—mathematics, individual scientific disciplines with which the world around us busies itself—all this remains. Rather, all this moves forward in this indicated manner; all this moves forward on the basis of phenomena into the depths of things, whereas we are interested in the *phenomenon as such.* Then we stop carrying out all this, stop living in these things, stop using them, and stop acquiring other similar things in the shape of natural phenomena, that means common things, judgments. What are we then to do?

I said that we are not going to doubt these theses. Our attempt is not some kind of skeptical one. We are just not going to use these theses; instead, we are going to *look at them.* We are going to look at their func- tioning as theses, as phenomena. We are going to look at *how* within these phenomena manifests what manifests itself, for example, the identity of objects in various manners of givenness. To this belongs the identity of objects from various sides, aspects, perspectives, and so on. What I am saying now is not some kind of thesis, but rather a *problem.* The problem is, for example, how is it that from various perspectives a chair manifests itself as one and the same thing? The problem then is: How is it that a present thing and a thing as not-present, or only alluded to in an indirect way of givenness, maintains its identity? This is the problem: in varieties of presentation, in varieties of presence the same is maintained.

So then you will ask me: How is this done?

Where will I find this answer? Understandably, I cannot formulate some kinds of conjectures, hypotheses. No, I just look at it, *look* at the *phenomenon as such*, which precisely consists in the creating of unity through various manners of givenness. Through determining how various manners of givenness are connected—through precisely this do I get the structure of the phenomenon as such. Of course, at the same time we naturally have to ask further: *What* allows for various manners of givenness at all, and upon what do they depend?

For example, we told ourselves, the core, the center of gravity of our sensory experience in which things manifest themselves most distinctly as they can show themselves, lies within a unity of possibilities. Or so we may say it entirely clearly: this room is the same for us who are in it as it is for the inhabitants of a house who are presently somewhere else. It is the same room: these things here, that table is one and the same for the person who happens to be looking at it and also for the person whose back is turned away, if he happens to know about it. Being turned away and being turned toward it presuppose some kind of structure that allows us all, so that in such absence under certain circumstances—we are concerned with determining what kinds of circumstances—we may determine the core coinciding with the core of possible congruence with this presence. But you see, who says presence and absence, he already says something else, he says: *time and place*. Presence, the present—this points to some kind of place, but at the same time it points to the present. Is the present possible in and of itself? The present is possible only so long as there is also the past and the future. The past and the future are present as the not-present. Any presentation, and that means any phenomenon, is not possible except on the basis, as we see, of some sort of structures of presence.

The phenomenon leads us to the structures of presence, to, as we see, *temporal* structures. But this is a peculiar time about which we are speaking here. Time—as we are used to speaking about it in history or in natural science—is a singular one-dimensional quantity in which a singular real moment is a present instant, a temporal point. But such a temporal point undoubtedly presupposes presence. It is not that the present about which we are now speaking is composed of these kinds of temporal points. A temporal point is comprehensible on the basis of the structure of presence, but not to the contrary.

What I have now told you is only a small specimen of that which with the science of phenomenon as phenomenon concerns itself. It seeks to find the structures on the basis of which something like the manifesting of things is only then possible.

Phenomenon, then, always presupposes presence. If something is to manifest itself, it has to manifest itself exactly here and now. To show itself means to come out of concealment, meaning there has to be a difference between showing and not-showing. And showing, coming out of concealment, then presupposes setting, a stage, on which only then things may step out. This stage is precisely presence as such. Presence though, as you see, is not composed out of instances, nor is it singular. In presence itself is something like *eminent presence*, and then there is something like *the presence of the not-present*. In the presence of the past, for example, the past is present like that which no longer can be present: and the future is present as such, like something which has not yet gotten to presence in the eminent sense of the word. What does all this mean?

We eliminated considering actualities, real things as such. Only when we eliminated reality as such and judging about realities as such, only when we eliminated the common use of phenomena for obtaining other phenomena and in them the structure of existence, and when instead of that we turned to the structure of phenomena as such, when we eliminated looking for the path to existence and its laws, its structures, characteristics, and so forth, only then were we able to grasp phenomena as such. Does this mean that we have found ourselves in some kind of entirely different sphere? Does this mean that we are in a different world? Does this mean that we will never get to things as they are in themselves? And instead of that we have only arrived at some kind of semblance, something in itself completely ephemeral, that has no material basis, something illusory? Have we given up investigating and searching for existence? But only through investigating existence can we find out something about existence—and have we put this aside in order to get a mere semblance, some kind of showing, and at the same time we do not know of what? Do we have some kind of philosophical will-o'-the-wisp that has gotten us somewhere into the clouds rather than into the heart of the matter, into the heart of existence?

Because we set aside a whole domain of investigating and examining existence as existence and its structures, this did not lead to that, that all this stopped existing. In fact we did not even stop believing in it, it only stopped interesting us, and we began to look in another direction. We cannot forget that the phenomenon is the very phenomenon of existence and should give us things in their existence-ness. Phenomenology, the science of the phenomenon as such, shows us not things, but rather *the way of givenness* of things, how to get to things, how to draw near to them, how they show themselves. But just *they* are the ones that show themselves. This then means: the world is two-sided. On the one hand, the world is the world of *existent* things, on the other the world of *phenomenal structures*— these also belong to the world. The world is not only the world that is, but also the world that shows itself.

This again seems so trivial and useless, but we saw that the world of phenomena, the world of phenomenal lawful order, is independent of the world of realities, of the world of actuality. It is never possible to deduce manifesting as such, as we said, either from objective or psychical structures. It cannot be done. At the same time, we also saw that manifesting as such showed itself to us in such a stance, in which we left reality as such to entirely run its course; we did not concern ourselves with it at all. This means that reality as such does not determine these orderings and structures at all; it does not come into consideration for them. The *universum* has this *unreal* side to it, which concerns how the *universum* shows itself.

If showing is to be a reality, then there has to be some kind of actuality here, to whose composition, to whose structure belongs manifesting as such. There has to be a kind of *real* being that cannot exist otherwise unless something manifests itself to it; but this does not mean that this real being is, so to speak, the creator of the phenomenon. No! The phenomenon as such is that which renders this being possible. The structure of the phenomenon as the phenomenon renders possible the existence of— what?—the kind of beings such as man.

But this is not enough. It is true that we will never deduce manifesting as such from the structure of real being. It is also true that we can never deduce any kind of reality from mere manifesting—from those kinds of structures as is presence and its givenness, various modalities of presence and so on—yet we know that actual manifesting is a fact. You yourselves are not any automatons, rather you are beings to whom reality manifests itself, existence manifests itself, and that in a certain sense in its whole. The world manifests itself to you—that is a fact. And if purely real structures—this means the structures of the material world, nature, spatial-temporal world of natural science—cannot tell us about manifesting as such, then still the opposite thesis is not valid, that is, the structures of the objective world would not be codetermined in a certain way by the structures of manifesting. In the kind of being that is man, this is absolutely clear. We also alluded that something like objective time presupposes something like *unobjective presence.* What time is will never manifest itself to us, will not be clarified from the purely objective world alone.

From these trivialities and banalities we got all the way to theses that I think are in no way trivial; they are, indeed, already too daring. What I have explained just now at the end is no longer phenomenology! *Phenomenology* as the teaching about phenomenon is the patient seeking in this nonobjective stance, in a stance that does not go after things, that does not use phenomena for the mere unveiling of things. But the phenomenon is, in fact, there to show us things; thus we go after this internal tendency of the phenomenon and lose the phenomenon as such from our sights. We lose it from mind and no longer have the possibility to get to it at all. Phenomenology realizes that the domain of the phenomenon as such is immensely extensive. This is not merely the domain of perceptual phenomenon; this is not merely the domain of analysis of how objects show themselves to us here, in our surroundings. This is not only the domain that shows us how, in perceptual givens, an object has to and cannot in any other manner give itself in the original. Rather, phenomenology is at the same time the domain of the examination of how, let us say, general structures of thought show themselves to us, how those near to us show themselves to us, and how society exists for us, how the past exists for us, and so on—all this is the domain of the phenomenon as such.

Underneath this, phenomenology then looks for the *presuppositions of the structures of individual showing*, the most ordinary and fundamental structures, those, such as is presence as such, the giving of presence in the most eminent sense of the word, temporal structures, structures of the most initial temporality—all this is the domain of phenomenology. What I have just told you about is already a certain *phenomenological philosophy.*

Phenomenological philosophy differs from phenomenology in that it not only wants to analyze phenomena as such, but also wants to derive results from this; it wants to derive *results*, as is said, that are *metaphysical*. This means to ask about the relation between the phenomenon and existence. You know that in phenomenological philosophy there is a superabundance of various conceptions: there are those kinds of conceptions that judge that the phenomenon as such is really just subjectivity of a sort, just life, experiencing of a sort. I suppose that this conception, this kind of phenomenological philosophy, is a not understanding, or a kind of slipping away from the proper problem of the phenomenon as such. The phenomenon must remain the phenomenon; it must remain an autonomous *unreal* region of the universe, which though it is unreal, in a certain manner determines reality. In what way? This is the question no science can solve, which is after all always within the framework of these naïve phenomena, even phenomenology that considers merely the phenomenon in itself: phenomenological philosophy can pronounce certain constructive hypotheses about this.

The phenomenon can determine objective being, the existence of physical things alone, in such a way that the phenomenon is somehow taken into account in their own structure and in the structure of their ordering. Not such the *universum* (whole) should be impossible without phenomena. The *universum* as a pure physical fact is within the framework of what is thinkable. At the same time, it is unnecessary and also not conceptually useful to think of the phenomenon as the purpose and meaning of this objective universe. Nonetheless, the objective *universum* is still somehow a priori determined, codetermined by the phenomenon, as it is possible to get something like the human being from the natural development of this physical universe or from something that is the proper concrete base of the physical universe. This is not a matter of some kind of immanent teleology or some kind of real factor that the phenomenon would realize with some kind of immanent purposiveness. The phenomenon as such does not have any strength; this codeterminacy has to lie in the very foundations of physical being as such.

From this relation between the phenomenon and existents that show themselves follows the peculiar situation of the whole. Existence—that which does not show itself—is undoubtedly the foundation of nature. Phenomena themselves lead us to this; phenomena themselves show us natural existence as something that is not itself something that shows itself.

Nonetheless the phenomenon as such shows us this existence at the same time as something that is lacking something. The *universum* without man, without mind—it is wrong to speak of mind, because mind comes into consideration for the phenomenon only as the *conditio realis*, a reality within which the phenomenon is realized, but that is not the phenomenon itself—is a universe conceivable without phenomenon, and that means also without mind and so on. The *universum* is in the end also the foundation of phenomena. The phenomenon is only possible as the phenomenon of the whole; and it is peculiar that the whole could be without phenomenon. But the very consideration that I presented for you here leads us to the conclusion that, although the *universum* without man and without similar beings, without mind and so on, is possible, somewhere within the foundations of the factical universe is a kind of *codetermining* of the phenomenon as the phenomenon.

This is at the same time a kind of peculiar and also precarious situation of man in the world. After all, man is a being, in whom is displayed on the one hand a predominance of the contingency of that not-manifesting universe and, on the other hand another side of the universe breaks through in man, it suddenly appears within him, it suddenly becomes real. Here is where we come out to our reflections upon the genesis of the care of the soul. For how we have been reflecting today, how Husserl reflected, and how we have tried to follow him—naturally man did not think in this way from the very beginning. Husserl's profound reflection about the difference between thinking about things and thinking about ways of how things appear, about phenomena as such, consideration about the difference between using phenomena to understand existence and using existence for the grasping of phenomena—that is something that required thousands of years of philosophical and scientific work. Clearly this was not there from the very beginning. But what was there at the beginning?

In the beginning this consciousness breaks through: that man as the exponent of phenomenon pays dearly for this privileged position in the whole universe. He pays dearly, for while he is conscious of the whole, that this totality shows and manifests itself to him, he also sees his own ex-centricity, that he has fallen out from the center, that he is only also a phenomenon, and a precarious phenomenon, one that of course depends on the rest of the world, and that as an ephemera. This consciousness—that man as the caretaker of phenomenon is at the same time the only creature who knows that its phenomenal domain has an end—is at the beginning of this entire reflection. An awareness that man is a creature of truth—which means of the phenomenon—and that this is his *damnation*—is already present in the mythical world, but not in every mythical world, not in all of them. It is in the mythical world at a certain stage. In the world of myths in the civilization out of which the Greeks arose this is the central myth. This is the meaning of the biblical myth of the tree of knowledge; this is the meaning of the myth of the cultural hero Gilgamesh and Enkidu; this is also the meaning of the myth of Hercules; and it is naturally also the central element in the Oedipal myth. All these myths have the same meaning: man is at the same time a creature of truth and this *truth is damnation for him.* Why? Because it shows his own precariousness, his place in the universe, which is overpowering in his regard. Of course, we have to imagine that in myths all this is not objectified. In myths there is not yet the kind of consciousness we have based on a refined natural scientific thinking about what an objective world means, what an objective nature means, and so on—that is not there, but this *problem* is there in this guise.

What is man to do with his situation, what is man to do in times of distress, in this *most fundamental distress,* that is not dictated by something external but that coincides with the very character of the universe?

The greatness—that which made Greek philosophy what it is and that which made it the foundation of all of European life—is that from this Greek philosophy developed a *plan for life,* one that stated it is not damnation, but *human greatness!* Of course, under certain circumstances: as long as we make this clarity, the phenomenon as such, the phenomenalization of the world, the placing into clarity—the program of all of human life. All this from looking-in [*nahlédnutí*]. Like in our thinking, so in our deeds, always to act with clarity.

Why is this such a *help* in times of distress, when after all mortality as such still remains here—this finitude and destruction of both the individual, the family, and so on? All Greek philosophy is always groping after something similar, which I have already indicated. Greek philosophy is always groping after that so it might show that the fundamental human possibility—this possibility opened up by the fact that we are at the intersection of phenomenon and existence—may leave us in the lurch so to speak, as far as the span of life is concerned. But precisely because (now I

will use my philosophical construct) the phenomenon and its lawful ordering is at the roots of the entire universe, man is not any worse off than the
being that would have the whole universe in its power, so long as it systematically pursues the phenomenon as such. Human life differs from the life
of the gods only in its quantitative dimension, but not in its essence: that is
the solution of Greek philosophy.

    This is, of course, only in possibility. This program presupposes a
fundamental transformation within man. What is told to us by myth is the
natural human stance. Human life is damnation, it is horror, because, as
Pascal said, "The end is always bloody, however famous the comedy may
have been."[1] This is the *natural* human stance. This is how it works,
so to speak, inside us when we surrender ourselves to instinctive self-
understanding, so long as it is not benumbed by consolations and fantastic
illusions. The Greek idea is the following: in just this situation it is shown
that man has *various* possibilities on the basis of this original situation.
Only then, in this situation, he has to prove himself; only then he has to
show himself as a creature who really does make phenomenon, that means
clarity, *truth the law of his life,* and with the help of this law in every domain
in which man is involved. *Given certain circumstances, man could make at
least the human world a world of truth and justice.* How this can be achieved
is the very subject of the care of the soul.

    The soul is that which is capable of truth on the basis of a peculiar, un-
transferable, only-in-man-realized structure of the phenomenon as such.
The soul is that to which things are revealed as they are, or that and what
they are. Our own being has to show itself to us by that, that the call, which
is encompassed within this situation, becomes for us also the impulse to
that, so that our own essence, our own being, our own being in that which
is its own, is revealed to us. We are also something that shows itself; we are
also existence that can show itself, but our own being can reveal itself only
as long as we understand that its core is the phenomenon as such, showing
as such, truth as such—and if we take hold of this. On the basis that he
stands between phenomenon and mere existence, man can either *capitulate
and degenerate into mere existence,* or he can only then realize himself as a
being of truth, a being of phenomenon.

    So this is the concept out of which grew not only classical Greek

---

1. B. Pascal, *Pensées,* ed. Brunschvicg, no. 210 (Paris: Garnier Freres, 1961).

philosophy but also Europe and our history. <u>*The history of Europe* is in large part, up until, let us say,</u> the fifteenth century, <u>*the history of the attempt to realize the care of the soul.*</u> We could talk some next time, if you were not too bored today, about how this looks *in concreto*, about how Greek philosophy shaped the care of the soul into two different express forms.

3

Phenomenology and Gnoseology—The Two Sides of Myth—
The Mythical Framework of Greek Philosophy

Last time I tried to describe for you the phenomenological conception of philosophy as teaching of the structure of manifesting as such. This
requires several explanations.

At first glance, it seems that manifesting is something like cognizance. Phenomenology understood in this way is a gnoseological teaching;
it is a theory of cognition. But as it is presented to us in its typical forms, a
theory of manifesting is always already an explicit teaching about *manifest*
cognition. Teaching about cognition, such as for example neo-Kantian
criticism, teaching of the neopositivists or critical realism, and so on, these
are all teachings that already presuppose the world is already in some way
revealed to us. But these teachings do not really speak about *manifestation
as such*, about the nature of the fact that things in their entirety manifest
themselves to us, and what this means. To the contrary, we can also say that
teaching about manifesting and manifestation as such still does not mean
that what it offers is any guarantee of cognizance and its foundation. It is
true that if we know the world, then it has to be, in a certain sense, manifest
and shown. But from the fact that we live in a world that is somehow clear
and manifest, that it is somehow revealed, that we are familiar with it, from
this it does not follow that we are cognizant of it. At most, from this follows that a path within it opens up through something like cognition. But
it also could very well be that we live in a world that is in some way
manifest, and yet—at least in its essential dimensions—not only *unknown*

but also *unknowable*. All these are problems only now coming into play. For this reason, as far as possible it is necessary to take care of a sharp distinction now.

The fundamental point of departure of gnoseology or the teaching about cognition, has the form of our thinking that we call judgment, because cognizance is an action that is concerned with truthfulness in the sense of concordance, in the sense of agreement of our thinking with its object. An action seizing upon a subject is in its elementary form a verdict, a judgment; that means, as you know, a very exactly definable structure of thought. It concerns a certain conception of predicative synthesis, usually subject-predicate, and this subject-predicated synthesis is something that *we* have to carry out *ourselves* by thinking. This is something created and shaped by ourselves through conscious and purposeful action. Judging creates judgment; a judgment does not exist without our judging. All our subject-predicate syntheses—all of our judgments—just as certain objective formations of our thinking, such as numbers, plurals, and so forth, are meaningful only in regard to certain of our own activities. All our cognitive activity takes place in systems of judgment and is thus the product of our conscious action, directed toward an end. This is cognizance.

But *manifesting*? Manifesting does facilitate our conscious activity. Conscious activities always have something within them, which on the basis of *certain forms of manifesting* only then is brought into syntheses; something like the perceiving of certain relations that are expressed in judgment, undoubtedly appeals to the level of manifesting and the manifestable. But the foundation of manifesting itself, the foundation of the manifestable—that the world not only is but also shows itself—does not result from any activity, does not result from this activity of judgment. The action of judgment must tie into this primeval fact, to the primeval situation that the world *shows itself*. For this reason there is a difference between, on the one hand, the manifestable and its opposite, which means its companion, not-manifestable, that belongs to manifesting as its correlate and, on the other hand, cognizance and unawareness, cognizance and its opposite. This first possibility of opposites is merely inadequate cognizance, that means a certain (privation) στέρησις; the other possibility lies in the synthetic activity of cognizance itself, which can either be right or wrong; there lies the difference between truth and error. In the realm of manifesting we also have a particular contrast, but not in the active sense of truth

and error, such as rightness and wrongness of judgment, but rather between manifestation and—what is the other term here?

It is not my intention to get into a deep explanation of phenomenology, but only in so far as it is a teaching about manifestation. The interpretation I have tried to give you about phenomenology is *not the orthodox
interpretation.* I again call your attention to this fact. The interpretation the
founders of phenomenology themselves give of phenomenology substan-
tially differs from the one I am trying to explain here.

Edmund Husserl defined his phenomenology as a teaching about the
transcendental subjectivity constituting the world and everything that is
encompassed by the world. What does this mean? I have explained Husserl's phenomenology to you many times, so I do not think I have to repeat
it. This difference, you might say, is merely terminological. After all, manifesting means that something manifests itself to someone. So some kind of
subjectivity is attendant upon it, and something appears to someone under
particular circumstances, the structure of manifesting is typical and lawfully ordered for every object. This ordering is just how these objects show
themselves with regard to subjectivity, and how they are outlined and
constructed, the very thing Husserl labels constitutive. The difference is
only semantic. Why are we so caught up in terminological differences?
Why do we not stick to the beautiful and tried-and-true formulations and
profound soundings of these problems by the master of phenomenological
analysis, unheard of profundity into the bases that escape everyday and
scientific views of reality?

We suppose that the formulation—that phenomenology is a teaching
about subjectivity, whether or not transcendental—*is insufficiently radical.*
In that aspect, it presents us with a definite existent, that means something
revealed, although very fluid and refined, instead of *the manifesting* of
existence. In our last explanation, we saw that just as in the beginning of
classical philosophizing in Plato, the following problem was always again at
the center of philosophical interest: What is phenomenon? How is it that
things show themselves? Again and again it was shown that instead of an
answer to the question what does manifesting mean, showing itself and so
on, we received evidence of some existent that is shown, that manifests
itself, that is the object of showing, but is not *showing itself.* That is also why
I suppose we have to lead the impetus to showing, to manifesting as such,
so far and so deeply so that we will not be stopped by anything that, as a
specific reality, could stand here and become a substrate of manifesting.

Manifesting has to emerge to us in its pure structure *without regard to any kind of reality*, to any kind of however refined reality that might serve as its underlay. The deepest and last of all philosophical explanations, the final answer to the philosophical question cannot be some existent. Rather *the structure of appearing must itself stand upon itself.*

For this reason I presume this most characteristic turn must consist in that very subjectivity itself has to show itself as something manifesting itself, as *a part of deeper structure*, as a certain possibility, which is sketched out in this structure and indicated as its component part. This does not mean that some kind of manifesting might be possible that does not manifest itself to someone. But it is not the case that this someone, that something would be its creator and bearer. To the contrary, the *bearer is that structure.* He or it, *the creator is the creation* to which is manifested that which manifests itself (existence), is the moment and part of this most fundamental structure.

While these last several remarks will not quench our thirst or dispel our hunger, because once we have seen this radical problematic in front of us, we should obviously like to throw ourselves into this direction and burn our way, so to speak, through this interpretation of phenomenology and take it up. Except that our task from the very beginning was something else, we did not give ourselves the task, as one might say, a supratemporal one. Instead our task was right from the start *supratemporal within time*; our problem was to *orient ourselves in our situation*, in the situation of our world, to pose the following question to ourselves: What might philosophy mean for us in this so characterized situation? We defined this position, or we tried to find its outline, by characterizing this situation as one of fall, ×× ×× decline that is evident in all things and that has so eminently demonstrated itself in our time because our entire spiritual sphere, built for two thousand of years and concretized in forms of state, law, and culture, that lived and ruled the rest of the world from the territory of Europe, in a short time collapsed. We live in a period following this collapse, and we live in an epoch of further and further decay of this past. We wanted to direct all our reflections so that philosophy would not be what it always has been and is—a fascination with the most amazing problems of which the human mind is capable and a pulling of our thoughts into this sphere. Metaphorically speaking, we are not concerned with the Platonic ascent from the cave, but to the contrary, with that second Platonic act—the *return back down into the cave*.

For this reason you might say this is all so illogical, for after all, first we have to get to what may clarify what philosophy is, its content has to be presented and unfolded for us, and it has to convince us, enrich us, it has to somehow fulfill us internally. Only then we can talk about a second act, of some kind of second task for philosophy. That is true. But *our reality*, to which we want to turn, which we want to understand, and in which we want to orient ourselves, is after all, at its foundation—and this is what I would really like to show—deeply *determined by philosophy*. Philosophy on its way out of the cave and on its way back down again carries out apparently two, although in reality *one and the same*, movements. We philosophize within the cave. And the philosophy we try to formulate in the impetus out of the cave is itself a part of the cave. This also means that the very *outcome* of this philosophizing is there, inside that cave. If we want to understand, or if we want to take philosophizing itself in its widest sense and meaning, we cannot do otherwise but respect the fact that philosophy comes out of a particular situation and then of course it can and has to return to this situation once again. So we leave aside the task of unfolding *phenomenology* before us as a real, systematically constructed philosophical problematic only for stylistic reasons. But we do not refuse this task, we do not jump over it; in a certain sense, we only *incorporate it into a context*, into which it belongs, which interprets it, and which allows that this context interprets philosophy itself. That is our intention.

First we want to demonstrate that this conception—the problem of *manifesting* and *manifestation*—is from the very beginning *the ground of all reflection* of European peoples reflecting upon their situation in a peculiar guise. Where reflection begins, where philosophy is still inchoate, not yet born, but we might say, about to be born, already there is our fundamental problem, already there it breaks through. It breaks through in the form of *prereflection*, which is myth—or at least in the form of certain particular and typical myths. Greek primeval philosophy, about which we are going to speak, and all of Greek philosophy itself, has a *mythical framework*.

I will try to work out this mythical framework a little for you. It is an enormous job, which I am not up to, for which you would need vast knowledge and a prerequisite philological and historical research that I can neither myself carry out nor even sketch out. Nonetheless, to a certain extent, it is possible to show *the basic mythical framework* in certain primeval fundamental facts of Greek philosophy, not only in the first philosophy but also in the classical, great philosophies of Plato and Aristotle, not to mention those following it, which are not in their fundamentals anything but their reprise, their repeating. As I have already emphasized so many times, myth is not something that mankind can shake off entirely and radically.

Please, I am not talking about myth in the now-carried-over sense of the word, myth in quotation marks. These kinds of pseudomyths, such as the "myth of the twentieth century," "myth of the general strike," or "myth of uninterrupted progress," and so on, are not myths in the exact sense of the word. These kinds of general, uncriticized, and uncritically accepted ideas, constructed out of or dependent upon ideological reasons, are useful cognitive motifs that pass themselves off as myths. They are often called myths in our present day, but this is not myth in the profound and radical meaning of the word.

As I am thinking of it, myth is something without which man can hardly live, not because of some kind of external need (which is just the ideological, when a human being somehow makes certain demands on reality, and so on), but because a human being cannot live without myth, because *myth is truth*. Real myth is truthful. And as long as a human being lives in truth—and it cannot otherwise, because man is a creature determined by its structure through manifesting as such and manifestation—then that first, radical, and still-*unreflected manifestation expresses itself in the form of myth*. For this reason, you see that myth never perishes in history!

Some positivists imagined that myth is a certain fantastical stage in human thought, as Auguste Comte says, a fictitious stage, followed by the stage of abstract thought, followed by the stage of reality, where man holds on to the given, massive reality, to which he can always appeal, to which he can always point, and which is by this evident, visible. Whereas myth—where there is some instance to which we can point—is always mere storytelling. And tales are told, and who wants to, let them believe them. . . .

In a certain sense, we still live in myth just because we live *in the natural world*, in a world that manifests itself to us. And the world as one that manifests itself—this is naturally *the whole* world. The world that I see from my perspective and in which in my period, my historical age, in my circumstances, I live, is the whole world, the whole world is the subject of experience.

But as to *the concretely experienced* world—notice this—what does it look like? This is, after all, your near surroundings, where, as we say, you are at home, where you have your own warm little corner, something like your own way out. There is something rather different there, something altogether distinct. In our modern world of university note takers, this *second* thing is rather difficult to take hold of. For we have become so rational, so abstract, that the sphere of the monotonous ever-repeating style of reality stretches out almost entirely all around us. But let me give you a little example. All of you have read *Grandma* by Božena Němcová. There you can get a good idea of what I am talking about.[1] This is a book written about one hundred and thirty years ago, describing a world that still existed until recently. When we read it, we still have the sense that we are reading something real. But there you see it, there is that *mythical* world, it is the description of the mythical world. There are two histories there.

One history of that which is *near*, true, and *everyday*; people are firmly rooted in the ground there. People are there in constant, daily, hourly, and every-minute contact with what is *good*, what is positive, and what *holds* when one stands upon it. It is what all people have accepted by and within themselves in some way, greeted it, and held on to it then in their joys and sorrows. He who holds on to this world does not go wrong.

You also find a protohistory there, another thing: a dark, *foreign*, hostile place, where lurks horror, madness, dark, indescribable *evil*. You know that Victoria's story is not told in its entirety, that is not possible, for in it lies something that is unspoken, because it is not possible to tell it, but it penetrates right into that other world.

These two worlds make up one entire world together—that is the difference. I use this example on purpose, I am not talking about ancient myths. This is a myth, this is the mythical world!—life space articulated in this manner.

In our rationalized imagination, this space is just what we are taught in school: the space of geometry and, at the very most, let us say, the space of physics and geography. But the concreteness of human life lies in this opposition. We do not live without this opposition. There is a whole host of these kinds of oppositions. The relationship between these opposites is *the problem of the mythical world,* which means of our life. The relation

1. Božena Němcová (1820–1862), *Granny: Scenes from Country Life*, trans. E. Pargetes (Westport, Conn.: Greenwood Press, 1976).

between these two terrible forces, between the power that accepts us into the world and the force that crushes and constantly threatens us—just think about all that is contained in this revealing.

On the one hand, we are given a warm, familiar world, that holds firm, keeps us warm, gives us sustenance although it is not comfortable, for we have to pay for it every day and every minute with hard, determined work and so on, and, on the other hand, that other horrible and somehow constantly present. While it is somewhere on the periphery, it can break through here at any moment. It is within all of us. Notice that history of madness begins with the most elementary things in our φύσις (nature), it begins where man flourishes and where he finds fulfillment. Suddenly something like that can break through in life everywhere. That means we feel that in our revealing as people there is constantly the element of what can drive us from one path to the other. We are left to blind wandering. Our human revealedness is the revealing of the world in its whole, but within it there is at the same time this element and this strange awareness of *problematicity*.

What is truly solid? Is this warm and near world that main power? It is near and holds just now—but is it *what* has the advantage, is *this* the victorious element? Or is it just provisional? *This is not revealed in that revealed world*! This is a problem, a horrible question present at every moment. You do see, after all, that the grandmother prays right from the first moment when she wakes up. This means that from the beginning to the end, she always has this duality present in her mind, it is part and parcel of the elements of her life. This most excessively sweet and most banal idyll that we can imagine in all our literature—in part *Grandma* is something like that—contains within it this element, this *mythical two-sidedness*.

And now imagine what I have just pointed to when the human condition is at its very beginning, when its power, strength, comfort, ability to manage in this world, all that makes this world manageable by us, is at its very beginning. Not in its completely elementary beginnings, that man would to that date be in dull half-dumbness, wasting away in half-animal life. Imagine it rather in a time of the first great urban civilizations of the Near East, where people began to construct a political life, a life of settled, no longer migrant societies. All around it, still the magma of half-settled neolithic life, which means nomadism, elementary agriculture with a mobile style of life. And there come into existence novel elements of life: there are cities there. If you think of the epic of Gilgamesh, for example, there you see this: the first thing Gilgamesh does is to build a city, the city that stands solid and firm, something that is not possible to move somewhere else. It is built with ascesis, with hard work. The entire style of life changes then, everything instinctive and elementary has to be broken and tamed. Men are taken from women, they become engaged in the service of an entirely different and differently hard passion: power, battle, war. But then arises a world much richer and more colorful, a life that has within it a much higher tension than the instinctual wasting away in which man is hardly aware of himself. Here is a higher consciousness of oneself, but not a reflected one. It is heightened precisely by this emotional tension, through passion, the holding back of all unrestricted instincts now in the man of discipline, ruling them, channeling them in one direction. In particular what becomes heightened is what characterizes mankind more than any-thing else: this consciousness of being threatened, a consciousness that while on the one hand we have much more that we can use and can therefore defend ourselves much better and, on the other hand, this very defense takes up so much space, that defense is to a large extent also offense, and this means that it constantly reminds us of the risk of death. This also means that this duality we saw in idyllic form in *Grandma* is formulated differently by the creative imaginations of these societies: in a manner of tension and tragedy. This, then, is the place of the birth of such peculiar myths, whose analogical source is the polarity we have already discussed—the polarity of that other, the strange, belonging to the night, and in contrast to the domestic, held fast, the daily, and the mediation between these two opposites. *This duality is at home in all myths.* This is not something that belongs, we might say, just to myths, but rather to myths, as long as it belongs to *the natural world* as the world of *good* and *evil*.

I have spoken so many times of these three kinds of myths that I will not be shy to talk about them one more time, the three myths that belong in some way to the first phase, from which, one day, arose Greek reflection. All of this is of course prior to the Greeks. I choose my examples haphaz-ardly. An ethnologist or a mythologist would do it systematically, but I just do it for the sake of illustration. The three myths that stick out and are particularly typical to my mind are (1) the biblical myth of the tree of knowledge and the tree of life; (2) Gilgamesh's myth of the search for eternal life; and (3) the Oedipal myth of blind wandering [*bloudění*] that is our own manifestedness.

I will just try to concretize my examples, these myths, and then I will tell you how I see the mythical framework of later Greek reflection. That will be enough for today. I will talk about the later development of the program of reflection next time.

Walter Bröcker analyzed the myth of the <u>tree of knowledge and the</u>① <u>tree of life</u> in a beautiful collection of essays in honor of Heidegger's sixtieth birthday, and his account is especially fine and profound.[2] He tells us that, as far as the version that we read in the standard biblical text, there are certain corrections there, in particular he considers it important to distinguish the prohibition of eating from the tree of knowledge from everything that concerns the tree of life. Why? Because the tree of knowledge is the tree of knowledge of *good and evil,* while the tree of *life* is the tree of *eternal life*, its fruit is eaten by the gods so that they may live forever, so that they do not die. The threat of this second tree is of course the threat that goes to the very core of life. <u>Man is revealed as the only creature in</u> the <u>whole world aware of this two-sidedness,</u> and this is what makes him special in comparison to all the rest. Only man knows this—apart from the gods. For it, for man, the world is revealed, uncovered. All these myths come from this duality, that this revealing is for man at the same time his damnation. All things are, and are in order. There is no division between them, no resistance against being, for within them is neither resistance nor not-resistance, within them is just so to speak mute agreement—from our point of view. But not so within ourselves, here there is this hard antagonism. What makes us what we are at the same time excludes us from the rest of existence. We are a creature that is not all right. This is awareness, awareness in the sense of the revelation of good and evil. Man—that is the creature to whom is revealed good and evil. But this revealing is at the same time—well, what? After all it was turned into sin, it became resistance to commandments, and this means that our *privilegedness* is simultaneously our banishment and our *ruin.*

Why is it forbidden to eat from the tree of knowledge, and why is the tree of life not guarded? It is unnecessary to guard this tree as long as the tree of knowledge is, so to speak, in safety. For only then, when man tastes the fruit of the tree of knowledge, when he enlists to revealing, which is a part of his being—only then does he begin to feel the desire for the apple of

2. W. Bröcker, "Der Mythos vom Baum der Erkenntnis," in *Anteile. M. Heidegger zum 60* (Frankfurt: V. Klostermann, 1950).

eternal life, which god reserved for himself. The gods are those who are immortal—ῥεῖα ζώοντες—the easily living.[3]

Banishment from paradise is at the very beginning of this myth, not at its end. This myth tells us a dramatic story, something that is necessary to see not as a story but rather all together at once.

It is analogous in the myth of Gilgamesh. Gilgamesh and Enkidu are those two who do what has to be done in the service of their deities, the good, sun-god Marduka. On the one hand, we have Enkidu, the example of man torn away from what is merely animal. Enkidu is a man-animal who goes with the animals to the watering hole, who grazes with them, who becomes tempted to go to the city, and who then becomes Gilgamesh's comrade, his companion on his adventures, and his comrade in arms against the horrible powers of that other side, among whom, of course, the goddess of the one who desires is most important. There, in that region, what constantly threatens man, what threatens the everyday and profound human order, is summarized. The rest you know about, and all of you have experienced that it is the truth. There really is that eternal volcano rumbling inside us. And these two humiliate this goddess. But the goddess is a deity, a force, which has its effect from that other side over us and is necessary to pacify in some way. The nature of this peace is determined by the gods: one of them must die! And Enkidu dies. This is revealed to him beforehand in dreams and so Gilgamesh lives through his comrade, who is in part closer to him than he himself, lives that which is the destiny of every human being, and then begins the search for eternal life, the futile pilgrimage after it. In this episode, no discovery is made.

Myth is not any kind of consolation, it is not some kind of support, it is not any kind of irrational injection; this is harsh awareness, or if you like harsh revealing of our revealedness/nakedness [odhalenost]. This is myth. Just so is the biblical myth, it also is *without salvation.* Everything further extends to and builds upon this foundation. In this poem it is carried off in an amazing way. Gilgamesh goes through the whole world until he comes to that person who has survived the Flood—those cataclysms which from time to time rip apart and transform the whole world—and from him he finds out about the plant of eternal life, which is somewhere, not for people, but for special, let us say, half-gods. He finds it and in fact picks it,

3. Homer, *Iliad,* VI, 138.

but at the moment this deed is carried out, fatigue overwhelms him, and he falls asleep beside this plant. A snake comes, devours the plant, and sheds its skin—and eternal life is wasted on this creature.

The third myth I should like to talk about is the *myth of Oedipus,* ③ which has at bottom the same meaning and is decisive for us. Oedipus is the man who represents human revealedness [*odhalenost*], the human knowledge of good and evil. But he represents this awareness in its *dual meaning.* He saves his city from the horror of attack by a terrible monster, one that demands a daily bloody sacrifice, and with his answers to it, he forces it to break its own neck. At the very moment that he becomes king, when he comes upon the stage of glory, this savior is found to be the outcast, the very last of all outcasts who committed and carries within him everything that shakes and rips apart human society in its foundations: he is a parricide and has committed incest. What this myth shows, what was its entire intention, is the exact opposite of revelation as revelation itself: it is the blind wandering after good and evil. You know how amazingly ingenious is the formulation of this story in Sophocles' drama, and how in his conversation with Teiresias, the mouthpiece of the gods, of those who have absolute knowledge of everything, not just like man who knows only one side, or one part of things, Oedipus imagines he knows about the good, and in actual fact, that good of his is the very opposite. The ground upon which he stands, what seems to him solid, can at any moment show itself to be the very opposite. But Sophocles' Oedipus, in that caustic investigative dialogue between Teiresias and himself, reveals himself as what he is. This is what is most typically Greek. And of course, then Oedipus is necessarily bodily marked as he really is, that means as *blind and wandering.* He leaves banished from the community; but at the same time, because he is the one in whom was shown this whole mystery of human revealedness, because he is this two-sided creature, of dual-meaning, a creature who is both damned and *sacred.* And from this, the meaning of his end, his death and his grave.

Why do I suppose that there exists a *mythical framework* in Greek philosophy? I will spell it out in detail next time, but here is roughly what I should like to say: Greek philosophy arises from the very beginning from the *primeval situation of human revealedness,* from that, that man is the creature who lives within the revealedness of the whole. The uncovering of the whole world by Greek philosophy is the continuation of this myth. Of course it is a great rendering, independent of this relation to the whole. But we still find in Greek philosophy this dual sense we spoke of above. Greek philosophy creates a relation to the whole that is not ordinary; it wants to penetrate behind the ordinary blind wandering, or behind the ordinary unclarity and unawareness in which we move, it wants to penetrate behind that we turn away from this revealedness. For that reason, there is great clarity about the whole, and for that reason the dictum of the ancient thinkers about that—as Heraclitus says, "What is common [that is, this whole], about this most people do not know even before they find out what this book shall say, and not even when its teaching reaches them" (fr. 1)— whether they find out or whether it is before this finding out—for them it is the same. But he, the philosopher gets into that condition, penetrates where Oedipus lies after his terrible experiences. With the strength of his mind, he breaks through to the other side. He holds together these two sides. What two sides? Those two sides of the world of our revealedness that belong together like day and night. Heraclitus' teaching lies in just that: *to hold these two things* that are separated otherwise, constantly *together*. This is that ἁρμονίη ἀφανὴς φανερῆς κρείττων—the unapparent connection is stronger than the apparent one (fr. 54).

It goes on. The investigating Socrates who constantly awakes from somnolence, is the continuator. And his fate is, after all, that kind of fate: the fate of sacrifice, which so to speak, necessarily has to be paid for by that looking-in to which it bids upon human beings.

The other thing is the grand philosophical project, that is the state of justice, where those like Socrates can live and do not need to only die—this is after all something that is also already built upon this foundation. What does it mean?

Here, after all, are laid the first foundations of human thinking about the state and about justice. This thinking about the state and justice comes *into reality*, after all, it is built together by later communities, it is built together in the Roman effort to turn itself into the state of right. And when it is not successful, it is created in other efforts, so that the state will be only under the light of justice and truth that is not of this world. But that is already the story of the historical construction that we call Europe. It grew out of this.

4

Clarity and Blind Wandering [*bloudění*] in the Mythical World—
The Birth of Philosophy as the Explicit Question Face to Face with
the Original Manifesting of the World—The Pre-Socratics

Last time we talked rather generally about myth. Yet we did not talk
about what myth is; nor did we discuss theories that have been created in
order to somehow clarify for us the phenomena of myth. No doubt, it is
one of the most difficult problems of the relevant sciences and also of
philosophy. I also do not pretend to give you some general theory about
myth. We are concerned with the idea of myth and the mythical picture of
the world only insofar as philosophy and philosophical reflection has in its
original form and in its successive development something that can be
called a *mythical framework*. Philosophy does not begin *ex abrupto*; it does
not come into the spiritual world where it merely fills in some kind of
empty space. Rather, it comes into the spiritual world where there exists
something that both helps and hinders its origin and development. It
hinders before it helps.

Otokar Březina once said the following peculiar phrase: in conversations we have with ourselves, the answers are given before the questions,
and the answers are always eternal and the questions wait for their proper
time.[1] These are deep and essential words. Philosophy is unthinkable without questions. But to develop or pose a question means precisely to find an
explicitly empty space, to find something that in a certain sense is not here.
But myth already occupies in some manner the whole world, it has already

1. Otokar Březina (1862–1929), essayist and poet, is representative of the
symbolist movement in Czech literature.

elaborated something like a whole notion, an entire picture of the world. Indeed, it can be said—and there are philosophers who also develop it like this—that myth is precisely this first elaboration of something like a *picture of the world in its entirety*. The first elaboration that is not yet capable of drawing any distinguishable line between itself and the world, not only between itself and the world but also between the world of understanding and the world of imagination, merely given, merely captured in imaginative variation.

Thus, answers are genuinely given prior to the questions, and this obviously hinders the development of something like philosophy right at its very origin. Yet, philosophy in its positive form has to have something that it can tie into, it has to have some kind of means, with the help of which it can place its questions and with the help of which it attempts to answer them. It cannot draw these means from that which is not, from itself, but rather from what is. Understandably it draws these means originally, primevally, from the very world of myth, even though it fundamentally changes their meaning.

As an example of what philosophy judges about myth and mythical thinking, I will read you a little passage from Ernest Cassirer from the second volume of his *Philosophy of Symbolic Forms*:

From the first most primitive appearances of myth it becomes clear that they are not merely the reflection of reality, but rather characteristic creative elaborations. The spirit poses its own independent world with regard to the factical world that surrounds it and rules over it. Ever more clearly and ever more aware, it confronts the strength of impression with the active strength of expression. This creation however does not yet have the character of a free spiritual act, but rather has the character of natural necessity, of some kind of psychological mechanism. Just because of the fact that at this stage there does not yet exist an independent self-conscious I, free in its reactions, because we are here on the threshold of the spiritual process which is destined to distinguish between I and the world, this new world, this new world of signifying has to be discovered by consciousness as a completely objective reality. Precisely because it signifies one of the first steps beyond that which is given, it takes on the form of the given once again as the product.[2]

I cite a philosopher with whose subjective philosophy I do not agree. I do not think that even the world of fantasy would not have an objectivity,

2. E. Cassirer, *Philosophy of Symbolic Forms* (New Haven, Conn.: Yale University Press, 1957).

in the sense of the presentation of something that is shown in contrast to those to whom it shows itself. I suppose that we see fantastic variations as objective because there really are something like objective elements here. You see that this author speaks about a spiritual process, in which the I itself occurs only then, the I itself has to be discovered only then, to discover for itself, so that it may draw a line between the original world and the world in its solely secondary and deficient manners of showing. All scholars agree on this, myth, on the one hand undoubtedly encompasses the expression of what might be described as the human or social world of a certain people, human group, certain society; on the other, it encompasses them in manners of fantastic varieties, always encompasses a whole row of specific themes, the meaning of which cannot be understood from individual myths, but rather only in comparison with other myths that are variations of the same themes, even in comparison with other myths that encompass certain overlapping and further extending references.

In this manner, and in an extraordinarily refined and often surprising way, modern structuralist sociologists analyze myths. They are near this sort of conception, which does not satisfy itself with the truth of common sense, that myth is fantasy, but rather they look for a certain material ordering within myth, a material structure that forms its own reality. They look for what shows itself within myth as its specific element and for that within myth which helps us get from our immediate surroundings, from the things of ordinary experience, ordinary need, to a capturing of the dimension of reality which transcends the immediate, above all sensible givenness, and heads toward capturing *reality in the whole*.

Last time I was saying that we were above all interested in myths in which the theme of humanity as reality shows itself, which has a narrow and fundamental relation to that, that the world manifests itself, that it manifests itself to us in its content and in its whole. This motive is captured in myths just in a mythical, and that means in a purely material, way. Manifesting itself is conceived within them as a certain domain, reality that belongs to the competence of certain existents, certain substances. Man appears in myths more as a participant in something that is in reality not his, that is not within the competence of his creative capacities, so that within the domain of manifesting he is really outside his own most proper possibilities. He is in some way let into it, allowed near it, but it is not really his, it does not belong to him.

In modern philosophers we sometimes hear that man is the being in which and through which takes place the breaking through of manifesting into existence, into the world of things. Myth understands this the other way around: man is the being that dares to penetrate into the domain that is not his, it breaks into somewhere, where from its origins it was really not at home. We exemplify this more closely in the myth of Oedipus, which we will examine several times more, and which is for us so important because we consider it the typical Greek version of the mythically conceived theme of manifesting, decisive not only for Greek poetical craft but also sovereignly important for Greek philosophy, as we will later try to indicate. I will not analyze it here in the version with which modern sociology is concerned. Modern sociology shows that the Oedipal myth originally belonged among the myths that were connected to particular cultic dealings, with what the French call *le bouc émissaire* which means the being onto whom certain societies transfer, which they weigh down with their own many and real sins, their own difficulties and which, so burdened, is banished from this society and, in this way, purifies it.

Last time I was mentioning how fundamental is the difference between *home* and *foreign*.[3] I pointed this out in a weakened and for us nearer form in *Grandma*, by Božena Němcová, in two histories, stories and counterstories, and tried to show how the two tightly coincide with another. The near world is the world of good, which is proven by a long tradition of human action in precisely tried and still repeated forms. Only within them is man capable of trust and living-at-home within existence, trust that does not disappoint. While at the same time, there is the constant threat of that which is unusual, not falling into these forms of rootedness, that which Germans call *unheimlich, das Unheimliche*, that is, what is *threatening par excellence*—the night element of the world. These two are in a close mutual relationship—the world as a whole manifests itself only in the form of this duality, which is in constant tension. This means that simultaneously even in the domesticated and the rooted there is the perpetual possibility of the breaking through of that other. At home there are elements of foreignness, precisely with which it is always necessary to make peace from time to time, somehow to reconcile oneself with them.

These two elements are shown, for example, in the Japanese life form and Japanese myths in an especially acute way. Japanese theater has a

3. The foreign = *cizina*, literally "the strange land."

peculiar phenomenon of wandering actors, who move from place to place and represent the element of the foreign, the vagabond, the strange within the rooted, basically traditional peasant world, old, not contemporary, rather Japanese society of long ago. In actual fact, these are weakened manifestations of this *bouc émissair*, the sacrificial animal, which takes upon it the particular function of representing that other and so to simultaneously purify from it the domestic. It is astonishing that in the Japanese world of myth there exists also a second instance representing the same thing on a higher level—rule, aristocracy, the ruler. He is also the representative of that which is not the every day, what has within it *fascinosum*, *mysterium, tremendum*, something before which man trembles, that is un- OTTO pronounceable, about which one does not speak, that is taboo and so on.

The Oedipal myth has within itself this element. Oedipus is, after all, the being who, so to speak, is here, although he should not be. He does not have the right to exist. The original oracle declared that the child was to be put to death, for with him is connected the fascination of the greatest horror, the loss of humanness in all its elementary foundations. This child should not be; it is to be annihilated.

All this is again sounded in a higher, poetically clarified form in Sophocles' version. There is that prophecy. What this prophecy means is important for us now. A prophecy, that is, after all, *clarity about what is.* Prophecy represents that which in reality is, things show themselves here in that which they are. And here we can see that the showing of things is not the domain of man but rather of the gods. Human beings do not *know*. Human beings are participants but in what sense? In such a way that they have wandered blindly into this world, that in this world about which the gods *know*, in which they are clear about things, man partakes, but as a *blindly wandering* one. He has lost his way there and so is constantly wandering.

Those who have mercy on the child blindly wander. Naturally all those who in some way come into contact with his fate blindly wander: his adoptive father, who deceives the child himself and who deceives himself and the others about what the child really is. They deceive out of good faith, out of their humanity, out of the goodness of the heart. For it is out of goodness that the shepherd did not kill that child. Of course, in Sophocles' version the thought of the *bouc émissaire* is no longer entirely purely executed: in several essential instances in this amazing drama—one of the most amazing ever—the child shows himself as an unruly being, without self-control, not mastering what is within him. In his behavior he legitimizes divine prophecy and divine knowledge. You know the scene: the moment when Teiresias first comes upon the stage, forced by public opinion, called by Creon, and provoked by Oedipus's more than brazen, importunate questions, and directly tells him that he is that damned one, Oedipus's reaction explodes from rage and all that hatred not only against Teiresias but also against Creon and all those around. This shows something about the essence of what grows here. This character is even more negative, for within it, through its fate is to be shown, what is the fundamental threat to humanity to be found within us.

Clarity is the domain of the gods. Man has blindly wandered into it, and man blindly wanders within it. Blindly wander those who had human sympathy for Oedipus, and blindly wanders within it Oedipus himself. He blindly wanders not only in the moment he commits those horrible deeds, first of all the murder of his father and then the marriage with his own mother, but also at the moment he apparently is completely victorious, when he frees Thebes from the kingdom of the Sphinx—and he frees it with the aid of knowledge, with the aid of enlightenment which he has, which the gods have inspired in him, which is not his.

This entire drama is, then, an illustration of the Greek wisdom, for us so often paradoxically sounding, that it is best of all not to have been born—but since this has already occurred, then it is best to return as fast as possible there, from whence man has come. For Oedipus it really would be better had he never been born or had he returned, following the prophecy, from whence he came. That is the motif of clarity. Clarity is something that *in reference to us* stands on the other side, and we have only blindly wandered into it. Our role within it is one of wandering.

Here we should recall one more modern mythologist, whose main work focused on classical Greek mythology, Karl Kerényi who tries to define myth as *founding*. It is often said that the function of myth, of fables, is to interpret or explain the origins of something. The etiology of myths is spoken about, that myths interpret, explain the origins of certain natural phenomena, human phenomena, phenomena of the moral world. But myth is something so immensely mobile, so terribly variable—as modern sociologists show—that it can accept with the greatest ease the most diverse kinds of functions. Etiological myth transforms itself with the greatest ease from the natural into the moral, and into myth reflecting certain quasi-historical phenomena and so on. Nonetheless, it has something to do with this fundamental. Myth founds in the sense that reality—which appears and reflects within it in fantastic guise—in a certain way *accentuates*, emphasizes certain things within it.

To explain with the help of storytelling, with the help of some kind of tale, help that tells of some kind of event—what kind of explanation is that? What kind of bizarre thought is this? If we take the myths of South American Indians—for example, how people discovered fire—there turn up characters such as the jaguar and the armadillo, and a story is told about how the jaguar took mercy on some little boy, and other things, which at first glance do not seem to have anything to do with the substance of the matter. Myth tells a history—why? And where is that etiological moment? It tells it simply because, because it tells it something like this: what now is, for example, that people use fire, is rooted in some kind of past, in something that *already* was here, that myth in its own manner emphasizes and on which it places certain accents. Precisely this can be called *fundamental*. It founds a certain custom, a way of life, the stereotype of our acting. A stereotype that obviously is capable of change. If we apply this to our theme of human dwelling in the sphere of manifesting, in the sphere where things not only are but precisely just where they discover themselves, show themselves, then this means that *the blind wandering* of man is *a fundamental trait* proper to man as such. Our manner of existing in clarity is just this wandering, but which is within the framework of a certain *clarity about the whole*, which *is not ours*, but which in our wandering we cannot wrench free from, and which determines the meaning and the path of this wandering in a way that is for us at first unfathomable. When it becomes transparent it is always exceptional.

The phenomenon of founding also means this: in its entire character, myth is rooted in the *past* dimension of time. The past dimension of time is from a certain point of view the dimension of not-actually real; it is the dimension of what is not actual. The entire mythical picture of the world, which myth really develops before us, is given in this dimension. In what manner, that is the business of mythologists' research. The structural study of myth often arrives at unexpected, amazing things. For example, Lévi-Strauss shows as the axis of certain mythical accounts what is apparently completely unrelated and for us at first glance entirely incomprehensible to the point of nonsense: the antithesis of what is raw, and what has been cooked, baked, and so on. This means at the same time the antithesis of the damp, the fresh, the cold and their opposites. With this is connected the antithesis of what rots and decays, and what is burned and turns into smoke. This is simultaneously to a large degree the antithesis between the world of culture and what is merely given in nature. In this way, when in the most various kinds of myths similar themes turn up, there arises something like a meaningful axis, allowing mediation between the greatest diversity and most distant dimensions of the world. The process, which we might label as a process of cooking, is able to mediate between heaven and earth. With this are then explained the most various folkloric beliefs and myths that have fallen into merely incomprehensible customs, as are for example the many customs of marriage. For example, in certain French regions, when a younger sister marries before the older, during the wedding the older one has to be on her guard that in a certain moment they do not put her on top of a hot oven.[4] Do you understand the connection? It is incomprehensible otherwise.

In my view, philosophy an entirely new possibility of the human spirit, a possibility that also did not have to be realized and in fact the majority of peoples, even the highly cultured, do not know it at all, originated in a shift to the actual present from the dimension of the past, which is the sphere of mythical fantasy, mythical, not distinguishing between being in the original and being in secondary forms, a certain kind of merely imaginative deficiency. Imagination is also existence, which is in some kind of way present, but it is a deficient form, not the form of its real, original presence. This means that the manifest which myth sees as the sphere of the gods, into which man has wandered, here becomes something that is not merely recounted, but what in the entire force of its stupefying presence *is here.* From the blind wandering of man into the sphere of clarity there arises the question: What is all this? Man really *is* in the manifest world in its whole and the manifest world genuinely is here as a whole, present here. We have experience of the world as the whole, even if we do not have it as the experience of particulars, from which, if you like, the world is composed. Just this manifest world is the problem from the very

4. C. Lévi-Strauss, *Le Crut et le Cuit: Introduction to a Science of Mythology,* trans. J. Weightman (Chicago: University of Chicago Press, 1983).

beginning. Ordinarily it is said that the first philosophy asks itself for the ἀρχή (principle) in the sense of some kind of fundamental element that in its certain variable possibility, that means the possibility to move in a certain sense, differentiate itself and then forms the ordered whole we call the world. But then things are spoken of which themselves do not have any manifestation in themselves, *manifest things* are spoken of, but not the manifest world, the world that shows itself. For philosophy in its beginnings it is characteristic just that it asks its question face to face with the amazing *primeval fact of the manifestation* of the world.

When Plato says θαῦμα ἀρχὴ τῆς σοφίας (wonder is the origin of wisdom),[5] and Aristotle speaks of how people started to philosophize διὰ τὸ θαυμάζειν (it is owing to their wonder),[6] out of wonder, amazement—this is what they mean. There is no amazement in myth; myth is not in wonder about anything, it knows everything beforehand. Just for philosophy it is symptomatic that it *is amazed.* It is not in amazement about particular real things, but rather about this primeval reality. This clarity is clarity about the fact *that* things are, that the manifest actualities are in the world before us and that, as a result, philosophy always has to take an interest in these actualities as such, and that it wants to reveal them in their *existence and structure.* To reveal them in their structure, in their existence, that is a problem that is also fundamentally different from all that myth does. For myth does not even dream that it would be possible to justify something, explain it, answer the question "why" in any way other than through some kinds of stories. But what does it mean to recount these stories? What is the answer? What is, is because it already was. There is nothing else to it. Once two went hunting and during that opportunity something important happened, maybe they brought fire home—and that was the end of it.

Philosophy has to find some kind of different way—and this is terribly important—yet what is interesting and fundamental in philosophy is that from the very beginning it sees these two things: *something shows itself, and this showing itself.* It is not always able to distinguish them with entire clarity, but it sees them both. It sees this peculiar dual sense that in this way

5. *Theatetus,* 155d.
6. *Metaphysics,* A, 2, 982b, 12.

gets into some of our rather fundamental notions—that <u>the world, on the</u> <u>one hand, *is* and, on the other, is also *manifest*.</u>

This does not mean that philosophy was from the very beginning subjective. I am presenting this whole account to show you how it grows right from such an extreme materiality, how (in myth) there is the <u>primordial</u> <u>way of</u> showing this manifesting and <u>manifestation of the fall of man into</u> a <u>domain that is not his property, but is the property of the gods.</u>

It does not mean, then, that there would be some kind of element of subjectivism here, some kind of reflection into one's own core and to the processes of the experiences of the core. In this process of discovering, man himself is only then discovered, he himself is also *manifest as a part* of this world or as one of the things among other things. And there is proof, I think, that ancient philosophy cannot be understood only from the perspective of seeking after some kind of structure of things. Philosophy can begin to look for the structure of things only as long as the question of the *structure of discovering* has already first emerged. It is impossible the other way around.

Without this we will not understand the birth of philosophy. We will not understand (Anaximander's) pronouncement, which is the first preserved philosophical dictum ever, the well-known pronouncement that we have so many times analyzed, about which we have spoken so many times already, and which we, so to speak, will never finish meditating upon. It is not entirely authentic, but is as it was preserved by later authors. It says: . . . ἐξ ὧν δέ ἡ γένεσίς ἐστι τοῖς οὖσι, καὶ τὴν φθορὰν εἰς ταῦτα γίνεσθαι κατὰ τὸ χρεών, διδόναι γὰρ αὐτὰ δίκην καὶ τίσιν ἀλλήλοις τῆς ἀδικίας κατὰ τὴν τοῦ χρόνου τάξιν (<u>and the things from which</u> is the coming into being for the <u>things that exist are also those into which their destruction</u> comes about, in <u>accordance with what must be. For they give justice and reparation</u> to one <u>another for their injustice in accordance with the ordinance of time</u>). Authentic, is apparently, the part from κατὰ τό "according to necessity, for they mutually give themselves fines and revindication"—τῆς ἀδικίας (for their injustice), that is, a sort of ἀδικία, κατὰ τὴν τοῦ χρόνου τάξιν (injustice, in accordance with the ordinance of time). You see, here all of a sudden these kinds of things are spoken about. Also authentic is the word ἄπειρον (the unlimited). At the beginning of a long period, the author who cites this, places ἀρχὴν τῶν ὄντων τὸ ἄπειρον (the principle of the things that exist is the unlimited). Ἀρχή (Principle) is certainly a later expression, not one at the beginnings of philosophy, but probably from Platonic-Aristotelian philosophy. Ἄπειρον (The unlimited) is however, apparently authentic. Why ἄπειρον? After all, ἄπειρον is not any kind of substance, any kind of thing, whose structure could be analyzed, ἄπειρον would rather be some kind of characteristic. But why is ἀρχή (principle) said? The most characteristic foundation of all—that is, ἄπειρον (the unlimited). But where is ἄπειρον really? It is in that world manifesting itself, which shows itself, in that world we constantly have around us and within which we are. This world goes on into boundlessness; boundless is that without which nothing individual can show itself. "This" cannot ever show itself all by itself, but rather *in the surroundings* which always extend further and further away, and then finally—where? Within what is it all? Every thing has its outline, and this outline distinguishes it from others; other things then have their own outlines and so on it goes. We will never get to the end. We will always have a thing, and it will have an outline. Each of these outlines will always point further on. What, in the end, *facilitates* each of these outlines is ἄπειρον. Only in this way is it possible to understand this dictum, and it cannot be understood the other way around—that there is some kind of substance that has as its characteristic ἄπειρον, and so forth.

The whole is here in this character. Yet it is somehow present in each individual thing. This is what is precisely important, that is the διδόναι δίκην καὶ τίσιν ἀλλήλοις τῆς ἀδικίας (to give justice and reparation to one another for their injustice). Each individual thing—we have to look at this entirely concretely—not only does it come into being and then perish, but also each manifests itself in that another veils and conceals itself. After all, each thing passes from the near to the far, from presence to unpresence, from presence in its original to presence in solely deficient modes. And in this is ἀδικία (injustice), committed by the present thing in its suppressing all others. Ἀδικία is injustice, but here it is not injustice in the moral sense. The thinker does not have any other, except this mythical way to express the thing, which for him from the point of view of his questioning about the present as present is supremely important. So he uses the words ἀδικία (injustice) and δική, διδόναι τίσιν καὶ δικήν (justice, to give reparation and justice).

So that we might move a little further, let us also take some of Heraclitus's dicta. Heraclitus's dicta, as is well known, are direct imitations of the pronouncements of the Delphic Apollo. You know how it was in

Delphi: a priestess sat on a tripod above a fissure out of which came intoxicating gasses; she uttered all kinds of shrieks. The Delphic priests who listened then translated them into dicta, in connection with answers to questions posed to the Delphic god, the prophetic god, to whom appertained the manifest world within the mythical world. For this very reason the oracle can utter prophecies and send down prophetic dreams and so on, because for him everything is apparent in the whole, the world is manifest to him in the original. Heraclitus's book—at least what we know from it—is full of pronouncements of this kind. Of course the Delphic pronouncements are in verse—Heraclitus's are in extremely refined prose. They have, for example, all the double meaning of Pythian dicta, among other things even that when you change the interpunctuation—and interpunctuation was not used back then—you change the meaning. What does this mean? It basically means as much, that the thinker takes on the function the god had there: he is the one to whom belongs *the function of manifestation in its entirety*.

Of course, at the same time, he also knows that man blindly wanders, that man does not come into the world of manifesting as into what has always been his assigned home. People do not have clarity about the world originally. Blind wandering is genuinely characteristic for people. What Sophocles says about Oedipus—this is human destiny. And it is a fundamental reality that the world always shows itself only one-sidedly, and always from our private point of view. This does not yet mean from our *subjective* point of view. Privateness has its *objectivity*. There does exist something like the point of view of the king, the ruler, and something like the point of view of the subject; there exists the point of view of the warrior and the point of view of whom the warrior plunders. And all these are—as contemporary phenomenology says—specific, let us say free decisions, that give us a choice from what we see as fundamental in our surroundings, what calls to us and what does not. The world always shows itself to us in these aspects—this belongs to human wandering, we *do not see the world in its entirety*.

And now let us take Heraclitus who says: Τοῦ δὲ λόγου τοῦδ' ἐόντος ἀεὶ (and of this account [logos], which is the case always) . . . (fr. 1)—τοῦ δὲ λόγου—What kind of logos does he mean? Τοῦ δὲ λόγου τοῦδ' ἐόντος ἀεὶ— "Because logos is ἀεὶ, always . . . " This can be interpreted in many ways. Ὁ δὲ λόγος (and this account [logos]) may mean this particular book (this is likely a dictum with which Heraclitus's book began). This interpretation is also supported by the following: "For this speech however, though it is eternal"—or better said "perpetual," "eternal" does not really completely fit here—or better said "though it relates to something that is at all times, people do not gain understanding either before they have heard this speech, nor even when they have heard it." This means: they will not understand it, not before reading, not even when they do read it. "And all this occurs according to her, and yet everyone acts as a complete novice, as soon as they start to try such words and deeds, such as those I proclaim here, analyzing, taking apart each thing according to its φύσις (nature) and says how it is with it. Yet other people do not know about those who lie awake just as from them is hidden what occurs to them when they sleep."

Heraclitus then, διαιρεῖ ἕκαστον κατὰ φύσιν (dividing up each thing in accordance with its nature), this is the most important: κατὰ φύσιν (in accordance with [its] nature), according to φύσις (nature)—he divides each thing according to its being. The being of a thing is not some kind of eternal structure; this is being that shows itself, the structure of *showing itself being*. To him being shows itself actually, as it is, whereas all others who try to speak about things, show themselves as novices and as sleepers, this means unseeing. For them things are not manifest in their φύσις, meaning in that which forms the whole from them. Everyone sees in the way we see only in dreams. And in dreams we always only see something partial, derivative, secondary, inauthentic. Here, what Heraclitus pretends for, is the *whole*.

Even with other dicta, for example τὰ δὲ πάντα οἰακίζει κεραυνός (lightning rules all things) (fr. 64), that lightning rules all things, it is not correct to understand from a material point of view that this concerns the structure of some thing. The guiding idea here is κεραυνός (lightning)— the flash, manifestedness.

We could interpret the first dictum forever. Let us take, for example, λόγος—here this word means the book Heraclitus is writing, but at the same time it is the λόγος about which we have spoken so many times, which consists with the λέγειν (to say, to collect) and with the Latin *legere* (to put together, to join). To join what is in reality πολλοί (many), those many, the disconnected, what is only fragmentary there, what is seen there only from their private points of view.

And further there is that peculiar dual sense, that it is possible to read τοῦ δὲ λόγου τοῦδ' ἐόντος ἀεὶ (and of this account [logos], which is always the case) or ἀεὶ ἀξύνετοι γίνονται ἄνθρωποι (men always prove to be uncomprehending), that is, according to where we place the comma. Just like in the Pythian dictum: *Ibis redibis non morieris*, depending on where we put the comma, after *redibis non* or before *non morieris*. So then we may translate here: "Because this λόγος *is*, perpetually incomprehending remain the people." Or, though this λόγος is *eternal*, the people remain incomprehending."

At first glance this seems to be just a dual expression of the same thing, but Heraclitus wants us to weigh both of these expressions, so that from them we understand two sides, or two parts of the same thing, on the one hand, *the being of* λόγος, which is that which it properly is and, on the other, its *constancy*, despite the fact that clarity in its entirety exists, that the world not only exists but also that it shows itself as a whole, people still remain within limits, and necessarily within the limits of their own private approach to individual things within it. We do not step out of our own particular world just by the fact that a philosopher comes and says: *Private* worlds are only part of *one* φύσις (nature). Nonetheless, precisely here is shown something extraordinarily essential, that is, the manifestedness of individual things is something deeply distinguishable from the manifestedness of the whole. The manifestedness of the whole—it, after all, *stands still.* Just because we never have the whole as such before us as a thing, just because the whole is for us always something *outside* the center, in which we have things, for this very reason in the entire changing of manifesting and showing of things, this whole remains standing still. Just as the horizon remains even when things that surface within it and fall back into it again are constantly changing, so it is with this manifestedness of the world in its entirety: this "in its entirety" stands. There is the ἀεὶ ἐόν (the always existing); there manifestedness shows itself such as showing once and for all. Whereas individual things—there is δίκη (justice) and ἀδικία (injustice), and the whole process of showing from up close, from afar, and so forth, all this, that we know.

I cannot lay out all of pre-Socratic philosophy one more time, I only hope that in some of the indications I have presented before you today, you see where our explanations from pre-Socratic philosophy were headed. And to this fundamental difference of being, Eleatic philosophy then appeals in a positively crushing way.

Eleatic philosophy tells us: negation can never be applied to the whole, τὸ ἐόν (the existent, what is), the "no" cannot be applied to it. If you like, "no" is only within the world. But τὸ ἐόν (or, the being of existence) is just that whole, and as a result the "no" does not exist here. Eleatism concentrates only on this element, that in such a way is everything within everything. It is not possible to apply any negation here—that is the fundamental path leading the researcher into the center of unshakable truth, into the center of ἀληθείης ἀτρεμὲς ἦτορ (the unmoving heart of truth), into the unshakable heart of the truth. And from this point of view you also comprehend why Parmenides says, or better said why the goddess tells Parmenides—this is again terribly important, this mythical objectivism—he comes to the goddess there, she gives him her hand and with this brings him into the realm of truth, into the realm of the manifest whole and at the same time tells him, "but now you will comprehend everything ἀληθείης εὐκυκλέος ἀτρεμὲς ἦτορ, the bounded unshakable heart of truth, ἠδέ βροτῶν δόξας, ταῖς οὐκ ἔνι πίστις ἀληθής but also the opinion of mortals, to whom does not belong any kind of πίστις [trust], any kind of trustworthiness." Here showing is in all its extent, manifoldness and so forth, in individual things, in actualities here; one part of the poem is about this and rather naturally this duality is explained. However, he does not call this being, those are βροτῶν δόξαι (opinions of the mortals), this is ὡς τὰ δοκοῦντα χρῆν δοκίμως εἶναι διὰ παντὸς πάντα περῶντα (how what is believed would have to be assuredly, pervading all things throughout), how appearance went through all of existence, penetrating it throughout.

Only the Eleatics Parmenides and Zeno thus proclaimed as only existent what is *always the same*, what shows itself as always the same. Only then, from that point of view and taking into account what other Greek thought had created, which in that period was already so actively unfolding, that is Greek mathematics, only then developed something like the capturing of existents in their own proper internal structure. This came out from this only then.

From this beginning, which I have tried to show, where one begins with the problem of the world, how it manifests itself, how it shows itself, how it unfolds before us, and from the question "what is this?"—this question in and of itself would want an explanation and explication, because it encompasses elements that in and of themselves are not clear after all. What does "to be" mean? What does it mean to say this "what is"? How does it differ from the question "why is?" and so forth? I have already spoken about the dual sense of certain concepts with which nascent reflection upon the world in its reality had to count, about the two-sided meaning with which it begins. Two-sided meaning, for example, furnishes the concept of motion. Motion is, on the one hand, a worldly reality, a reality in the world, that is the passage from a certain enduring object through a continual row of spatial and temporal phases, or if it concerns the process, then also qualitative and temporal phases; on the other hand, motion is, after all, also manifesting. Motion is also the passage through these peculiar phases of manifesting, of approaching and receding, coming into presence and leaving from presence.

This dual sense is proper to a whole row of elemental concepts, questions and answers, and for this reason, from this primeval beginning is also born a *dual* movement of thought, which has many points of contact, but which is in its entire essence double, dual, and is in its strongest guise represented by the pair of chief names in Greek philosophy: Democritus and Plato.

Democritus, first with all consequentiality (it is not a question of primacy but of this consequentiality) and in a grand manner (so that Aristotle was able to say about him that he first wrote about everything, about everything that is at all) set out on a quest for the whole, that means after what is eternal, in such a way that he applied this eternal to reality in the world by means of mathematics and geometry (which equally sees everything that it sees as once and for all unchangeable, eternal). In this way, Democritus created the concept of philosophy as *science*, and if you like, as a system of scientific explanations. For Democritus the meaning of philosophy is the structure of existents in the world. And naturally, during this, he is interested in the *eternal* in them. The eternal—what is it? From it comes the concept ἀρχή (principle), not that it is called that in Democritus, but the foundation of the thing is there. Ἀρχαί (the principles) are two: ἄπειρον (the unlimited)—this is the empty geometrical space, homogenous, isotropic, and so on; and τὰ ἄτομα (the indivisibles, the atoms), which are able to move within it, but in themselves are completely unchangeable, eternal, and for this reason form the foundations for possible constructions.

Also for Democritus, man got himself into the world of truth really

by losing his way. Human beings do not know. One such of Democritus's)
pronouncement was preserved, and Sextus Empiricus cites it: Γιγνώσκειν
τε χρὴ ἄνθρωπον τῷδε τῷ κανόνι ὅτι ἐτεῆς ἀπήλλακται (a man must know
by this yardstick that he is separated from reality) (fr. B6)—"on the basis
of these explanations, these reasons, it is possible to notice, that cognizance of ἐτεῆ [in reality], the truthful, of that how things really are, is
foreign to man, he is alienated from this." Similarly, other fragments:
Δηλοῖ μὲν δὴ καὶ οὗτος ὁ λόγος, ὅτι ἐτεῷ οὐδὲν ἴσμεν περὶ οὐδενός, ἀλλ'
ἐπιρυσμίη ἑκάστοισιν ἡ δόξις (this argument too shows that in reality we
know nothing about anything; but for each of us there is a reshaping—
belief) (fr. B7), and Ἐτεῷ μέν νῦν ὅτι οἷον ἕκαστον ἤ οὐκ ἔστιν οὐ συνίε-
μεν, πολλαχῷ δεδήλωται (now that in reality we do not grasp what each
thing is or is not in character, has been made clear in many ways) (fr. B10).
In Democritus it is often stated that φύσις is ἐν ἀβύσσῳ, that truth is
concealed somewhere in an abyss. From this sum, Karl Marx deduced that
Democritus has within him a skeptical element, in contrast to Epicurus,
whom Marx so raises over Democritus in his doctoral dissertation. (Marx
wrote a very interesting dissertation on Epicurus that is still very worthy
of reading.[7])

The most ingenious move in Democritus's thinking lies in this: just as
Heraclitus says, most people, the normal human being is (ἐτεῆς ἀπήλλακται
[separated from reality]), but the philosopher can carry out such a deep cut,
which will convert all of reality from the motion of manifesting into
constant manifestedness, which consists in that, that we penetrate beyond
the region of what is visible in the ordinary sense of the word. And geome- 2
try teaches us how we shall penetrate beyond the region of what is visible.
For example, in the teaching about the similarity of figures. Anaxagoras's
pronouncement is familiar, ὄψις γὰρ τῶν ἀδήλων τὰ φαινόμενα (appearances are a glimpse of the obscure) (fr. B2a), what is unclear we see through
τὰ φαινόμενα (appearances), through what shows itself. When I draw a triangle in the sand, then I demonstrate upon it precepts for all triangles, even
for those invisible similar to the visible one. In this way, through the teach-

---

7. K. Marx, *Differenz der demokritischen und epikureischen Naturphilosophie*,
in K. Marx and F. Engels, *Werke* (Berlin: Dietz, 1974), Ergänzungsband 1. Teil, str.
257–373.

ing about geometrical analogies I can get all the way to the invisible. That the invisible has its end somewhere, that it is not as Anaxagoras said, that there is no end anywhere, is evident from that. Were we to apply this geometrical teaching, this geometrical abstraction, to reality, then we would never arrive at the opposite process, to the process of synthesis. Were the process of progress from large to small, the process of division, to actually go on for ever, then it would never be possible to stop anywhere, never turn it around, and naturally the reality of the world, which is nothing else but the construction from "atoms," would not be possible.

This is, however, a thing that interests us only in part. We cannot now lay out Democritus's system and this whole first amazing human attempt to carry out a genuinely systematic, and multileveled explanation of the structure of all things. But, you see, that it is something altogether different than myth—it is *science*. However, for us, it has its anthropological side, which is immensely peculiar and of interest here. Democritus is a materialist. This is materialism! If there is somewhere a conception of matter as a thing absolutely unchangeable, autonomous, not determined by anything else except by that, that it is, without any other further meaning, then it is here! And the mechanics of atoms and their possible enchaining and so on. But why does this thinker do this? What interests him in this? What is the attractant in this whole? Of course, the human spirit thirsts after explanation—that is certain. But where does this thirst originate? That is more evident in Democritus than in anyone else.

Democritus's thirst is a thirst for the divine, for the divine—that is, the eternal, the permanent, ἀεί (eternal)—and for this reason, Democritus says: "Who takes care of knowing, for matters of the soul, he takes care of the divine: and who takes care of other things, practical, primarily bodily, then he takes care solely for the human."

What is behind this? In connection with this, Democritus created a whole morality, or, so to speak, a whole theory of self-discovery, a road to oneself. One's own also manifests itself to him in this process. One's own soul—that is that, which thus goes after the eternal and constantly passes through the universe under the rule and plumb line of the eternal. And for this soul, which wants to see τὴν ἀλήθειαν (the truth), which wants to see the unconcealment of things, the first rule is to maintain absolute purity of sight and purity of its internal substance. For this reason, we read in Democritus the kinds of pronouncements that we read in Plato's *Gorgias*:

"Better to suffer injustice than commit injustice." The impulse to the ✗✗✗ ✓ eternal leads in Democritus to the discovery of one's soul, to the care of one's soul. Here, of course, the care of one's soul is the gateway to the victorious march to the explication of the universe as a whole and its structures.

Next time we will see in Plato that there exists still another way of care of the soul, which comes from manifesting as such, and we will see how it essentially differs. Democritus's way is essentially separate, individual, and private. Democritus also warns him who wants to take his path, for example, against family bonds, community ambition—not to dedicate himself to community affairs, not to dedicate himself to what tempts there. In Plato we will see how a second way of looking at the universe and at the care of the soul unfolds.

In both thinkers we see what is the soul; the soul has become here something essentially different from all it had been within tradition. The soul in the entire tradition up to these thinkers is in essence the soul from a foreign point of view, from the *other's* point of view. It is a soul-shadow, soul-image, a soul requiring a corporeal balsamized receptacle, a sculptural picture, if it is to exist, if it is to endure, for example, word, writing, signs, and so forth. This is I for the other. But even the soul of the mysteries is a soul for the other. Even the soul renewing itself in organic cycle, through which it is led in the Eleusian mysteries, the soul consisting in that everything in nature is born and renewed again and again: that is in newer and newer guises, new stalks grow up, Adonis is here once more, and so on. What does it mean, that the same stalk is here again? This means form. However, form is something I see, it is the soul for the other, not the soul that I *am*. The soul that I am—it is for the first time in Democritus and in Plato. This is the soul that lives in contact with the eternal. According to ✗✗✗ ✗ Democritus, it lives briefly, but this does not matter, because this contact with the eternal is the same in man and in god—that is the divine. That is why the soul is in its own way eternal, even if it dissolves into atoms. Next time, we will talk about how it is according to Plato.

For this peculiarity, there is created something in European life that has never been created anywhere else in the world. Do not take my explications as some kind of idealism, I do not imagine that philosophy would be the driving force of the world and that it would even ever have any chance for this. But this is how it is. As soon as this human possibility once emerges, it steps into the radius of all other human possibilities. Although philosophy as clarity, as radical reflection about the world in its whole, evidently will never be realized and who knows whether it could even be realized, it forces all the other possibilities of man, the not-philosophy, to reflect. And by this it brings not-philosophy itself onto another level and into another state than it had been prior to reflection. That is the task of philosophy. Philosophy is a certain idea. This idea depends upon the capacity of individuals and ages to comprehend what philosophy has been concerned with and when, to tie into a certain tradition and eventually to progress in it further, to repeat it. In this is the peculiar stamp and distinctiveness of European life, in this is also its continuity, that this possibility arose here. In this sense I will try to show you that Europe as Europe arose from this motif, from the care of the soul, and that it became extinct as a result of that, that it forgot about it.

5

The Philosophical Problem—Conception of the Soul and Care
of the Soul in Democritus and Plato—The Principle of Freedom
in the Greek World—Socrates—Care of the
Soul and the Heritage of Europe

Last time we talked about an extraordinary awakening that signifies
the passage from myth to reflection. Myth is not as impractical as it may
seem; it is not just some kind of fictitious thing, a fairy tale. As we saw in
the examples we went through, it is close to practical life. For example,
something like a calendar has a mythical origin. But the last reason for our
interest in myth should be mere curiosity about beginnings. Because of its
tie to ritual, the main function of myth is to provide human beings with
safe ground beneath their feet, a ground of conviction, faith on which they
may move about with certainty. This faith is not the work of any single
individual, and, as a result, every individual feels involved in something
objective and given. We characterized the passage from myth to reflection
as the passage from *the past to the present*, because myth is something that is
received and passed on from one generation to another. Here, the past also
plays a thematically important role, because it follows that things *are* from
the very fact that a story is told. A story is something that tells us about a
past event. Yet, upon reflection, the *present* world as a whole, the world in
its entirety, suddenly appears before us. The showing [*ukazování*] of the
world in its totality—this is the incipient moment from which reflection
arises. And this manifesting of the world in its entirety, its showing of itself,
is not something practical. At first glance it seems to have nothing in
common with human action. The world shows itself: but we are passive in
this. This is not a matter that depends on us. The world shows itself—this

means that in the world *there is* something like the phenomenon or manifestation of showing itself. Of course, it shows itself, but we are not the authors of this showing, we are only a part of this extraordinary, awe-inspiring occurrence.

Whereas the world really does show itself to us in its entirety, every present individual element also clearly forms a part of the greater presence. And in its entirety, this presence has peculiar characteristics: what is present completely, originally, so that it shows itself to us in its qualitative form, shortly creates space for a sole unity, but is again followed by change, and then further and further transformation. But we know that even there—where such changes leave us in awe, where we enter unfamiliar surroundings, the complete unknown—there will be some kind of continuation; even there the same things will happen again and again. We know this without a doubt. At the same time, this means that there are deep *differences* of givenness in what is given to us as a whole. But to be given as empty or uncertain does not mean not to be given. The two must be sharply distinguished. The world is given to us in its entirety, but this does not mean that it is not given to us *perspectivally,* that it is given to us in its full completeness. After all, even at its best, this completeness denotes a certain perspective because it is completeness from a certain point of view. The world shows itself to us in such a way that we ourselves are included in it, and that just means that it shows itself *necessarily perspectivally.*

ↄↄↄↄ   Last time we tried to show that these differences in the showing of the world in its entirety, in their original form—meaning everywhere realized in the same way—are exactly what is sounded, of course besides other things, in the very beginnings of philosophical reflection. We noticed this in several examples. We found it in the ancient dicta of Anaximander and in certain words of Heraclitus: there is present the primeval fact of the revealing of the world in its entirety. You know that the ancient philosophers who already began to reflect upon their predecessors—such as Aristotle, and he was not the first—noticed something like that in their predecessors' thought. Already Plato used to say: θαῦμα ἀρχὴ τῆς σοφίας (wonder is the principle of wisdom), wonder is the beginning of that σοφία (wisdom) for which philosophical reflection strives.[1] And Aristotle, who, like everything he took into his hands, already considered his predecessors systematically

---

1. *Theatetus,* 155d.

and as comprehensively as possible, also said that the very first peoples to philosophize did so out of wonder. Of course, he includes mythologists as well, whom he takes to be philosophers in a certain sense. But above all he speaks of philosophers in the more precise sense of the word.

What is this wonder about which Plato and Aristotle speak? Aristotle himself does not say it would be wonder about the entirety of the world, about the primeval fact that everything is revealed to us. Aristotle gives other examples. Nonetheless, the shock entailed by the discovery of philosophy is not a shock equivalent to the wonder over some kind of individual thing, wonder over some curiosity, some kind of striking, surprising, and yet still only individual thing; rather, it is a shock really signifying the passage from unreflective faith to the sudden challenging of faith by the fact that something reveals itself, that things are intelligible.

That the world shows itself to us does not by definition indicate what philosophy will do. If the world shows itself in its entirety, then, at first glance, it seems that the question is answered the moment it is posed. The world shows itself and shows itself to us in its original form. What shows itself is not a mere picture, as things that are themselves in their own presence. Then where is the source of any activity, some kind of work that philosophical thought might do? Where does what we take to be the fundamental characteristic of philosophy—the question—come from? How is the philosophical question formulated? What does philosophy really seek, when after all, this whole, and everything, is given and shows itself?

The problematicity is in this: although the world shows itself, and shows itself in its entirety, it *never shows itself in the same way twice*. It shows itself in such a way that alongside what shows itself, accompanying what is urgent for us, near, obvious, and qualitatively complete, there is also incommensurability in uninterrupted continuity with what directly shows itself in its completeness. And what reveals itself in its completeness *is not the whole*; these are just individualities, changeable details, varying with our movements, the diversity of perspectives. Naturally, I can go back to the same thing, but my own internal perspective at the same time changes, and so forth. Yet at the same time this whole remains as it is. The fundamental, the grand, through which everything else only then becomes what it is, endures. But this whole remains concealed.

Where is this grand presence? Where is that which makes things what they are? Where in the present is that which reveals them in their real being? We cannot derive or accept it from anything else other than from *the present as the present.* We cannot go on the way myth does; we cannot simply make up the answer to this question. Naturally, the answer to this question will be the work of philosophical thought. But this does not mean falsification; this does not mean even the unconscious falsification practiced by myth—myth falsifies without being aware of it, myth draws its certainty from a tradition that is not self-reflective. We will not find the answer like this. Rather, it will come from the present, from, as far as possible, the most present. This means that we do not want any answers to our questions, posed as sharply and precisely as possible, that would not be eternal, that would not be drawn from what shows itself. But of course this showing, as we already know, is problematic, multiform, manifold, taking on different appearances.

In our daily praxis, ordinary life, it is sufficient to come to terms with the immediate things in our environment. But the question of what is really all that makes up its core, what we know that somehow underlies this whole, but whose essential reality we do not understand—just because things in their entirety are here and show themselves to us perspectively—we must try to answer differently. Precisely here, in the diverse ways that things are given to us, ranging from the changeable to something which is always here also encompasses the specific human moment of showing: we are those to whom the world shows itself, but it shows itself in an extraordinary two-sided way. To a certain extent, here philosophical reflection can be tied into myth that says man is only admitted into the world that shows itself, into the world of the manifest, into the world of truth. This is not originally his world, but rather the world of the gods who see everything not only partially, from one side, only in passing, but rather in its real entirety. So it becomes philosophy's effort to come to a view of things in an analogous way, one that gets to the fundamental, to what itself forms the permanent foundation in what shows itself.

We already saw signs of this effort in several examples from the beginnings of philosophy. It occurs in Heraclitus who separated everything that is given to us into two categories: the immediately given, and what is not immediately given. This is that simultaneity of *uncovering and concealing* we have been describing. We also saw how Parmenides' grand thought that being in its entirety is something to which any "no" does not apply was still an effort to penetrate behind the changeable to something which remains and endures. He then tries to somehow characterize what is endur-ing and entirely positive—what remains, endures, what cannot be negated in any kind of way, what does not accept any kind of nonbeing, any kind of "no," that has characteristics such as "without beginning," "never aging," and so forth—and he tries to make some order out of these σήματα τοῦ ἔοντος (signs of being), as he calls them, into signs of that which is. Because it has no beginning, on this basis it can then be designated as never aging, and so on, so that a whole row of these signs is built one on top of the other. One stands upon the next, one justifies the next.

This justifying is the philosophical task that concerns us. To find something upon which stands the rest, and to find it in such a way that we might build in a solid, unshakable, tapped from the presence of existence itself, way everything that surrounds us, is the program.

It was long before philosophers were able to formulate this program, before they got to the point of somehow attempting its realization. Before something like this program was realized, more than one hundred years elapsed between the world's showing itself as multifarious and devoid of unity to its showing itself in its totality. Only then, thinkers who stood upon the shoulders of those who first had seen reality showing itself in its entirety, where the presence of the world as a totality was fundamental to their words and thoughts, were able to construct a project justifying what is most present of all. The most present is what is most enduringly present. And what is most enduringly present cannot be further questioned—from either the outside or from within. Thus it is elementary, as simple as possible, and, in its simplicity, lasting. Only then, on the basis of these philosophical ideas, such thinkers developed a project justifying present existence from itself, from its own principles, from its beginning, from what is most original within it. Only they were able to descend from the great presence of the whole to the concreteness of what shows itself. These thinkers, about whom I would like to speak today, these two great thinkers, two opponents and at the same time, we might say, quarreling brothers, are Democritus and Plato.

I already said a few words about Democritus last time. What are the beginnings from which Democritus arises? And what does Democritus really expect for his efforts? What is his intention? What goal, what pur-pose, weighs upon his mind? What is the point of this stroll through the universe from its incipient beginning all the way to the concrete things which show themselves to us like the things here around us? What does it mean?

In the very first thinkers, such as Anaximander and Heraclitus, this particular shock, this grand passage from the past to the present, was something new that did not need closer justification. It was a new creation, as when a person wakes from a dream into reality and cannot sleep again. Suddenly we have *purposeful* reflective activity here. What is the purpose of this activity when it is not practical, when, after all, it concerns just pure, deepened knowledge of the whole, worked out, shaped and formed by thought? What is its purpose? That is our main question.

You all know of Democritus. So I will not go into his system in any kind of depth, although it would be exceptionally interesting to show the link in his thought between the apparentness of the world in its entirety and his atomism. The apparentness of the world shows itself, for example, in Democritus's teachings about knowledge. As he naively says, and as the whole atomic tradition repeats after him—things themselves—which so to speak come to us, come from the outside, sending their images, their parts directly to us, into our soul, which somehow, it is not known how, accepts them into itself—that spirit which according to Democritus is made up of atoms, and so by definition cannot accept anything into itself. But fundamental here is the thought about the whole, a whole which sends us its messengers and who show themselves as such, even if in a misshapen, distorted way. The whole cannot but reveal itself to man except in a distorted way. This is the meaning of Democritus's statement, that everything has to be apparent, that ἐτεῆς ἀπήλλακται ἄνθρωπος (separated from reality) (fr. B6), that man is deprived of the true path to how things really are, precisely, without perspective, without distortion. For this reason the philosopher tries to somehow remedy this misshapenness and this distortion. Democritus is the first to grandly and universally harness mathematics for his enterprise. How?—I will tell you that right away.

But so I do not lose sight of the question we are concerned with: What is the meaning of this whole? What is the meaning of Democritus's intellectual work? We will see that in a moment. After all, we realized that the world of the present is something altogether different from the world as people ordinarily understand it, and as they used to understand it, particularly in the mythical world. Those peoples moved about on the ground of a mythical world. There they had firm ground below their feet. What are we concerned about now? To get firm ground under our feet again! Because what this is really about is finding in what shows itself to us the truly fundamental, the fixed, what can carry weight, and so forth. But we have to sort this out for ourselves. It cannot just be received from tradition. So that we might be able to achieve something like that—from what is present to explain the present, from what is deeply, eternally present, to explain even what is ephemerally present, to show how it is based upon it, how it is justified by it, and so on—we need a certain strength. For that we need something capable. *The agent of this deed of all deeds* is our soul. For all the ✗✗✗ ground over which man moved and to which man adheres and adhered hitherto is no more. There the human mind was half-asleep. But now man has to remain awake [*bdít*]. This is about such a completely *vigilant, wakeful* [*bdělou*] *soul* and its power. So that we might be able to carry out this completely new, and in a certain sense, merciless task discipline of the soul is needed, care for the soul is needed, so that it may be capable of ᵇᵘʳᵃᵘˡᵗ something like that. For that reason, although at first glance it might not seem so in a philosopher who is always—and rightly so—held to be the prototype of all materialism, at the center of Democritus's teaching is the *care for the soul*. Those words do not occur in Democritus, those words appear in Plato: τῆς ψυχῆς ἐπιμελεῖσθαι (to take care of the soul). Nonetheless, the idea does exist in Democritus.

Let us explain the *method* of care for the soul right away. The soul is focused on the unconcealing of things, on their complete unconcealing, on the truthfulness of revealing things. For that reason the soul must constantly care only about the truth in the way that we have indicated, that is, to live from what shows itself as present, not perhaps for some outside instrumental reasons and so on, but rather because it is focused on what is. The soul that gives up this principle is corrupted. It destroys itself, becomes incapable of the task that is required. And so who is concerned about this great abrupt change to *the present as such*, is first of all bound to the morality of truth. For that reason, we find in Democritus the following statements, such as that a human being should always be truthful, whether or not it seems to his advantage, whether someone knows about it or not, whether someone is present or not: it is better to be the victim of injustice rather than commit it—these are Democritus's statements before Plato's. This is about a soul capable of this kind of deed. In Democritus to care for the soul means to care for it so that it might be able to live near what is eternal, so that it might be capable of a life in that grand presence. That will naturally be a life of thought, that part which precisely states what is, what is present.

Of course, the soul has *degrees* and various *manners* within presence, how presence may be present. If we call knowledge the presence of what is, the γνώμη (knowledge [thought, judgment]) of our soul, then it has to be said that the soul has at the least two γνώμη, that it has that γνώμη which we might say is not the true legitimate son of the soul, but rather some kind of bastard—what Democritus calls σκοτίη γνώμη (bastard knowledge) (here σκότιος [dark, obscure, bastard (=not from legitimate wedlock)] does not mean darkness in the literal sense of the word, but rather means an origin that is not-good, dark, unclean), and then it also has a noble γνώμη (knowledge), of good origins γνησίη γνώμη (legitimate, lawful knowledge).

Nonetheless, σκοτίη γνώμη shows us things that are, and in a certain sense, also how they are. When we see colors and when we taste things, and so on, then all this is very changeable and imprecise. For example, color changes with the light and who knows with what all, and how hard it is to pin down! And yet in color, just as in taste, something of the nature of the thing manifests itself. You know how evanescent are things like taste. Yet still we do speak of something like a sharp taste, which already in and of itself points to some kind of form somewhere underlying this quality. Perhaps behind something like color there also lies a certain configuration of what is before us here. At first glance, Democritus's view of things seems to be extremely impoverishing, simplifying, and excluding every quality. But that is not Democritus's intention. His intention is to show what underlies, what is the foundation of that which shows itself in this way, that which is solid, permanent behind the changeable. To teach the human soul to become a soul capable of this γνησίη γνώμη as profoundly and as far as may be possible—that is Democritus's goal.

Yet, after all, we still have to mention his doctrine itself. There is no doubt that it is connected to what his predecessors saw and intuited from the totality of the world. But except for Melissos, none of his predecessors discovered that this great revealing whole is *never-ending*; that things which are here, in our proximity, are encompassed within something that is endless. The same story is always repeated over and over again: near, far, near, far, and on and on. And when I take hold of this thing in its entirety, I have something like infinite space before me. Democritus is the author of the idea of *empty space*. While Melissos completed the Eleatic thought of one being, or better said, disagreed with Parmenides' conception by characterizing this one being as infinite, in his thought it still remains an infinite being in Parmenides' sense: one that is full. Yet, Democritus is the first for whom there exists something like *never-ending empty space*. For that reason, Democritus is also the first for whom there exists *a plurality of worlds*. In older thinkers we know about, the plurality of worlds is a successive plurality, not a concurrent one. But the plurality of *concurrent* worlds in *infinite* space is something fundamentally different from the mythical plurality of successive worlds. There, thought of many worlds is a mythical thought of beginning and end, of a world periodically repeating itself, which has, we might say, its own solemn beginning and thus also its own end, followed by, in a way, the same thing again. This is a principle existing, for example, in the idea of feast days and sacred holidays. Feast days and sacred holidays are nothing other than a return to the first day of creation, that most powerful day when all things were created the way they are. For this reason the sacred day of celebration has extraordinary strength and power. The plurality of Democritus's worlds is of course something completely different. It is a *plurality within the present, a contemporaneous one.* Democritus is right to call it *not-existence* because it is empty, because it is nothing but the idealization of something akin to a geometric body or a solid, firm measure, which can homogeneously move about. But at the same time he maintains that not-existence in a sense is. Yet, he calls that other principle, other beginning, no less permanent, *existence*. What is, we might say, is drawn from the character of the thing itself, what is distinguished by the fact that it is solid, impenetrable, unlike that space which in and of itself contains nothing that would somehow characterize and distinguish its parts.

On these two principles—the principles of empty space and of the solid—everything else must then be based. But before it is possible to found everything else, it is first necessary to make that firm and solid existent completely firm and solid. Naturally, the existent, the things which surround us here, are not without change and malleability. They can be renewed, transformed, and so on. But what if their changeability and malleability could be attributed to something made up from space, something absolutely inflexible, absolutely specified, determined with absolute geometric precision. And the element we finally come to through this method, unbreakable and absolutely invisible, will also be absolutely solid.

I already told you last time that Democritus also penetrates from

what appears to us as visible to what is not visible with the help of geometry, with the help of the principle of *mathematical analogy* and the principle
of similarity. Geometrical precepts about the area of a triangle apply to
triangles of any size. Using this method, Democritus gets from what can be
seen to what cannot be seen. This is the achievement of γνήσιη γνώμη.
Naturally, penetrating to the invisible cannot go on infinitely, the way
Anaxagoras wanted to. If we followed this path then we would never arrive
at any end, and then naturally the way back, the way to assembling complex things out of the elementary, would also be impossible. It is necessary
to stop somewhere. The minute, but solid, geometrically precisely defined
parts that are finally indivisible, these are ἄτομα.

The world can then be explained from these two principles, from
atoms and empty space, the world as a moving whirlwind of atoms in
empty space. Because these atoms are suitably shaped so that they can fit
and join together—Democritus is clearly not aware that other principles
would be needed for this here—all the incredible shapes that we see around
us when we look up into the sky are created.

But this principle of forming things out of the elementary, from a
certain number of fundamental shapes, is repeated again and again on a
number of different levels in Democritus's thought. Because Democritus
does not explain merely the origin of the world and the things within the
world as the mutual combining of atoms in empty space, but rather he
explains everything, he explains as well—as I have told you—*the qualities* of
things. In what way? Above all he tries to find the elementary, and so
convert the richness of all kinds of nuances into several simple principles.
For example, when one is talking about colors, to find the elementary
colors, those which are most fundamental, which can then make up the
others. Another similar example is the explanation of language out of
phonemes. The entire limitless variety of expression, capable of giving
voice to all things, about the whole world, even history and society, is made
up from only several phonemes. Under certain circumstances, simple, elementary human results can lead to refined and complex results.

On a whole host of levels—of which the most fundamental is the
most precise, geometric—a trip through all of existence is launched, based
on what is present, what is most present of the present. And because of this,
the soul capable of something like that must be cared for. The soul capable
of this journey is also capable of living in such a world in *the best way* that is

at all possible. It may ultimately confront what is eternal, the presence of the eternal. For the Greeks, the eternal is that which is divine. The soul lives in a divine way even if it lives only for a short time. The difference between short and long is no longer an essential difference. The soul that has been scattered into atoms, in its γνησίη γνώμη, has lived a divine life. For that reason the goods of the soul, as Democritus says, are something divine, whereas he who busies himself with things of the body, occupies himself only with the human.

Things are completely different with Plato, despite the profound affinity with Democritus. In Plato as well, at the center of everything that he does, is the care of the soul. But this is not so that the soul might journey through the universe just as what is eternal. In Plato the soul journeys through the universe just so it will be what it is supposed to be. We do not care about the soul in order to understand, but rather we understand so that the soul *will become* what it is not yet completely, *what* it *can* be!

The meaning of these two doctrines is in a way turned around even if the care of the soul is at the center of both. This difference and opposition surfaces especially in the fact that while Democritus advocates the morality of truthfulness, at the same time he also advocates a sort of intellectual selfishness, intellectual isolation. He warns whomever wants to have a pure soul to avoid involvement in practical affairs, to avoid starting a family, so that he might have to care about his progeny, and if it must be, that he rather adopt than have his own children. He also should not try to become prominent in his city. The city is certainly something very important, it is impossible to live without it; care of the soul is only possible in a well-run city. But Democritus never considers that philosophical effort is necessary for the organization of the city so the soul might be capable of something like this. Besides, Democritus's own city was a bit of a *procul negotiis* (most remote of things) in comparison with the global and historical center where Plato lived and about which his philosophy is really a perpetual reflection—that is, in comparison with Athens. Plato's philosophy is a reflection on Greek life in his age and on Greek life in general. For him the quintessence of Greek life is Athens—and rightly so. Why?

For Plato, Athens represents a unique principle belonging to Greek life as such. In political life, Plato sees a sharp opposition between the principle we might call the principle of ruthless centralized rule, and the principle of freedom. And for him the Greek world is the representative of the principle of freedom. But of course, we have to understand this in the Greek sense of the word: this is the world of free nobles, that is people who are—as Hannah Arendt nicely phrased it—despots in their own home so they might be equals in their city. They are absolute masters of their households, but in the *city* they are *equals*. Of course the city, if it is going to be capable of functioning, has to maintain certain very rigorous rules. There every one of these mutually equal lords has to guarantee the sanctity of these rules. He has to stand for and guarantee not only his own freedom but also the freedom of everyone else. This has to take place either entirely from instinct and tradition, in an absolutely unquestioned religious-mythical form, or, once the solidity of this ground is shaken, it has to take place on the basis of *looking-in* [*nahlédnutí*]. The Greek world is not united. It is organized into independent tiny city-states (πόλεις), and these have various regimes, such as democracy, such as aristocracy where only a certain group rules, such as tyranny where only one rules. And of course, tyranny is already a retreat from this Greek principle, it already is decline. Yet in the Greek cities, tyranny can only last for a short time. Of all the Greek cities, Athens is the most Greek, because it is the guarantor of freedom for every other city. That was shown in the Persian wars.

The Persian wars were the manifestation of a global conflict between the principle of a great centralized power, the Persian colossus, and the principle of a free city. And Athens had to bear the brunt of this conflict, because Athens became the target of the Persian attack, while the other cities just helped out. And they hardly helped. The deciding events occurred on Athenian territory or were decided by the Athenian fleet.

This situation demonstrated *the principle of freedom,* the principle of the city life of free nobles, to be more powerful, to be, in fact, *the most powerful* on earth. The Persian monarchy, which encompassed every previous oriental despotism—the Persians ruled over the entire Near East then and over Egypt as well—was wrecked by Athenian determination, by Athenian ingenuity. And yet this new world power was not able to turn itself into a real power. Instead it very quickly destroyed itself. Within fifty years, this summit of humanity, achieved by Greece in the years 490–480 of the fifth century, culminates with a horrifying fratricidal war lasting thirty years from which the Greek world leaves destroyed. Plato is its witness in his youth.

Plato lives from Athenian tradition already because of his family: on one side Solon, the lawgiver, who gave the city its constitution, an aristocratic-democratic constitution, the rule of the best; on the other, Codrus, that fabulous king who sacrificed his life to save his city, as a result of an oracle who pretty much recommended this to him.[2] This is Plato. For this reason, the tradition of the greatest deeds of the Athenian city-state, the victory over the Persians, lives on within him. When in the Peloponnesian War, things end with the horrible humiliation of Athens, which is forced to destroy its own naval power, everything on which it stands, this catastrophe also takes place around his nearest relatives. After the fall of the city, his closest relatives played an often terrible role amongst the so-called thirty tyrants, or guardians of Periraia. Plato lived this historic catastrophe from close-up, as something of his own.

When he describes the history of his own life in the *Seventh Letter*, above all his political life (because life for the Greek man is a political life, for a citizen of the city-state life does not exist outside the city-state; the first Greek people, who lived the entire content of their lives outside the city—and this was absolutely revolutionary—were philosophers: Democritus's recommendation is completely at odds with Greek morality, with Greek habit and tradition), Plato begins this letter telling us about his relatives who, during Athens' fall and its newly installed aristocratic constitution, bid him to join them—naturally Plato is tempted. But he resists. When this regime falls and Athenian democracy returns from exile, Plato again turns away from politics, again he does not submit. In both cases the standard for why he does not submit is one and the same: the reflective thinker.

This character also has something in common with the greater framework of myth, which we have already talked about several times here. Socrates, whom Plato followed, and who served as a warning that he not enter political life in this kind of guise, is an old Athenian who lives in a new age, but who also knew the city-state which lived on the firm ground of tradition, of myth, where all free noblemen upheld divinely sanctioned rules: not to harm others, not to interfere in their own private sphere, to leave them alone, not to enslave them, not to take, and not even attempt to take what does not belong to one.

2. King of Athens, eleventh century B.C. During his reign, the Dorians invaded Athens, having heard from Delphi that they would be victorious if Codrus's life was spared. Finding out about this oracle, Codrus—in disguise—invited death by starting a quarrel with the Dorian army and so saved his city.

In a state of war, political change, and philosophy, this awakening into the present, especially in the vulgarized manner which already then had become widespread, a manner insidious and quick to impose itself in the form of spiritual comfort and cynicism, when the present qua present means, why should we care about tradition, about god, and about everything that is far off and not present? Who knows, whether it even exists and probably it doesn't at all. In this situation and this atmosphere, Socrates defends *with new methods* the old; he defends the thought that it is important not to harm, that it is better to undergo injustice than to commit it. This is the principle without which something like consensus in a city-state would not even be possible. But he upholds it not just with tradition, but rather with something else. He supports it by talking with his fellow citizens. And he uncovers them, reveals that they are *errant* people, *blindly wandering* [*bludně*].

But you know that according to myth, such wandering is the fate of every human being. To be lost is the element in which we all live. After all Oedipus, who thinks that he is living perhaps best of all, is lost in this way. So lost were tyrants who thought they justly ruled for their own personal benefit, that they ruled better than those who led the city into catastrophe. Lost are also those who, exiled by these tyrants, returned from exile and thought their old methods could be sufficient in an age when everything was, as was a public secret, already shaken up long ago. And now Socrates walks around such an Athens and talks to every one who thinks they know how to manage things, and that includes everyone. Everyone knows what is good and how he should live. After all we read in the *Meno* (92e) how Anytos tells a foreign guest who asks how he might learn about civic virtue and from whom: why from any decent Athenian! Everyone knows about it and everyone will give you advice. And Socrates goes around and shows everyone that they contradict themselves about the good just as soon as they start to think about it, just as soon as they start to talk about it and analyze it even the least bit systematically. For he who knows what is good, what is truth, has to have an enduring kind of knowledge. Here we see the return of that philosophical motif what endures in constant presence, what is maintained without change: to maintain opinion without change; not just on the basis of opinion, but rather because it has survived eternal investigation, investigation of what shows itself as existent, as present, in philosophical investigation, in real reflection.

Because Socrates, that man who several times showed that doing injustice is worse than sustaining injustice at the risk of his own life, stands firm during the rule of the tyrants. Yet this man gives speeches that knock over those who think they have knowledge of the good—he shakes up the ✕✕✕ certainty on the basis of which the city has existed hitherto, and at the same time he does not say what is good, he only invites people to *think*, that they think like him, that they search, that everyone *responsibly* examine their every thought. That means that they should not accept mere opinion, as if it were insight, as if it were a looking-in—to live from true insight into what is here, what is present. For that reason Socrates represents both the old and the new together. The reflective Socrates, who confounds all those who think they know the truth, focuses his attack above all on those who think they can deduce new principles of life just out of the present, out of what is self-evident and given. Just those kinds of principles of life, for example, it is good to pay attention to one's own self-interest at any cost. The incredible paradox of Socrates' actions is that he fights with present means against another present, with what is given against another given. He tries to prove never before formulated paradoxical theses, implicated in traditional life but never formulated there. Socrates himself is constantly investigating, for that reason he also does not think that he is a man of any kind of special wisdom, but he is the one who risks his life for certain principles, or, better said, for that insight that certain principles are not truthful. In this sense, as the representative of the ancient, he is the messenger of the gods, of that god who knows the whole truth, the Delphic Apollo. For that reason the Delphic Apollo says that he is the wisest of all: σοφός Σοφοκλῆς, σοφώτερος Εὐριπίδης, πάντων ἀνθρώπων Σωκράτης ὁ σοφώτατος (Wise is Sophocles, Euripides is wiser, but the wisest is Socrates).[3] This is the pronouncement that Chaerophon brings from Delphi, and that is the meaning of this pronouncement. Socrates is still the representative of the ancient divine world, but *through new methods*. His revealing of others' ignorance is based on revealing their secret dispositions for tyranny. Athenian democracy is in fact eaten through with the poison of tyrannical leanings. That is how Socrates is portrayed in the marvelous Platonic dialogues, the *Gorgias* and in the first book of the *Republic*, which was originally named *Thrasymachus*.

What is this investigating, and what is this call to reflection? Just what

---

3. *Apology*, 21a.

Plato says, following Socrates: the care of the soul, care of the soul. Only through it does the soul become what it can be—harmonious, not in contradiction, no longer running the risk of shattering into contradictory pieces, thus finally joining something that endures, that is solid. After all, everything has to be founded upon what is solid. This is the basis of our acting morally, and this is also the foundation of thought, for only thinking that shows what is solid, stable, shows what is. That is the identical principle we saw in Democritus. For that reason care of the soul manifests itself in three ways: in one way as the complete plan of existence, in another as the plan of a new political life, and in yet another as the clarification of what the soul is in itself. The care of the soul is manifested in these three ways.

Today I would like to present this entire thing, but I think that I will not be able to pull it off, because each of these points needs a thorough explanation. So today I will restrict myself to showing the meaning of the figure of Socrates and the meaning of his *fate as a philosopher*, because this is the foundation for every other domain of reflection and every other direction we might take. For Plato, Socrates is almost always on his mind, a constant goal for his reflection.

The care of the soul is something completely internal. The care of the soul does not intend to teach some kind of outward success—let the sophists do that. The care of the soul is the internal forming of the soul itself, forming into something unyieldingly solid, into existence in this sense, because of the very fact that it is occupied with thinking. And it is a precise thinking, a bounded, limited one. For that reason the soul gets a certain form, it does not become dispersed. Whereas the soul of man who does not concern himself with questioning and answering—what Plato calls an internal conversation, thinking—the soul of man who dedicates himself to sentiment or who dedicates himself to enjoyment, this soul dissolves in the uncertainty of pleasure and pain, which naturally go hand in hand. This uncertainty lies in the fact that pleasure and pain do not have any defined limit, any defined form. They always want more and more—and there is never any end to them. The life of this dedication is something like the net of the Danaids.[4] The soul that really cares for itself takes on a solid form,

4. The fifty daughters of Danaus, compelled by their father to kill the fifty sons of Aegyptus, to whom they were to be betrothed. Notwithstanding purifica-

just as every thought worthy of the name is *a defined* thought, specifying ideas, having a specific thesis about those ideas.

This is not at all a kind of pallid intellectualism, although it is countlessly interpreted in this way. This is the attempt to embody what is eternal within time, and within one's own being, and at the same time, an effort to stand firm in the storm of time, stand firm in all dangers carried with it, to stand firm when the care of the soul becomes dangerous for a human being. For without a doubt, the care of the soul in a lawless city endangers a human being, it endangers the kind of being that stands for the care of the soul, just as that being endangers the city. And it is altogether logical that the city then treats it accordingly.

Nonetheless, Socrates does not provoke by his care of the soul. You know that he places particular emphasis on this point in his apology. He does not provoke, but his whole *existence* is a provocation to the city. He is the first who, face to face with secret tyranny and the hypocritical remains of old morality, poses the thought that the human being focused on truth in the full sense of the word, examining what is the good, not knowing himself what is the positive good, and only refuting false opinion, has to appear as the worst of all, the most irritating. While in actual fact he is the exact opposite. And who takes the side of the many has to appear as the best, even if in his most profound essence he represents the exact opposite. Between these two there will be inevitable conflict, which cannot end other than with the destruction of he who is good. Socrates is aware of this.

But after all, Socrates is the *messenger of the gods*, he is the one who Apollo entrusted with this mission, he is the one who proves it with his life and his death. In the moment that it occurs, the judges themselves become subject to the court, and in that moment the city becomes subject to the wrath of the gods. The whole world is in evil, because the city which prevailed over the most powerful, even in its decline, in its humiliation, is still a *potential victor* and calls upon itself the wrath of the gods. The world is in evil.

And what is the philosopher's reaction, not Socrates' any more, but rather his inheritors'? Socrates leaves a heritage. Socrates did not help

---

tion of their crimes by Hermes and Athena upon the orders of Zeus, it is said they were punished in Hades to forever pour water into a vessel full of holes. *Gorgias*, 493b–c.

himself, but he helps others. In what way can a philosopher who is in such dire straits help others? In a philosophical way, through the outline of a city, where the *philosopher can live,* where the man who is to care for the soul can live, the man who is to carry out the philosophical thought that it is necessary to live and think on the basis of looking-in [*nahlédnutí*], nothing else but that. To create such a city is the work of his successors. That is the city where Socrates and those like him will not need to die. For this a world of experience is needed; for this a plan of what is truth is needed, an outline of all of being. For this a city must be planned out. What is its essence, and what the soul is capable of must be examined. That is the meaning of the figure of Socrates.

From this situation, from reflection on this catastrophe arose the first systematic reflection on the state—Plato's *Republic.*

It is impossible to fully appreciate what this writing signifies. That philosophy came upon the scene, that it came into reality, does not mean that from that time on it actually became some kind of ruling power. It is not and was not a ruling power. Philosophy is reflection. At the moment when reflection breaks through, when people awaken, this does not mean they stop falling back into slumber. They will live in myth again. Plato himself knows that, which is one of the reasons why he also creates new myths (there are also other, deeper reasons). But from that point on, even the unphilosophical life is forced to somehow make its peace with philosophy, it is forced to reflect, and in this way itself incorporates certain elements of philosophy.

This is that singular thing about Europe: as I told you, *only in Europe* was philosophy born in this way, in the awakening of man out of tradition into the presence of the universe, only in Europe, or better said, in what was the embryo of Europe—Greece. After the catastrophe of the Greek polis, it became important that this *inheritance* remain alive, an inheritance of thinking about the state where philosophers might live, about a state of justice founded not on mere tradition, but rather on *looking-in* [*nahléd-nutí*]. Again, after the catastrophe of the Greek cities, when the Hellenistic empires of the Diadochs arose, from which then eventually Roman monarchy emerged as the last great Hellenistic power, then philosophers arrived with the program: this state should be the ground of justice, this should be the state of philosophers. And with all their energy, putting every possibility into this task, the Stoics really did educate mankind about the universal human tasks of a universal empire. And this empire again was destroyed. This empire succumbed to catastrophe just as the Greek polis before it. In the final analysis, it fell because, just like the Greek polis, it was not capable of convincing its public that it was a state of justice. The moment this great empire was wrecked, the primeval example of all empires, it left behind a heritage—if we have states at all it is because this empire existed.

This heritage goes all the way back to the Greeks, especially to Plato, because when mankind in its new form tried to bring the city of justice into reality, a city to be founded not on the changeability of human things as Rome was, but rather on absolute truth, so that it would be the kingdom of God upon earth, then the guiding thought of this other kingdom, this other world, which is the world of the real truth, is after all Plato's thought. It would not even be possible without it. In this way, one heritage leads to another, and through catastrophe, despite their destructive consequences, this heritage is spread throughout the world. After all, the Roman Empire is something more general, something more encompassing; and Europe, which arose from the development of one version of the idea of the kingdom of God on earth, is again something more encompassing than the Roman Empire. In that way, through catastrophes, this heritage is kept alive, and that is why I suppose that perhaps it might be possible to dare suggest the thesis that *Europe,* especially Western Europe, but even that other one, arose out of *the care of the soul*—τῆς ψυχῆς ἐπιμελεῖσθαι. This is the embryo out of which arose what Europe used to be.

Of course, Europe wasn't just that, and for long periods of time, the care of the soul transformed itself in such a peculiar way, that it became pretty much unrecognizable under the weight of something, something that might be deemed a concern, or care about *dominating the world*. That is another, also unique and incomparable history, but one that more than anything else contains the germ of what has taken place before our very own eyes: *Europe has disappeared*, probably forever.

How I have described Socrates, his fate and his necessary conflict with the city, his divine calling and at the same time the divine anger his fate called into the world—that of course calls to mind something else. Usually it is said that European civilization rests on two pillars: one, the Judeo-Christian tradition, the other, antiquity. On my understanding, as I have tried to depict it, Europe stands on *one* pillar—and that is because

Europe is a looking-in [*nahlédnutí*], Europe is life founded upon seeing what
is. To become what it is for Europe, the Judaic element, which is obviously
extraordinarily important in the European Judeo-Christian tradition, had
to be Hellenized, it had to pass through Greek thought. People speak of
Christian dogma, but Christian dogmata were *justified.* Christian dogmata
were not mere myth. And the very thought of that world, the other, world
of truth and divinity, which is the divinity of pure good—occurs in *Plato*
first, it is not present anywhere else. So, in a certain sense, it is possible to
say as Nietzsche did, although his meaning differs from my own, that
Christianity is Platonism for the people. Nietzsche despises the basic thought
Plato formulated, of some other world. And from this hatred of the beyond, he overlooks what is most fundamental about the phenomena of
Socrates and Plato, that is, the care of the soul. When Nietzsche himself has
to tell us what positive thing will help us out of ethical nothingness, out of
our present-day nihilism, he speaks of the eternal return. The eternal
return interests him because eternity is what this is all about—eternity is to
be found once more.

But how to find eternity in a world of decline—as we told ourselves in
our first lecture—in a world fundamentally characterized by temporal decline? How to find eternity there? Is not Nietzsche's search for eternity, his
attempt to leap from history into what is beyond time proof that it is
absolutely necessary to *reiterate* care for the soul even under new circumstances? However, to reiterate does not mean to do the same thing that was
already here once before; to reiterate means to attempt to, *through new
ways*, new words, new methods, say the same thing. *We have to say what is,
again, over and over, and always in a different way, but it always has to be the
same thing!*

6

The Examination of the Soul—Ontocosmological Modality
of the Care of the Soul in Plato: The Teaching About
Ideas and Mathematics—Introduction to the
Problem of the Platonic State

Let us again briefly repeat the difference between Plato's and Democritus's care of the soul. In Plato we do not care about the soul so that we might penetrate right to the ultimate reasons, to the first causes of everything, and to look into the essence of things. This was Democritus's purpose. To the contrary, we know the world because through this we want to care for the soul. In the care of the soul, thinking is important as a positive, determining, enriching organ, as an organ of its goodness, its perfectibility, the heightening of its being. For this reason care of the soul is important: it opens the character of the soul itself. We can only understand the nature of the soul, comprehend its substance and see it, only as long as we carry out this care, when we dedicate ourselves to it.

From this, at the same time it is clear that *the soul* forms the *center of philosophy. Philosophy is the care of the soul* in its own essence and in its own element. And for this reason we think that the Platonic teaching is really something that circles around the notion of the soul and around the care of the soul. The care of the soul really opens up the concept of the soul. Suitably clarified, this concept gives access to all the other dimensions of philosophical thought and questioning. The care of the soul takes place through *questioning thinking at all.* The form of this questioning thinking is such that one of the participants in a conversation allows himself to be questioned. It has the form of a conversation that is ordinarily divided into two persons, but it can also take place within the core of the soul itself.

Accompanying this, a readiness to let oneself be problematized is important, to allow the question to arrive. On the one hand, encompassed in this
willingness to let oneself be questioned is the certainty that this regards
only the thing itself; on the other, there does not exist any end, any closure,
for here there is also the experience that even what seems at first glance self-
evident can be made the object of questioning, of problematization, and
becomes a requirement that it has to be done in this way. Only a completely clear and unified, not contradicting itself, but rather consistent
speech about everything, about anything at all, about which it is possible to
think meaningfully, only this kind of absolutely coherent speech then may
mean the existence, the creation of the internally unified soul, which,
because its thoughts are *binding*, is not split apart, torn into various mutually contradictory opinions. Because we are not sure of this beforehand and
can only certify it through inquiring, *inquiring itself* creates a special unity.
That is the stance of constant inquiring and searching, inquiring searching.
This stance of the inquiring searcher is in a way *certain* in the face of
contradiction [*rozpor*] and its spiritual consequences. It is—one might say
using a later term—a kind of ἐποχή (suspension of judgment) that is exceptionally positive.

   Here, ἐποχή does not mean the suspension of all judgment. Rather, it
means provisional hypothetically fixed opinion, which is exposed with all
loyalty and all good will to further and further research, and that with [the
intention] of arriving at a coherent discourse, achieving an opinion which
means looking-in in the fullest sense of the word, looking-in, which does
not have to be disavowed, which does not have to be taken back, which of
course means the presence of the ideal, which in factical life need not ever
be realized. In the end we want only what we can answer for in this manner,
what we either see with such clarity that it withstands every kind of imagin-
able inquiry, in such a way that it is either so initial, so elementary that the
questions we would pose about it themselves presuppose it, or such that in
the exploration of opinion it withstands the crossfire of questioning: these
form a *unified ideal*, which this investigating, this care of the soul, seeks.

   But notice this is not merely about this content. This is not in the first
place about looking-in. Rather this unified looking-in has meaning mainly
because in it is asserted the *binding character of thinking*, an obligation
which only then makes something from our being, from this thinking reed,
something which cannot be disavowed, which is then certain, has a stable

form and, in this sense, having a stable form, it does not dissolve and disappear the moment it presumes to be.

So develops the environment of the philosophical movement unknown to prior philosophy—even the Democritan, even if, as we say, Democritan philosophy is philosophy of the care of the soul—a philosophical environment that in its actuality *cannot remain limited to one thinker*. Here arises the philosophical thought, the philosophical ideal that *does not depend* on a particular philosophical opinion, on some kind of philosophical thesis and thought, on some kind of system. Right away, we shall see that Plato first gave the grand example of what this stance means.

I brought your attention to the most important idea to *the formation of the soul itself* by itself. This means that this soul turned the experience that *it does not know*, the experience of *knowing its not knowing*, into experience about its own being. At the same time, it also experienced that it is brave because it exposes itself to problematization, that it is *wise* in knowing not knowing in the form of temperate and disciplined investigating, because it submits all other human affairs to this thinking struggle. It is just by making its own what is binding for it, nothing other than, as we would modernly say, its own responsibility; it does not claim anything apart from what is in this way its own. So it obtained a certain standard for what is its own being. It gave itself this *standard*: it is what is unified, constant, and exact. Once the soul tasted this standard and obtained it, then it also knows that, just as common life in political allegiance, so common handling of things and people around us *does not answer to* this standard. Here a schism opens up. The regular, natural, naïve contact with people and things is uncertain, inexact, shaky, unawares, full of contradiction [*rozpor*] and not unified—it is sunk into semblance δόξα (opinion/appearance).

Care of the soul then, discovers *both*: δόξα as well as the unitary ideal. It discovers the irreconcilable as well as the permanent, the passing as well as the precise—both discoveries are equally fundamental. The care of the soul is, simultaneously then, the discovering of two fundamental *possibilities* of the soul. Within these fundamental possibilities is simultaneously the discovery of two regions in which the soul moves about.

The soul of everyday dealing with things and people is a thing, to say modernly, of *undetermined immediacy*. Its surroundings are demanding, such that they captivate us, but at the same time are uncertain and evanescent, without firm contours and boundaries, becoming indistinguishable. This is the δόξα soul. Just as it applies to our immediate contact with things, such as for perception, so also for our acting. After all, the immediate contact with things teaches us that things as they show themselves to us are fleeting; they have only the *semblance* of form. The surface of a table is in its own way rectangular, but in the right sense of the word it is obviously not a rectangle, obviously it is not any kind of geometrical shape, however complicated, in its own way it is an *uncontoured thing*. For you know that one of the discoveries of modern art is the possibility to present things surrounding us in such a way that we recognize them as these things—in the most variable ways, and this is always such that it is possible to choose a *certain style* from what de facto takes place in our perceptive experience. At the same time, it cannot be said that all these things are not actually within unmediated contact. How utterly differently an impressionist sees the visual world around us and how utterly differently a cubist sees it!

In contrast to this, the soul of self-questioning investigating is the *reflected soul* remaining at what is *firmly delimited*, what is pure and precise. The soul that takes care of itself is then in motion from immediate uncertainty to circumscribing, delimiting reflection. And philosophy is in this motion, and this motion is something actual. Philosophy then captured and proven through deed. There does not exist any purely objective evidence of philosophy, as there exists objective evidence of mathematical sciences, mathematical theorems, which do not touch our being, do not have anything to do with it and are independent of it. In contrast to this, here, in this motion, remains proper philosophizing because its matter cannot be built upon anything on heaven or on earth, nor can it be suspended from it. Rather, it develops in the manner of a *spark* that catches fire once—of this Plato talks about in the *Seventh Letter*—and then feeds upon itself.[1]

At first glance, it seems that this concerns objective thoughts themselves, that after all in the Platonic dialogues Socrates never speaks about things either mysterious or somehow deeply speculative. Socrates presents even what regards the deepest teaching, the teaching about the ideas, pretty much in continuity with how he speaks about art, or better said, about the craftsmanship of shoemaking and the craftsmanship of medicine and

1. *Letter VII*, 341c.

about the things connected with it. The Platonic Socrates bids himself and the partner with whom he is conversing, who wants to converse with him, everyone who wants to break into the flow of Platonic dialogue, to *look-in*, to look-in just as we look-in in mathematics and in all cases where we have before us some kind of objective structure that everyone can control and with which everyone can reconcile themselves—to reconcile themselves with it. For that, there is positively a summons—despite the fact that it all takes place in the milieu of the objective—it is objective in that it is possible to go back and it is possible again to bring about the same thought within oneself, to control it, to pose new questions about it, and so on—for all that, it must take place in something that is *capable of looking-in*. To look-in means to *see*. This means it all takes place in a being to whom the world manifests itself. The being has its own special privilege in contrast to all other worldly beings of which we are aware and which at the same time draws a certain *directive* from this privilege. All this nevertheless occurs in some kind of alternative. That alternative is: to *be* or *not to be*. This is the difference between dissolving where I submit purely passively to what seems truthful and real to me, and that which endures examination and investigation *in extremum*.

This new thought, this completely *new ideal*, that everything man does and thinks has to be answered for in this kind of way, means a *new forming of the self*, a new forming of that which man, so to speak, is by nature a being to whom the world shows itself, manifests itself. In some way, this forming is within our power; we form ourselves in some kind of way.

Here, Plato shows that in his account the care of the soul is articulated in *three* grand currents, the care of the soul manifests itself in a threefold manner, this philosophical self-forming shows itself in three kinds of ways. Three manners in which each of them is in a different way close to one's own core, that which I am.

Most distant from this core is what we could call the *ontocosmological* way of philosophizing, the *ontocosmological project*. If we care about the soul, then we care about something to which the world manifests itself. And we thus want, as far as possible, to establish upon *looking-in*, which can also be answered for, this world, which originally gave itself to us as an *uncertain tradition* rooted in an *uncertain past*, coming from some place and rooted somewhere, in some kind of past to which we do not have access. Although it is always present in that it founded this world of ours, it itself escapes as much our looking-in as our intervention. Plato never systematically presented this ontocosmological looking-in in any of his dialogues. In this consists the grand *far-sightedness* and grand peculiarity of this philosopher. I will try to tell you something about this design. As we have it before us today after extremely laborious reconstructions that are the result of the most exigent study, this design allows us to look into a philosophical system that hardly has any equals, it is so immensely deep, thought through, full of ideas and profound soundings. What is most peculiar and most profound about it is that <u>Plato *did not write it down*</u>. Plato *did not want* to pass on this system as something completed and capable of becoming tradition. This is the *far-sightedness* of a thinker who understands philosophy as a *living work* of someone who cares for the soul in thought and who avoids every final fixing of what he somehow advances, what he lays before us not just for acceptance or belief (belief in the sense of δόξα [opinion/appearance]), but rather for examination, for further work.

It might be said: this is illogical. If I want something to be discussed further, then the first thing is to make it somehow public. And Plato did make this public—by debating, lecturing about what was most his own with his most intimate pupils whom he considered most able to reconcile themselves with something like this. And these lectures all bore the title "On the Good" (Περὶ τἀγαθοῦ). It is said that Plato once held that kind of lecture. No. Instead it was a systematic deed, it was a *systematic of his own ontocosmological philosophy* that bore this title, and it remained unwritten, as it stands in the *Seventh Letter*.

In the *Seventh Letter*, among other things, it also says that this most singular content remains unwritten because the care of the soul, which takes place through constant examination, also has within it even this *ideal*, that means this *spark*, which nourishes it. In this spark there is something that manifests itself, something shows itself, in it there is a kind of *vision*— and this vision cannot be entrusted to mere word because the word is fundamentally two-sided, double-meaning. The word *simultaneously* means opinion and insight, it means opining and looking-in. That is why what is in the profoundest sense looked-in by the philosopher, very easily becomes the object of a discussion that in reality is no longer a philosophical discussion, because it is not guided by that to which I look-in, but rather is guided by merely verbal opinion. But in the discussion not intended as an honest battle about *what is*, but rather so others look at it, so they may be entertained, where someone is to eventually win, in such an agonistic discussion, even the most profound and most reliable view can be torn to pieces.

So then there are *three* currents of care of the soul: the first is ontocosmological; the second is *care of the soul in the community as the conflict of two ways of life.* Into the sphere of this conflict belongs the death of the just and the truthful as the end of the traditional polis and the sketch of the new community founded upon a philosophical final truth in what we might call absolute truth. The third current is *care of the soul regarding its inner life,* its relation toward the body and incorporeality, the problem of death and immortality. This is the third, most intimate, most inner current.

Each of these three sides of the care of the soul should require such a thorough account that it should really demand a lecture just for itself. But after all, we only want to get from Plato somewhere further—even if I judge that in the founding of this peculiar ideal, the *ideal of philosophy* as *living in truth*, in truth that wants to be capable of being looked-in at and obligates us, and as a result of this absolute obligation teaches us absolute obligation, there is genuinely something so fundamentally important, so fundamentally new, that man lives from this, in a certain sense, right up to today. Today we live from this care and concern for the soul, but in a certain sense, in decline. Why in decline?—We will talk about this later. The objective side of the care of the soul has become so immensely hypertrophied, and has become so especially attached to its practical application, that this other side, this fundamental side, of *forming of the self,* has been forgotten. To this day, the care of the soul is the ground upon which we move, from which we live, and within which we are—without our even being aware of it.

I would like to at least indicate something. You all know that Plato's teaching is always labeled as the teaching about ideas and that characteristic of Plato's philosophical thought is the peculiar hierarchical division of the world, or rather let us say existence, because what Plato calls the world, is not all of being, but rather only its certain part, that part that is not comprehensible in itself, is not intelligible. Above this world exists something that only then makes it comprehensible—and that is just that true world, true existence to which belong the ideas.

What are the ideas? Everyone assumes they know something about

1　this. Some say the ideas—this is the first attempt at a theory of concepts, they are generalities, what we call general concepts, except that Plato in his naïveté somehow became confused, and from these generalities, which we know do not exist and are only our means of thought, he made a lot of permanent, otherwise worldly and immaterial existents.

2　　Others instead tell us: the ideas—this is just what allows us to understand things around us, what we always already have to know when we want to see individualities around us as something. When, for example, we want to call "a glass" what is shining here and what, when I touch is hard and rounded and so forth, then after all, I need something that is not encompassed by this shining and roundedness and so on, in and of themselves, I need something that gives all this *unity*, what only then shows all this as a meaningful whole. And what only then somehow orders all my impressions and tells me what they really are—do you see in this roughly the Kantian teaching? Those are the ideas.

3　　And then there are those who say but the ideas—after all, those are genuine beings in the essential sense of the term that are unknown to us in this world of constantly changing and decaying things, these are concentrations of all possible meaningful content within a unity, which we will never be able to encounter with our own eyes, and so on, which we can never meet in our surroundings. It can be somehow ascertained only through immense concentration of philosophical thought. The ideas—this is an entirely *different way of being*, eternal being, where there is neither birth nor extinction and where it is impossible to speak of something like time, and so on.

　　But just because there are such difficulties with all this, there are such an immense variety of interpretations, and each of them has something to them. Because the idea is something *general*, that it is a *unity*, which is, as Plato says, one above the many, we have to, in a certain sense, always pose the idea as some "one"—that is certain. It is just as certain that Plato genuinely imagined the world of ideas as some kind of peculiar concentration of being, as *a different being* than the one here. There is equally something to the third interpretation, that the ideas serve to give us clarity about things, that in a certain sense this *manifesting* of things is tightly connected with the ideas, that things cannot manifest themselves to us other than on the basis and through the mediation of the ideas, that manifesting is something other than what manifests itself, that it is an entirely different kind of structure.

This is where we arrive from our initial explications. In and of themselves, things that manifest themselves, after all, have within them neither near-ness nor far-ness. They do not have within them something like distortion nor perspective; they do not have within them something like an authentic way of being in the original and deficient way of givenness. But things cannot manifest themselves to us without these oppositions; they cannot show themselves to us. Manifesting is of its own kind, a sui generis field, a structure that is structured in these kinds of peculiar oppositions. There always has to be something *more* here than what manifests itself—if it is to manifest itself. And we know that *manifesting* is manifesting of *unity within the many* and within many manners of givenness and so on.

Plato, no doubt, has before him this fundamental thought and has a peculiar guiding thread for his own peculiar way of thematizing this thought, that things can manifest themselves to us only on the basis of something else than what they themselves are. In Plato this guiding thread is *mathematics*, mathematical structure. This teaching is immensely difficult to comprehend, but I will permit myself to explain certain of its simple foundations.

So that something should be at all and should be manifest—it must be *one*. Fundamental within everything that is, is: that it is one. If we considered broadly everything that is needed so that whatever kind of thing manifests itself to us, that it is, for example, also necessary for this that it distinguishes itself from others and yet is similar to them and so on, all these threads of meanings, in which a thing only then starts to sketch itself out as what it is—if we were to reflect in this way, then we would never get anywhere today. I will only briefly tell you in what sense for Plato mathematics is the key to the structure of existence, and even its manifesting.

In the world around us, we constantly have spatial things before us. But spatial things are, after all, limited by surfaces. If we should erase surfaces, we should erase bodies. Surfaces themselves presuppose something prior to them, they presuppose lines. Erase lines and you erase surfaces. Lines themselves in turn still presuppose something else, at the very least a plurality of points. Points have to be at the very least two if they are to determine a straight line. But this means that points presuppose number. And so we get—as you already see—a whole particular scale: numbers, then points, lines, surfaces, bodies.

In the cosmological dialogue the *Timaeus*, Plato enigmatically says that when our world was created, *indivisible*, unmoved and eternal *being* was somehow forced, mixed and incorporated with *divisible*, becoming, and material *being*. Thus, the *same* and the *manifold* were also fitted together at the same time. What does this peculiar strange formulation mean?

We said: indivisible being. You see, we took our point of departure from spatial forms and we went to always higher and higher presuppositions—until we got to those peculiar, primeval ones, which can no longer be broken down, which are in this sense absolutely simple.

What do you mean simple—you will ask—when they are numbers? For numbers are made up of units. Yes, numbers are made up of units. That is clear, but they are *paradigms of composition* made from units. But, added is the peculiar Platonic teaching, not in Plato himself—as is known, he does not write about these things—but rather in Aristotle, who says that Plato held *ideas* to be *numbers*, the most fundamental, most elemental numbers, and that these elemental numbers cannot be put together, arithmetical operations cannot be carried out with them. In this sense they are really also not made up of any kind of homogeneous identical units. Also added is the teaching that there are only ten of these elemental ideas (nine or ten—opinions about this are a little divided). Numbers as we know them, as we operate with them, where there are infinite, endless examples of every kind of number and where familiar operations can be carried out with them—these do not belong to the realm of ideas, they do not occur in the realm of proper ideas, they only occur in a certain lower domain, which is no longer a domain without any kind of presuppositions, but rather one that really presupposes the ideas.

In Plato's *Republic*, in the teaching about the state, at one point, where it speaks about how the philosopher must be able to capture *the one above the many*, it explains that existence is divided as a line sectioned twice into two parts.[2] When I divide the line twice into two parts, in such a way that each of these parts are unequal and mutually proportional after division, then, on the one hand, I get *the visible* world—that is one half of the line—and on the other, *the invisible* world—that is the other half of the line. The visible world is made up of, on the one hand, what is not real—from pictures, from the imagination, and so on. In a certain sense there is much more of this than of the real, that is, the second part of the line. But then, when I want to firmly determine somehow what is real, I have to take

2. *Republic*, VI, 509d–10a.

recourse to this second, invisible part of the line, and there I have something like triangles, squares, rectangles, and so on, in the precise sense of the word. Rectangles, squares, and circles in the precise sense of the world cannot be seen; they do not exist for our perception; they are accessible only to our logos, meaning they exist on the basis of definitions and these definitions are at the same time *idealizations*. Something like a circle, a line, that has no breadth—this does not exist in the visible world. Just as a line does not exist in this ideal sense. Let us say edges exist but not lines in the geometrical sense of the word. Thus we have to take recourse to the higher, and there I can determine *precisely*, for example, the circumference, volume, and certain other relations between individual moments of this kind of ideal form.

This, then, is the domain of mathematics. Numbers exist in this domain in our sense. They are numbers that can be added together and with which all kinds of logical, as the Greeks say, which means calculating, operations can be carried out. But the invisible domain also has within it just these kinds of diversities. It encompasses things such as the point, line, surface, and so on. Plato does not say point, because for him the point really does not exist for certain reasons that I will not explain here. Instead of the point comes the unit that can be multiplied infinitely. And so we have the point, line, surface, and a stereometric body; it does not go further, only three dimensions and number.

The most fundamental, most important problem for ancient geometry, geometry of Plato's age, is the problem of *the relations* within the mathematical domain. Relations within this mathematical domain—such as one, two, three, four, as dimensions—are really *graduated* in a peculiar way. We have quantities that are mutually incommensurable and quantities that are commensurable. But with the discovery of incommensurability, relations in the domain of mathematical entities do not end. And, it is shown that under certain circumstances, when we cross to another dimension, commensurability is possible between quantities that are incommensurable. For example, a rational relation is possible between quantities that are in and of themselves irrational when we move them up to another power. Should I have a triangle whose sides are irrational, then nonetheless it is possible that the square of one side will be in a rational relation with the square of the other side. Thus, it is possible to get to a gradation of relations between the rational and the irrational in the domain of mathematics.

This means that dimensionality does not only have the sense of passage from one dimension to another, but rather that it simultaneously has the meaning of the mixing of the *comprehensible with the incomprehensible*, that it simultaneously means the mixing of *two various principles* that Plato sees in the foundation of all things. But how do *quantities* originate at all? Every quantity has within it a dual principle. On the one hand, if you take a line, then you can—this is an old theme of Greek philosophy—divide it into two different parts. The smaller part you can keep dividing on and on; the one part will keep getting larger while the other will constantly become smaller. That is, we have before us a couple, always two parts, a pair of quantities that can infinitely grow and diminish. In this line is encompassed an infinite possibility of growth and diminishing that is indeterminate.

What is made from a line that has, let us say, two parts? A certain relation, a certain specified relation, the ratio 1:2. This means that the principle of indeterminacy, this potentiality of constant growth and diminishing has to be somehow directed, legalized by something else—and this other principle, that is the principle of *determinacy*, unity, *limit* whereas this first is the principle of *unlimitedness*, continual growth, and so on. These *two principles*, this is *the beginning of everything*—so holds Plato. And in these *primeval numbers* we have nothing but the *first models*, the first paradigms of this joining of two principles. *The ideas* are nothing but the first relations, *original relations* between this couple: between *indeterminacy* and *unity*.

But because these original relations are *numbers* and numbers are the presupposition for lines, lines for surfaces, surfaces for bodies, bodies for material things, for this reason encompassed in these original relations is really what is necessary so we may understand everything at all that is in the world. That is why this outline of existence, the thought that *ideas are numbers,* is the foundation of all the rest of understanding of the world.

Here comes yet another thought. We have numbers, lines, surfaces, stereometric bodies within the domain of mathematics. Four geometric spatial representations in total. But these four spatial representations are simultaneously, vertically conceived, the model for the hierarchy of existence: at the bottom the material world, then the mathematical, which mediates between the material world and the higher one, and finally the archetypes of the linking of the indeterminate and unity—these are the *ideas*. The mathematical is contiguous with the *ideas* and this *mathematical* is at the same time the *soul*.

At first glance, this seems immensely abstruse, peculiar and impossible. But we cannot forget about one thing, that in Plato the soul is obviously something interior, and this interior does not show itself to us. What shows itself to us, that in which the soul manifests itself to us, is just that, in whose light things show themselves to us. Our soul manifests itself to us precisely in these mathematical formations, it shows itself to us in how we *measure* things around us, how we determine them, how we reconcile ourselves with them in thought. Of course, we reconcile ourselves with them also aesthetically; we reconcile ourselves with them also with our senses. But the senses belong to the domain of the body; this is nothing but the result of mutual causal action among things. But what shows the activity of the soul in its proper sense is our relation with the mathematical world. There, in mathematics, in *thought, thinking* shows itself to us, in thought *thinking* is present. That is why the soul is in this intermediate domain.

of course the soul is intermediate — phenomenology studies the intermediate

In the cosmic projection, the soul genuinely is a geometrical formation, it is that X there, in the sky, it is that surface which embraces the world, and that surface is determined by the principle circle, the equator, and then there is also a second circle there, an interior one, that is an ecliptic one, and these two circles determine not only the shape but also the movement of the heavenly vault.[3] Plato himself called this part of his teaching myth and fantasy; but not that part touching these two original principles, the indeterminate which is forced into the determinate, *contemporaneously* with identity and difference. While in the domain surrounding us, *difference* prevails, *identity* prevails in the domain of principles and the mathematical.

No doubt these Platonic reflections encompass something that philosophy has forever intended, that it has sought for ages up through today. Whether the *manner*, through which Plato leads this thought of his, the thought of *appearing existence*, is really adequate and pure—that is another, further question. That Plato considers that, which is the principle, indivisible and permanent, as at the same time *higher existence*, not just what facilitates the manifestation of existence—in this Plato undoubtedly succumbs to the tradition of Greek philosophy, or better said, to the philosophy of that time, which considers as existent what is most present and most enduring. In this Plato's reflection becomes something other than mere

3. *Timaeus*, 36b–e.

reflection, it becomes a teaching about *absolute being*, it becomes the teaching that we call (metaphysics) This means both teaching about *manifesting* and about *existence*. That which manifests existence is in turn another, higher existent, and so on. The philosophical ideal of *life in truth* is formulated here as *a metaphysical ideal*, but it remains grand that Plato did not rigidify this into some formula, that Plato did not pass it on, that Plato merely debated about it with those closest to him. You know that among those closest to him belonged those who rejected this entire method, that two of the four references we have about the lectures *On the Good* come from Aristotle (in an indirect way), from that thinker who accepted the teaching about mathematical entities, because—as he says—the mathematical can be isolated without us committing an error. Nothing changes about the mathematical, whether it exists, whether it moves or does not move. But where the ideas are concerned, for example, in something like the idea of man, the idea of a living being, essentially a living thing—to elevate such an existent into the unmoving and indivisible means to falsify it—so according to Aristotle. That is one of the directions.

The other is life in the community life *of the philosopher in the community* Important for the life of a philosopher in a community is that the philosopher poses the question of the lawful arrangement of life in the community from the point of view of the thought of the just life. The community is traditionally administered by certain rules. In the community that is administered as it should be, justice rules. But this justice should not be apparent justice, meaning justice for the exterior, justice for the consequences of justice; rather, it should be justice for the sake of justice, because it is understood that justice is something good and right. This is the understanding at stake. And naturally, understanding this matter means coming into conflict with ordinary perception, which understandably looks at right and justice and so on entirely differently, which looks at right and justice as a matter of utility, an external utility, as a matter that can be put to a specific test. No ordinary citizen is going to behave with regard to others as he would behave by himself and for himself. In ordinary perception, right and justice is regard for others. Justice can be understood either as the ideology of the weak, or as a certain tradition that is preserved because it brings advantages. Justice is simply not anything written by nature in the core of things, but rather a matter of convention (νόμος). Who is of this opinion—and naturally all these sorts appeared in these times—comes into conflict with the philosophical conception according to which (justice) is not rooted in convention, but rather is something that allows for human coexistence at all, and that exists just as much in the individual soul as in the projection of the individual soul into the social whole that forms the proper axis and structure of public life.

What is said about justice, this really applies to human (ἀρετή) (excellence/virtue) in general. Justice is only the all encompassing title that is used for ἀρετή in general. Ἀρετή is what makes man in the good sense of the word—that is, indivisible—even if he has four distinct moments.

This dual way of seeing, the common way of seeing and the way of seeing of the philosopher are inevitably in conflict. And the entire traditional community, even the present community, is of course disturbed and disquieted by the philosopher. The philosopher brings all public and secret ways of regarding things into difficulty. I say public and secret because in the ordinary way of regarding right, justice, and ἀρετή, in Plato's polis, something like absolute hypocrisy rules. On the one hand, the traditional way of existence is upheld, and it is put forth as the ideal. Precisely those who returned after the end of the rule of the thirty and installed democracy in Athens again, they after all, wanted to reestablish the old mores, upon which rested that great community of Miltiades and Themistocles, that is to say the community that drew upon a solid tradition and from an absolute reliance on the loyalty of its citizens, on their will for equality in front of the community, from the reliance on their honesty, that will not want to take possession of anything more than is in the interest of such a community, where all want to take part in an equal manner in responsibility and rule.

They want this ideal, they do have this ideal in mind; but somehow they are not up to it. In reality, a rather different kind of opinion already rules, in reality, a *tyrannical* opinion in the extreme. Everyone knows and everyone imagines that all this is just a convention that must be preserved, if the state is to remain barely wobbling on its feet. But in reality, it is advantageous for everyone to take power of as many goods as possible, and this means ultimately to seize hold of the other citizens. And to seize hold of the other citizens means to become a tyrant. And to be a tyrant is the highest ideal of every ordinary Athenian democrat of those times. And Socrates reveals all this. This is contained within the *Gorgias* rather clearly; this is contained within the first and second book of *The Republic*; these things are spoken about rather openly there. In the discussion with Callicles in the *Gorgias* the topic of conversation is nothing other than this problem.

These circumstances naturally lead to the conflict with that philosopher who sees justice and all other ἀρετή as the relation—remember what we just laid out about cosmo-ontology—as the *internal relation* within man himself between distinct moments from which man is composed, from which is composed his ψυχή (soul). The soul is in relation to everything; the soul is in relation as much to the sensible as to what is above it. The soul is just what is capable of taking care of itself, capable of drawing itself out of decline and forming itself into something solid, determined, precise, to find solid relations between each of its components. To establish such precise relations signifies justice.

Let us then project this into the community itself: we get four conditions without which the community cannot exist, that is the condition which comprehends to whom is showed what is truthful, the condition which helps him in this, and the condition which serves finally for mainly bodily needs and all other needs that are not merely elementary but also luxurious, that is the state of the nourishers. It is now a matter of getting to an analogy between what is the solid relation between the constituents of the soul and the constituents of state life. That is the problem of the Platonic State.

This problem is—as you see—the problem of *the intermediate*, again a problem similar to the one in ontology, where something always must mediate between extremes, where ideas mediate between these contrary principles, where specific kinds of relations, from the purely rational through the simply irrational and complex irrational extend all the way to complete indeterminacy. This problem is again the problem of the intermediate and is embodied in its essence in this intermediate state, in the condition of those who have both the ability to comprehend what is just and turn to those who take care of everything that is bodily as their guardians, as their advisors and protectors against external and internal enemies. This is the problem of the intermediate in the completely concrete sense of the word.

These people, these guardians who get the highest education, the highest παιδεία (education), who arrive at an understanding of what is, and from whom is chosen the government, these guardians are at the same time constantly on the battlefield. They are those who must constantly be prepared to risk, to sacrifice their lives and at the same time must be prepared for the most self-abnegating discussion and for the most self-abnegating kind of life. Upon them, upon this intermediate, rests the whole state; upon their asceticism, upon their sincerity, upon the soul of their self-abnegation rest the mores of the social whole. They are also the model for all the rest. And those who live the life of the community, meaning to live for the community, for the whole, for others, only because they live in this kind of way for others, render possible something such as *the state of justice*. This then, is the second current of this reflection.

As you see, this is the problem of the state as founded upon *spiritual authority* that is simultaneously joined to justice as founding ἀρετή (excellence/virtue). In the rulers who are chosen from these guardians, the soldiers of the body and the spirit, ἀρετή-σοφία (excellence/virtue-wisdom) predominates; in the rest ἀρετή-σωφροσύνη (excellence/virtue-moderation) predominates, this means discipline. For them it is property, of course within certain limits; for them it is the family; for them it is the continuation of their existence by others, through their descendants, whereas for the first nothing else exists except the community, they exist only within the common.

We will leave this third current for next time, because I think that a lot was laid out today. And now I should just ask if you have any questions. They do not have to be about today's material, they can also be about other things.

Last time I told you that within this care of the soul I catch sight of the essential heritage of Europe, that is to say, what in a certain sense made European history what it is. This does not mean that these thoughts were realized here, it only means that they were a certain ferment, without which we cannot conceive of European reality, that the unphilosophical, especially the neo-Platonic, reconciled itself with this and was to a certain degree forced by this to reflections often of an entirely different stamp. But from this impulse something constantly remains here and this original impulse is returned to again and again. Do not think that I would assert this thought in some kind of dogmatic fashion. I would only like to show that in the conception of the care of the soul is encompassed something like *the ideal of the truthful life,* that is a life that, as much as in praxis as in its activity of thinking, always directs itself by *looking-in*. The way in which man carries this out, how the philosopher sees it, is understandably subjective, directed by his capacity, it directs itself by his particular circumstances, but precisely in the fact that care of the soul lies in that proximity of the problem, in this exposing oneself to criticism—in this is already given the *self-overcoming* of the philosopher.

Finally, it could also be said that discussion takes place, on the one hand, within philosophy itself and, on the other, between philosophy and not-philosophy. The most important is just this discussion with not-philosophy, because as we shall see later, philosophy tries to discuss, for example, with such an enormous and hard reality as is the only great power created by antiquity, that is the reality of Rome. And that philosophy tries in a certain sense to discuss with what rejects every philosophy, and [rejects] it in the name of something that philosophy itself helped to conceptually formulate, that is in the name of the absolute, absolute being, and so on.

7

The Care of the Soul in the City: *Politeia*—The Transformation of
Myth into Religion—The Care of the Soul as Movement:
The Discovery of Eternity—The Metaphysical
Foundation of Europe's Heritage

Last time I said that in Plato's work the care of the soul is applied in
three directions. First, in the general layout of being and existence, that is,
in the grand system of principles of the world of ideas, which itself is the
principle of the world of mathematics. This is the framework of our world,
both concerning its components as well as its movement. In regard to its
composition, the cosmos is the beatified spirit and all its parts are the
harmonic parts of its structure. This is one perspective. The other is how
the care of the soul is applied in the plan of life in the community, that is, in
our common-historical life.

At the center of each these three reflections still is the concept of the
soul. The soul forms the center of the ontological-cosmological schema,
there the soul is the center that mediates between being as the foundation
of all existence, between principal being and the weakened being of things
around us. Already, the first point of view, the first layout of the problematic, encompasses a kind of answer to the question: What is the soul? The
soul is the center mediating between principles and between principiates,
between what is absolutely eternal and what is close to nothingness in all its
character and all its stamp of being, to what, just about, does not exist. The
soul is what is movable, but movable in the sense of lawful ordering and
orientation to the higher.

How then does care of the soul play out in our social life? I already
started to lay this out last time. This playing out naturally is connected to

the way Plato looks at the contemporary decline of his community and its relation to the traditional community, to its past and eventually to the future, because Plato looks at the historical process as something that can be the object of philosophy and that is tied to the fate of mankind and the human soul in general. The contemporary decline of the Athenian community is, as we know, represented by the fate of Socrates. Socrates' fate is for Plato the criterion, from which it is clearly evident that the contemporary city that wants to be traditional is no longer capable of this today. And in reality latent tyrannical opinion rules over it.

For this reason the community of that period is no longer capable of carrying out the synthesis for which the Athenian community had been renowned—the synthesis of authority and freedom—which was characteristic for it and which made the community become the very example of the Greek world and showed its superiority over all else in the world. The most powerful that had hitherto ruled over the world, the synthesis of all eastern monarchies in the form of the Persian Empire, destroyed itself in its aggression against Greece, above all against Athens. But this great historical moment was substituted by a situation of decline, which manifested itself in what Thucydides called the great war, in what signified in actuality the catastrophe of the entire Greek polis, in what ended with the catastrophe of Athens and the convulsions of Athenian constitutional life after the end of the war, convulsions which manifested themselves in the actual tyranny of the thirty. This did not end even with the return of democracy to Athens. Despite the fact that those who were returning were pacified, just after this return, the trial of Socrates began and ended so tragically. Not that Socrates' trial was something tragic for Socrates—Socrates was a seventy-year-old person when he had to bid life farewell—but it was tragic for the community itself, for it showed its blindness, its incapacity to see both its own duty and what the community could be in general and what it ought to be.

The community itself does not see that the philosopher, who is the thorn in its side, is in reality—mythically spoken—the envoy of the gods. The tragedy of the entire situation is that this divine envoy, this mouthpiece of Apollo, the god of enlightenment and self-knowing—γνῶσι σεαυτόν, "Know Thyself," is the Delphic utterance—is accused precisely of ἀσέβεια—of atheism. From there follows the program for those who outlived Socrates: it is no longer possible to participate in life in the community, in that actual community, rather one's strength has to be reserved for the planning and laying out of a different community, one where the philosopher can help himself as much as others, in which the philosopher does not need to perish.

This philosophical-political schema, where the philosopher does not perish, but rather where his constant examining, whose unwritten, because unwritteable, layout was that first ontological cast, which we encountered last time, this problem of the city also revolves around the problem of the soul and care for it. The state, as Plato describes it, is only a specific pretext, a specific impetus to develop and treat the problem of the soul. We do not know the soul, we cannot know the soul, because it is something invisible after all, something with which we do not come into contact the way we do with other things. And that is the reason why, in his considerations about justice as the fitness of the soul, which opens his treatment of the problem of the state, Plato introduces this connection to political life in context of the state.

You know how the problem of the state is introduced in this work, which is really the first preserved systematic of the problem connected to political life, its development, decline, and possible renewal. It originally begins in the separate dialogue *Thrasymachus,* which is analogous to other dialogues from Plato's youth, which are concerned with the definition of a certain ἀρετή (excellence/virtue), a certain human excellence. Just as the *Laches* speaks about courage and the *Euthyphro* about piety, so the dialogue *Thrasymachus* is about justice. Right at the threshold of this whole conversation, when he intervened in the developing dialectical discussion between Socrates and Polemarchus, this sophist pronounces a certain insolent and entirely tyrannical opinion representing the thesis that justice is in reality the interest of the stronger. What people ordinarily understand as justice is in actuality a mere simpleminded naïveté, or let us say stupidity, and it is an affair of the weak and powerless. Whereas real ἀρετή is the exact opposite: the ability to, as far as possible, take power of everything that is at hand, and this means above all to take advantage of all others. When Thrasymachus pronounces this thesis, Socrates is initially busy just purely refuting this thesis, and this with not always above-board methods, because against a sophist, Socrates is not choosy and calmly uses means equally sophistical.

But this whole discussion led only to show with a certain probability that justice is not what the sophist says. It has entirely different qualities: justice is really what strengthens society and what gives it cohesion, makes it healthy, and so on. This is shown, but at the same time, the character of justice, what it is, remains in the dark. Only at the beginning of the second book, where Plato's brothers come onto the scene and make these two amazing speeches, which in one stroke take the whole discussion to a high level, the problematic starts to develop in connection with the problem of the soul. Both of Plato's brothers require Socrates to separate the problem of justice from connection with those kinds of questions such as whether justice is externally profitable, whether it strengthens society, or whether it is the other way around, and that he concentrate attention on the question what is justice in and of itself, meaning within the soul, with that within us which is the object of philosophical care, with that within us capable of truth and falsehood, and what, as a result is then able to furnish in its very essence that side of truthfulness encompassed in justice as virtue, as human excellence.

These two speeches are in peculiar opposition. First, Glaucon makes a speech that Thrasymachus could or should make, had he not been occupied with tangential concerns, but rather genuinely deepened his thesis, that justice is nothing else but weakness. Or let us say that in a certain sense it is something that benefits certain people, or even the majority, but in some kind of negative sense of the word. You see, in this speech is made that grand distinction between what is good in itself and in its consequences, and that which is merely instrumental. Thrasymachus, the representative of latent tyrannical opinion, takes his point of departure from common opinion, which holds that justice is not good in itself, nor even the good we like for itself or for its consequences. Rather it is only a means, which follows from that, in and of itself, it would be best of all to be able to want and have everything we may desire, without regard to whether it is ours or not, whether we commit a wrong or not. In that case, as can be seen, to commit wrong also belongs to what is good. Against this, the factical human situation is that to be in a situation where we are wronged is obviously understood by us as evil. This "to be wronged" is a much more burning, a much more pregnant evil than "the ability to commit wrong" is a good.

You understand, to be able to commit wrong is a splendid thing, but we do not feel it to that positive degree as we feel negatively the wrong committed to us, especially when we are unable to take vengeance—and that is usually our situation. Because this is the way it is, people establish conventions among themselves: they will not mutually harm each other, and they consider this instrumental good as the norm of human conduct, the rule by which they will guide themselves in everything. Because in actuality everyone is of this opinion, justice has to be comprehended as something that has its validity only in this convention and in this social consensus. As soon as we look at every person individually and from within, what do we discover? Nothing other than tyrannical opinion, the desire to take power of everything as far as possible within our grasp. This is then shown by the thought experiment in the history of the ring of Gyges, which is to be evidence that everyone holds this opinion in their soul, that in actuality the character of our soul is given by nature. Here the problem is already articulated: what is justice in regard to our soul?

Then comes another thing, a confrontation of two kinds of life, the life of the just person with the unjust. So we may be able to carry out this confrontation, we must first put before us in idealized form—idealized not in the sense of some ideal, but rather in the mathematical sense, as is a line, a certain idealization of something which in reality lines, and so forth, only merely approximate. Ideally the unjust will simultaneously be that person who is able to realize his injustice perfectly, and the perfect realization means that he will never be a sucker in his injustice. This means he has to take care that he never manifests himself as unjust, because injustice is seen as something negative in human society. The peak of injustice will be to actually be unjust but at the same time to always seem just. This is injustice in its pure form. In the same way, justice in its pure form is where the just can never be even suspected of acting from reasons of external gain. For these reasons he will act thus even when he will constantly seem unjust, although he is just.

Socrates is the case of the just who appears as unjust. Socrates is the one who is the constant thorn in the side of the entire community. He performs the constant task of unselfish caring for the community, in the sense that he is constantly thinking only about its good. At the same time, he does what has been assigned him, what is his function, and he does not mix into what others do. In this sense he realizes the Platonic definition of justice τα ἑαυτοῦ πράττειν, to do one's own to do what is my own proper task. Yet his constant examining, his constant nagging, so to speak, is what

reflexive

makes him the object of hatred of everyone—his showing that the community is in a bad way.

How do these two end up, how does this comparison end? The man who is perfectly unjust will be successful in everything, will attain the highest success in the community, will rule, will attain such riches, such distinguished posts, will marry his children into the best families, will realize all his aims and yet will always be focused only on his own, and in actuality does not care about the community. The other will neither have peace nor success, and all the failures of the city will be blamed upon him. He will end up being accused and brought before justice. Because it is impossible that this man would not come into conflict with the community, he will necessarily be accused and will end up in horrible agony upon the cross. This is the comparison of the two. The man of perfect truth and justice has to necessarily perish in a community of this kind of opinion, where this kind of image of justice rules.

And then Plato's second brother comes and says: this is still not enough. This still is not that strongest thing which burns us the most. The defense of justice Glaucon pronounces is still not everything. Even more important is the way in which justice is praised in our entire tradition. It is no better than this praise of injustice, it is in actuality identical to it. It is praise not of justice for itself, as it is in our soul. It is in actuality praise of external consequences, social results, δόξα (opinion), semblance. In this way, the old poets Hesiod and Homer praise justice when they show that he whom fortune favors is just—the just king about whom Homer speaks, that his flocks multiply, that bees bring him honey and his granaries overflow, and so on.[1] This opinion is the same even today. Justice is thought about in the same way, even more so, in present times.

What is a young person to do in such circumstances, who sees before him the choice between the life of justice and injustice? Both are something difficult, on the one hand bidding the grand life of success and, on the other, resembling something akin to shipwreck. Of course, it is difficult to live this unjust life so that a person escapes detection, but nothing great is gained without difficulty. He who once takes this path has to develop a great art. After all, he will not escape the sight of the gods—but what if the

1. *Odyssey* XIX, 109–13.

gods do not exist? After all, today—this speaks from that entire age—we are so far along that we can be explicit about this skepticism: whether the gods exist, we do not know, and if they do exist, then we only know about them from the poets, who render the gods like beings who can be moved in their interests to justify the unjust. In addition to that, we also have mysteries, initiations, sacrifices, all kinds of ritual and god-mollifying practices that cause the unjust to accomplish what they want not only in this world but also in Hades. What to do under these circumstances?

These two brothers offer such a culminated attack on justice and at the same time require Socrates to tell them not about justice and injustice in relation to social success and failure and to δόξα, to semblance, to what brings consequences of particular acting, but rather in relation to the true character of the thing, to that, how it is within our soul and how it shapes it. You see, the problem of justice is the problem of the soul, its internal shaping and its form.

What does Socrates then do? He says: I am in a big quandary, I cannot say either yes or no, you just carried out such an amazing apology for injustice that I cannot but admire you. Although you are able to speak in such a manner, nonetheless you do not think like that. Apparently, there is something divine within you, because it is divine to take the side of truth, almost from the character of one's own inner being, although I am not clear about what is the truthful. And I am supposed to defend justice at your behest? This is difficult in the highest degree for me. Of course, it is no less difficult not to defend it.

What to do? The question is: What is justice in the soul? The soul is something invisible, something I am unable to see. Where do we encounter the soul? Perhaps something that already helped other philosophers to get from the visible to the invisible would help us. When we spoke about Democritus, I told you how he got from the visible to the invisible— through a geometrical analysis, through the similarity of triangles or other geometrical forms. When I sketch a geometrical form in the sand, I can demonstrate certain theorems upon it, for example, the sum of its angles, or the Pythagorean theorem. Because I know about the similarity of triangles, I know that what counts here for this shape sketched in the sand counts even for those I do not see, which are not apparent. Atoms are kinds of stereometric forms that I do not see but for which geometrical theorems certainly apply, that I can demonstrate on the visible.

Where do I have some kind of model in which I see the soul in its action? I do not need to carry out something, such as a mystical look into oneself. This model is there where justice and injustice are visible—*in the community*. Only for this reason the conception of the state is brought into this entire examination. That state comes into the investigation of justice, of the soul and of what is its nature, through this turn. For this reason Socrates brings the community into genesis. Let us see how the state is constituted, how it is formed, and from what it is made up. Perhaps during this forming we will come upon what in this great visible model is justice and what is not, what is its opposite.

The genesis of the ideal community, naturally the community according to reason, is carried out here. What Plato explains about how the state originates is not the genesis of the historical community. The historical community obviously comes into existence from injustice, out of violence. But we are concerned about the genesis of the rational community, which comes into existence through agreement. By that agreement there exists something like a reciprocity of interests rooted in the reciprocity of our needs. No one is completely self-sufficient, precisely on the basis of our absolutely basic needs—these are named there in a certain order, the most basic is the need for food, the second is the need for shelter, and the third is the need for clothing, all these are physical needs. On the basis of these important physical needs, then, it is possible to construct the elementary community composed of four or five people. There it is shown that it is advantageous if everyone does what is his own, that everyone does not look after all their own needs. Rather, each individual looks after the needs of exclusively one kind; he specializes and furnishes some one thing for everyone. The city then lives in this kind of reciprocity. Only a very elementary community is going to satisfy only physical needs. Even when this community grows, when all the individual needs within it naturally expand (because this community will not be completely self-sufficient, contacts with the outside through trade and with someone who mediates between these needs, through internal trade, will arise there, and there will also be people who are not specialists and who will only be workers, and so on), all these people will make up an elementary and simple community, healthy, but absolutely primitive.

We know how Glaucon jumps in here and says that this is not any ideal; this is awful. If you wanted to make a community for pigs, this would be about right.

Socrates draws a picture of life in this community where people will live on the whole decently. They will have bread and even all kinds of simple cakes, they will live long lives and will be able to reproduce only to the extent that no one lacks any of these basic needs. In this they will be rational, so that all their mutual services and needs be in complete equilibrium. But it will be a primitive and modest community. No one in it will have any, so to speak, higher aims other than the maintenance of elementary life on this level. They will live ahistorically, in a constant idyll; no one will try for preeminence over the other, everything will be in calm equilibrium.

Then, when Glaucon proclaims this is not human, the problem arises how the properly human reasonably gets into the community. The question is posed in this way: Where is justice and injustice in this community? Justice and injustice—says Adeimantus—is possible precisely in this reciprocity, in mutual accommodation of favor. Everyone does what is his, and gives from it what is due to the other. To this, Socrates says maybe there is something to that, but we have to go on. In the elementary community there is also justice in a very elementary form—justice of exchange, where for equivalent, equivalent is obtained. Everyone in this community has the same, so that in its own way, it is the community of justice. Of course, it is the community where the higher is lacking, where all functions are aimed at the maintenance of physical life and its needs. For this reason, the transition to the πόλις τρέφουσα (the nurturing city) is necessary, to the city that becomes hypertrophied and demands luxury. The introduction of luxury into the community turns it into the unbalanced community rather than the community in equilibrium. Within the elementary community, basic needs are clearly defined; in the community of luxury, they are not. There they grow without limit—here is the antithesis between πέρας (limited) and ἄπειρον (unlimited). The community of growing and ever multiplying needs, the passionate community—Plato at the same time calls it the bloated community, the hypertrophied one—is in its way a sick community. This leads to need to constantly expand. The community has to distend itself externally, and for economic reasons alone, this leads to war. War demands a military state. This community is sufficiently reasonable that the principle of specialization—that everyone does their own—rules in it. The community so organized will demand a special army. Here, Plato simultaneously sees a possible turning point. Those who manage this matter are not on the same level as the rest; they are people who deal with life and death. They risk their own lives and at the same time give death to the enemy. They are people whose specialization is to risk and to threaten life. These people can again bring equilibrium into this community, whose needs grow in a precipitous and unlimited way, and they are capable under certain circumstances of transforming it into a healthy community again. For this reason the entire problem of the community rests within them, within this class, in their formation. The community in new equilibrium will naturally not be the primitive community, but rather the community in which the infinite element will be in a certain way occupied, *tamed*, handled. At the same time, mutual exchange and equality will not rule in this community, the mutual exchange of the equivalent. A certain hierarchy will have to rule there, for the whole problem of the community is focused in the class of those who risk their lives and give death. When they risk life, they have to be courageous above all. But what does it mean to be courageous? You see that justice first wants something other than *this* excellence of the soul: it wants courage of these combatants, it wants a class of people who feel they are on the battlefield in every moment, and in every moment they really are upon it. But courage in Plato is naturally not blind courage, rather it is something regulated through *looking-in*. To be courageous means to know when I have to risk my life and when I have to threaten others.

In Plato this class is called *the guardian* and in this is already encompassed the thought that these people guard rather than attack; they guard and protect the community. But so that they know under what circumstances to defend—this is not simple—at the same time they have to be aware, they have to know, they have to be clear about this most horrible and least daily occurring thing of human life. They are the ones who in every instance represent the extreme human possibility, which man in reality never escapes, he just does not think about it: that man is a mortal being and that life has its end. They constantly have this in mind, constantly are in the field of this extreme human possibility. For this very reason these people have to be specially educated, they have to be a kind of paradoxical combination of the man of extreme insight and extreme risk. They are people who are seeking wisdom, that is, insight; and they are brave at the same time. This joining of knowing in which instant a human being has to risk his life, with knowing about all of life and all its relations— because knowing is something indivisible, which means insight into the whole of all things—the joining of these two only then makes up the guardian. The guardian has to have the profoundest philosophical training of which man is capable at all. And in this is the problem of the state, so that these kinds of people vouch for it. These people, who are the only ones able to understand what it means to be a guardian, what it means not to live for oneself, to abstract from oneself entirely and to live only for the whole—they are the true political people. Political responsibility is not everyone's affair. In this lies the hierarchy within the community. Responsibility comes into the hands of those who are singularly ready for it.

The choice of the guardians is a terribly important thing. Not everyone has the natural character that determines that he is to be a guardian. Here, it is necessary to select them and then give them the appropriate preparation, the appropriate education. From the guardians themselves are in turn chosen others still, from the guardians are chosen those who answer for the guardians themselves, who represent their own decision making. The entire body of the guardians cannot be determining, only a small group can decide for the community, or in the end only one, and this one or this small group is determined by another selection from the entire body of the guardians.

In this way we arrive at a peculiar hierarchy. Here is a community that takes care of physical needs, no longer in a primitive sense, but rather in a somewhat cultivated sense. Here we have the body of guardians and then, above this, those who decide what the community will do. They are those who will have the sharpest insight; naturally they will also be people of the highest responsibility and this means they will also constantly have to live on the battlefield. It is, so to speak, intelligence on the battlefield, eternally on the battlefield, never in peace. There is no longer exchange in the ordinary sense of the word.

There is nothing, as it were, to give these people from the rest of society. The rest of society cannot give them anything other than elementary nutrition. They also cannot accept anything else from them. Any other advantage cannot exist for them. As soon as something else should come up to them, they would no longer be guardians in this strong sense of the word. They can only be this. Just that is "to do one's own." This means that the principle "to do one's own" leads in this case to hierarchy, not to equality.

What do we see then? The city brought in this way into equilibrium again from the endlessness of constantly augmenting needs, the community in this way again tamed and disciplined, gives us a picture of life, where reason—that is to say, insight—directs action—that is to say, defense and attack, protection of the whole. To all of this the normal organic exchange of all functions regarding our bodily needs is subordinated. What is this in reality? Here we have a picture of what each of us individually is within himself.

✗ ✗ ✗   The picture, presented for us in this way, is in reality the soul in its projection into society, into this grand whole. The same thing is in miniature in our soul. There is also something that is capable of disciplining everything else, showing it the way. Further, there is what causes that we can dispose of our life in agreement or disagreement with insight. Last of all there are functions regarding our needs and our desires. Needs are necessary, but there are also needs susceptible of growth into infinity. To maintain them within the framework of πέρας (the limit) is the affair of these higher functions. This is the soul.

In society we then see a picture of the soul, and also the reverse (for we already have concern, care for the soul). Care of the soul is that which Socrates does, constantly examining our opinions about what is good. Each of our acts, each of our thoughts and each of our deeds is in the formal sense aiming for something, for some kind of goal. This goal as such, in its formal guise, we call the good. Examining what is good is care of the soul. We examine also in order to keep that of which we have once had insight.

The care of the soul consists in that we constantly examine our speech. Thinking is internal speaking, an internal conversation, dialogue that takes place within the Platonic dialogues between the discussing individuals and that in reality takes place also within the soul of each of these ✗ ✗ ✗ ✗ individuals who take part in this conversation. The care of the soul is something that transforms us internally, that at once makes us from instinctive and traditional beings; beings who look at what is normal in society and spiritually nourish themselves with this, into beings who entirely reverse this course, who are constantly examining. And only in that which resists this examining do they take on their own form. In this the soul becomes something determined, in this it elevates its degrees of being. Of course, the soul always is, even the soul of that ambitious person who falls into the sphere of ἄπειρον. But the soul that is cared for *is* more, it has a higher, elevated being. This being is, so to speak, thickened, concentrated, it is always the same, it does not dissolve, does not blur.

Because care of the soul is possible, the state is also possible, and the community is also possible. In the grand model of the state we saw what the soul is with its own internal tensions, with its internal contradictions, with tendencies, one of which aims downward and always wants more and more, and the other aims toward the most possibly intense being. The center there is θυμός, or let us say bravery, the organ of courage, capable of listening to the highest and risking at the same time. In this we discerned what is our soul. Yet, from the cultivating of our soul arises the possibility of forming the state, the community that is necessary so that a person like Socrates does not need to die. *yes.*

You see, then, that the question of the polis and its constitution, its constituting, is again the question of the soul, its character and its examination—care of the soul.

The most important side of this whole process of the transformation of the community into the true community of justice is, of course, the education of the guardians. This is the most proper subject of this work. When the question of law-giving comes into the new community, Socrates says that these are small details, with which he will not concern himself. We are interested not in law-giving in its entirety and in its details—it does not concern what will be, let us say, taxes, and what punishments will be meted out, but rather that most important thing—the only one this is about—the regulation of upbringing, education, which leads the guardians from the first moment of their existence to their end upon the battlefield, or until that moment when spiritual leaders will be chosen from them and when finally they abandon even this ruling function so that they dedicate themselves in the end only to themselves, and that means to the care of the soul in the sense of self-philosophical examining. Self-philosophical examining is the affair of the chosen, mainly in the situation where they no longer have to care about the community and when they can care about the universe in its entirety, for its harmony and its deep foundations.

I said: the regulation of education from its very beginnings. This beginning is formed in a peculiar way, it is the beginning of musical education. As you know, in his education, Plato is steeped within traditional Greece. The *bonne* class in Athens enjoyed this dual education: music and gymnastics. Musical education began earlier according to Plato—Plato ironizes this in part—it began with children's tales. And the first reform arrived at is, then, reform of children's tales. Children cannot be told all tales. They cannot be told certain children's versions of Hesiod's theogeny; they cannot be told children's versions of Homer's heroic histories. At least not without consequences. Why? Because behind this reform of children's tales lies something enormous: *the transformation of myth into religion*. Plato is the classical thinker who carries out this transformation.

In Plato's age, myth is in full decay. Myth is in decay already in the tragicians. Above all in the last of the great tragicians, Euripides, myth is already a matter that is reflected upon. But in its own full character, myth is there where it lives from afull, something unreflected, something that has us in its power as, let us say, a dream. We are not able to free ourselves from the power of the dream that lays before us certain quasi realities as if they were things themselves. Likewise, myth treats us in such a way. Myth is a grand passive fantasy—a fantasy that is not aware that it is fantasy and that answers to certain deep affective needs of man. Myth is practical in its entire character. In contrast to this, religion is something after all, which demands a personal act of faith; it is something actively carried out by us. And the Platonic religion is the first purely moral religion.

Greek philosophy was headed in this direction from its very beginnings. In Heraclitus, in Xenophon, and so on, we have dicta, where a philosophical-moral critique is posed in regard to the mythical, although perhaps moderated mythical world, for example, the Homeric. Behind Plato's reform of children's myth lies the thought that guardians, if they are genuinely to be guardians, cannot live within myth. Rather, from the very beginning they have to get used to living with an entirely different imagination of what is the divine than that of myth, with the imagination that the divine is the principal, the good, for which everything in the world is aimed. The divine is innocent of all that is insufficient and bad in the world.

This principle leads not only to the thought of reform of traditional myth but also to that whole side of Plato's critical activity, which is very often interpreted as something barbaric, amusical: his attacks on Homer, castigation of the poets, elimination of passages that do not fit into the Platonic scheme of what is heroic and divine, what is in actuality brave and heroic. Of course, we have to realize that the notion of the autonomous work of art is a purely modern thought, which the nineteenth century successfully fought for, and in the nineteenth century this notion also had its own reality and you all well know that this reality never really established itself. When art lived in constant relation with myth and religion, when art was not independent, no one ever hesitated to proceed as Plato proceeds. During the age of classical Greece, we already encounter similar phenomena long before Plato. For example, in one of his elegies where the distribution of human actions and human ages according to decades is given, Mimnermos says that in sixty years, everything is finished in man and he should die. Solon bid him to rework the poem and put eighty there instead of sixty. This is an example of how the task of the poet was perceived back then.

Of course, the poet in Greece of the classical age was considered a wise man who not only entertains the public but whose words also have weight. And they had even a law-giving weight. The poet was cited in court as testimony of certain juridical opinion.

I am not going to portray the whole progression of Platonic education. That would lead us to repeating what we have already spoken of in that first outline: the Platonic education of the guardians and of those who are chosen from them as rulers encompasses within it the ascent to the highest principles, encompasses the path out of the cave all the way there, into that clarity, to that domain from which the reality of the world around us is clarified. We spoke about this outline last time.

Now I want to note that because the problem of the community is in actuality the problem of the soul, not only the origin of the state of perfection but also all other forms of the state, the state of imperfection, are naturally explained in relation to the activity of our soul. There must exist a correspondence between the perfection of the state—what makes the state in the eminent sense of the word—and the state of the soul of those who take part in this constitution. And just like that the correlation between the decadent forms of the state and the condition of human mind exists. All this psychosociology of state life—this soul of the social group—this is the proper subject of Plato's work.

But then, there is also a third motif, a third substantial problematic that Plato lays out and that follows from the care of the soul, which from communication with others in the community draws itself back into itself and concentrates itself on the individual, on the relation of man to himself, on the relation to his φύσις (soul) and to his own eternal fate.

Cosmology has shown where the soul stands in the whole of existence; it is the origin of movement, it can only be understood in movement. The movement of the soul in its most proper sense of the word is precisely *care for its very self.* Neglect also belongs to care as its modality. Originally and most of the time, man is such that he neglects this care. The proper, positive care of the soul is somehow the concluding of something that is sketched into the nature of the soul, but is not always explicitly captured.

Teaching about the community showed the soul as a structure of contemporaneous moments that are in mutual tension, a structure that has to be stabilized, developed so that the soul acquires, as far as possible, the highest being.

Being means not merely some kind of positing of certain characteristics and certain structures; rather, in being itself all things are differences, there exists something like the ability to elevate being by degrees. The soul, which moves between principles and ideas and which is unitary, which cultivated itself by care of itself, is more than the soul that does not care for itself, that neglects itself, that eventually, just as it commonly is in pseudotyrannic perception, surrenders itself to desires, which are such that they grow without bounds, and succumbs to that ἀπειρία (unlimitedness, unboundedness), that second principle, the principle of multiplicity and indeterminacy. Indeterminacy has within itself just that negative, and as a result diminishes being, whereas care of the soul, by its efforts for unity, concentrates being, elevates it into a solid form.

The soul can be comprehended only if there exists something like being which is not physical, not bodily, not a thing, is not the world of things and material things around us. In this domain of being, the soul discovers itself, through its own movement, through thinking self-definition and reflection on this defining: precisely this is care of the soul, care of oneself. In this way the soul arrives to the realm of the ultimate, original reasons and origins. The realm of reasons and origins is at the same time the realm of causes and their order. Being teaches us to comprehend from what originated things, instead of taking care and dedicating ourselves merely to those constantly repeating and forever surrounding us actualities of common material surroundings. By that, we again and again encounter things, we do not arrive at any understanding of them, this is always only constant repeating of the same, getting to know further familiar, but not comprehended things.

During our experience, with which we get to know the proper character of the soul with the movement, through which the soul itself shapes itself, through which it has the capacity to shape itself, we also comprehend that when we do not shape ourselves through this way of conscious reflection, in reality, we still shape ourselves in the opposite way. We are the authority of our own decline, we are responsible for our decline. This experience of the soul about it itself discovers at the same time that there exists a depth of being, which we unveil only when we swim against the natural current and against all general tendencies of our mind and all our instinctive equipment directed to reality, to materialness.

This materialness is the realm of indeterminacy, which we do not know originally. We comprehend things around us in their indeterminacy only when we begin to measure them with precise measures, which are given for example by mathematical knowing. Behind mathematical knowing lie the ideas and behind the ideas lie their principles. Only then do we see that these are not any kind of precise forms, that everything around me is the domain of the undetermined δόξα (opinion). But δόξα means that this is not only the domain of the undetermined, but rather at the same time the domain of something constantly changeable and evanescent. Here is the philosophically conceived common experience, which Greek man always knows, that everything somehow melts away, that human life is not the only thing which is constantly declining. Rather all things are somehow in decline, all are decaying, all are being worn out in time.

The impetus of the soul to discover what is precise, pure, and does not succumb to all these changes and oscillating is, at the same time, a battle against time. While this is not explicitly articulated and thematized by Plato, it is factually constantly present. In relation to it itself, the soul is the discoverer of eternity. It tends toward eternity, and its most proper problem—the problem of the status of its own being—is the problem of the relation to eternity: whether in its being it is something fleeting, or whether in its depths it is not something eternal. This is that third current, third grand problematic, which follows from the care of the soul—the question of the eternity of the soul. Plato works out this question in a peculiar dialectical way. In the grand dialogue *Phaedo*, he tried to present something like the reasons speaking for the immortality of the soul, for immortality that is understood as enduring even after death, independence with regard to bodily existence, independence with regard to the world of decline. The soul is something that moves between these two domains, between the domain of principles and the domain of that principiate, the indeterminate, that itself it can embark on this indeterminacy and yet it can concentrate itself in such a manner that it gets a solid shape. In this effort for a solid and eternal form, it focuses upon its limit, to the limit which it wants to achieve. That the soul has this capacity provides the axis around which revolves Plato's thinking about this tension.

This is then placed into a peculiar atmosphere in Socrates' last conversation. The philosopher stands there before the situation that this world will stop existing for him in the next instant. What will be next? In the *Apology* is it said: if it is not-being, then something like that would be a gain. There it is, as if Socrates were not speaking of a high probability of surviving. But in the *Phaedo*, there is a fundamental change in this matter. That great change consists in that Plato is just the one who changes myth into religion and transforms traditional myth in its essence into myth of the immortal soul. He is both the first and the only one of the philosophers hitherto who understands the immortality of the soul in a way differing from tradition, for which the existence of the soul after death is a common fact. But you know that in Homer and in all those poets, the soul survives in the form of a mere shadow. I also said that even in the mysteries and ecstatic religions, immortality is always conceived as existence for the other. There the soul that exists in Hades is a mere picture, what can be seen, for example, in dreams. In dreams I see the long departed, but he himself does not have any core, he is only an image. In the mysteries, where he, the hero or god who dies again comes to life, like Dionysus or Adonis and so on, this also regards the vegetative cycle where the same renews itself in some kind of manner, but it is generically the same, that means form, something that I again see from the outside, that I can look at, whereas from within this problem is not posed.

For Plato, because he discovered the principle of the care of the soul, for the first time the soul is something that even in its fate after death is something that lives from within. Its fate after death becomes a component of its entire concern and care of itself.

We already said that in Plato the soul is the principle of movement, and movement is fundamentally the movement of the care of the soul, the self-directing of the soul by its own questioning, the effort to shape itself into a solid form. This is what the soul essentially is, but for this very reason, the soul is the only thing that brings itself into motion. Plato also conceives it as the source of all movement in the world. As a result of this, the soul is then in its most original form housed not in the human body, but rather in the body of the universe, and that of the universe, which is responsible also for the physical movement of all things.[2] In this way the theory of the soul also became the principle of some kind of fantastical physics. That is why it is also necessary to ask about the fates of the soul before birth and after death. The new Platonic myth answers to that. Almost all the grand Platonic myths talk about this question—about the question of the life of the soul before and after. In the end, this is a matter of faith, which is the principle no longer of mere myth, but rather religion. Here a certain individual act is required, what Socrates does in prison, when he offers a proof of immortality to his friends.[3] Of course, the reasons do not convince us and of course did not convince even the participants of that conversation—that is evident from the entire conversation—even when Socrates in the end is able to win against all counterarguments. There is a certain act of trust that is philosophical in that sense, that at least it shows how something like that is conceivable, and in that sense, perhaps, accessible to looking-in. This third principle is what in Plato's teaching also influenced an entire future, which takes place in the birth of something like religion. Religion, which, in contrast to myth, relies on myth only in the sense of a certain concretization of a fundamental ontocosmological conception of what the reality of all things stands upon.

In all three of these directions, Plato's teaching is the grand metaphysic of the Western world. All metaphysics, says one contemporary thinker, is Platonism.[4] The future of European life will show the profound effectiveness of all three of these motifs we articulated here and which basically are rooted in the thought of the care of the soul: the systematically cosmological motif, the practical-state motif, that is, of life in the community, spiritual power and spiritual authority, and last of all, the problem of how to convert myth so that in its place steps something like religious faith, religious faith in the sense of a purely moral religion.

2. *Timaeus*, 34b.
3. *Phaedo*, 66.
4. M. Heidegger, "The End of Philosophy and the Task of Thinking," in *Basic Writings*, ed. David Farrell Krell (London: Routledge, 1993), 427–49.

The Jewish religion, for example, is not purely moral. In the *Deca-logue*, and so on, there are undoubtedly moral precepts, but the Jewish God is the wrathful god who punishes in a manner beyond all human measure. And among human measures is also the measure of human insight. Apart from that, the Jewish God is not a matter of a purely moral religion; he is a god in this world, from that other world. Something like the difference between the two worlds, between the true world, the world of true being, and the world around us, the apparent world, the world of seeming, δόξα (opinion)—that exists only in Plato. This difference crossed into Christian theology from Plato. It did not cross there from the Jewish religion. Only here, on this basis, was something like the theological conception of divinity of transcendence able to arise.

When we realize all this, we see that what is usually said—that European life stands upon two fundaments, on the Jewish and the Greek—this applies only conditionally, so long as the Jewish element passed through Greek reflection. The Jewish element is only formed by Greek reflection so that it may become the ferment of the new European world.

You see this, for example, in what I told you about the myth of Socrates. The grandest Platonic myth is the myth about Socrates as the representative of the gods, who carries out his divine commission through examination—that is, the care of the soul—and necessarily gets into conflict with the power representing the highest that had been attained in the historical world, with the community, that had once been victorious over the Persians. And this community now destroys that man who is the man of divine dispatch. Here, there is this conflict, and as a result the whole world lies in evil. Here is the opposition between those two, between what is completely unjust and seems to be just, and what is completely just and seems to be unjust. As a result, it succumbs to the judgment of the world and necessarily brings upon itself that consequence. The sinfulness of the world falls upon his head; this culpability falls upon the head of the one who is just. Here in reality we have before us the outlines of the Christian myth. Already in the Epistle of St. Paul to the Romans it is said, after all, that the world lies in evil. This is here, in this myth.

Of course, the Christian conception the soul and care of it is disengaged from the intellectualism of Greek dialogue, Greek dialectic. In Plato, after all, the care of the soul takes place during conversation. Of course, not only in conversation but also in other moments there. Today I laid them out for you. Those who regulate the community and who have spiritual authority in the end have to be not only people of insight but also people of unconditional responsibility and courage. But in the Christian method all this is insufficient. Or better said, the moment of insight is further embedded in something peculiar, foreign. In Christianity, the moment of insight occurs in that Christian dogmas are not considered as something to be accepted blindly. Christian dogmas are something that man will never comprehend in their ultimate depths, but he can comprehend at least that much, which is the right and the wrong path. These dogmata have meaning, they are meaningful. In this, there is something that no other spiritual domain has. Again the Greek is reflected here.

The seeds from which it is possible to live off in subsequent difficult transformations are encompassed in what we have now portrayed as the grand metaphysic of the ancient world. Metaphysics itself grows out of a particular historical situation, from the situation of the decline of the polis, the decline of Athens. It creates a heritage that can survive in the declining polis, and survives even the decline of Hellenism, and helps so that after the decline of the Roman Empire still another formation is conceived, that is, Europe in the proper sense of the word. The surviving of the heritage is obviously also its change, but this metaphysical foundation still endures. And surprisingly, upon it the domain of European life is spread out, is generalized.

It is understood that we should not imagine this in such a way, that this metaphysic should take hold of reality in some kind of way, that people should explicitly reflect what we talked about here today. In those actualities such as the Hellenistic empires, there always existed people who grew out of this tradition, and they just about forced reality that was of a completely different origin to reconcile itself with this heritage, so that this difference itself was reflected by this, so that from its unreflected form it transformed into something which reconciles itself with this heritage. This process is our concern. This is not a one-sided reception of points of view; rather, it is always a discussion of philosophy with unphilosophy, with unphilosophical reality. In discussion of all this metaphysical epoch, this reflection has an active, attacking character. Back then, philosophy actually meant something that brought ferment into reality, that hitherto had not been in it, which is a situation entirely different from today. Today, philosophy is something playing an ever diminishing role in spiritual reality, which itself has to defend laboriously its own justification, its own autonomy, and so on, beside that which arose upon its foundation and which is no longer philosophy—science and technology.

Science and technology naturally coincide with a certain state of our entire society, which is more and more becoming a mass one, and with the thought of quantitative progress which carries this society. You remember that in the first lecture we talked about how according to certain signs it seems the thought of quantitative growth, which is implicated in everything occurring today in the world, is decisive in agriculture, in the organization of life, in technology and in science, is somehow at an end. The question is whether, under these circumstances, there does not exist for philosophy perhaps again some chance.

8

Being and Phenomenon—Rendering More Precise the Account
of Myth: Philosophy as the Surfacing of Problematicity—
Care of the Soul and Finitude—Discussion

Before we move to the discussion, allow me several remarks that
perhaps will clarify some possible objections.

Above all, here is the problematic of the second and third lecture, *question 1*
where we—as you certainly remember—spoke about the problem of the
phenomenon, about what *manifesting* really is. We tried to formulate the
problem of manifesting to avoid every reduction of phenomenon to something like an existent, to that *which* manifests itself. Certainly many of you,
who are familiar with the problems of current philosophy, asked yourselves
the question: Why is the question of the phenomenon formulated here
without his mentioning the common, and in a certain direction of philosophy, fundamental conception of being?

Vulgar phenomena are those phenomena of things, existents, those are
existents that show themselves; but this fundamental phenomenon is the
phenomenon of *being*, meaning the phenomenon that at first glance does
not show itself. We tried to show that we do not get the phenomenon into
our hands by looking at what manifests itself, at its characteristics, its
properties, relations, and so on. Rather, we come closer to the phenomenon when we leave all this aside and start to pay attention to the *ways of
givenness*, the manners of revealing itself. We should not become fixated
on these kinds of ways of givenness, but rather when we discover their
internally meaningful structure—only then something not originally in
our program will start to show itself to us, what we did not have in sight,

and what in reality led us to experience things, their relations, their connection with their manifoldness and in their various determinations. Even for us this duality revealed itself here, only by this the phenomenon in the proper sense of the word, that *deeper* phenomenon, showed itself to us. Is this not exactly the same as when Heidegger says: the actual phenomenon, the deep phenomenon has to do with *being*, not existence. What is the difference?

What does being really mean? That things show themselves is obvious to everyone, this is common. But what is this being? At first glance, this is a mystery for everyone. Being is an abstract concept. How is it that the real, substantial phenomenon is to be the phenomenon of being, and not the phenomenon of things, existents surrounding us or that we are ourselves?

This has to do with how something is to show itself to us in its *internal* character, then in some kind of way we have to have *sense* for what shows itself. To say that we have sense for something means that it does not leave us indifferent, that it does not leave us insensible. The word sense denotes the sensible organs and everything capable of sense. To have sense for what manifests itself to us means to have an understanding of things that is required so something shows itself *to me*. And manifesting and showing are always showing to someone. This manifesting *for me* presupposes a certain kind of sense for something from the thing, for the thing itself. Of course not so that sense for a thing should be by something given case by case within me. This sense is something characterizing us both constantly and globally. We understand not mere individual things, but rather we understand the whole stamp of a thing, we have a sense for their internal, substantial stamp—the *sense for being*. This sense for being always has to lead us when we understand any kind of thing, when any kind of individualities, individual things, their aspects, characteristics, and so on manifest themselves, when they show themselves to us. To bring to light this peculiar internal aspect, this sense within us for the fundamental of a thing, the sense which is only then *the condition* so individualities manifest themselves to us, this after all will be something substantial for phenomenon in the deeper sense of the word—for the *phenomenon of being*.

Why did we not use this terminology? Why did we not use this already formulated structure of thought? Simply because we are posing the question to ourselves: Is not the conception of being excessively weighted

down by the great philosophical traditions? Are not many old philosophical themes encompassed within it? While it might have certain advantages,
yet we ask ourselves the question whether the problem of showing or the
problem of being is *more primary*, whether the problem of being is not just
a part, a moment of *showing*.

We have specific reasons for this. Showing always presupposes a
certain manifoldness, a manifoldness of structures of showing. For this very
reason, I emphasized that the *one* within many ways of showing always has
to show itself to us, in various manners of givenness, from many sides. For
this reason, for example, we also see that in contemporary thinkers being
is nonetheless necessarily distinguished, for example, between being and
what is absolutely necessary so that the comprehension of being gets off the
ground at all, so that it plays itself out, that is time—between original *time*
and *being*. But if that is the case, then the problem of *showing itself* is in
reality *more fundamental* and deeper than the problem of being.

Undoubtedly *being, time,* and *showing itself* are tightly connected
with each other, but they are not identical. How are they related? That is
just the question that must be solved in the end.

The second question I should like to call attention to is this one: in   #2
some of our previous considerations we talked about myth and we maintained that myth is insufficiently considered in rational philosophy and
that it is necessary to consider also something like the *truthfulness of myth*.
In other reflections we also said that myth is *the dream of reason* and that
philosophy is related to myth as waking is to dream. Of course, contradictions can be noticed in this. This question is also extremely important for
the whole question of the further development of philosophy and the
relationship among philosophy, myth, and religion. I would like to sum-
marize here.

When we talked about how myth is in a certain sense the truth, that
there exists something like the truth of myth, we wanted to emphasize
above all that myth is in the wider sense something touching truthfulness
and untruthfulness, just as every manner of clarity about the world touches
truthfulness and untruthfulness. Myth is a certain manner of clarity about
the world, about existence in its entirety—about this there can be no doubt.
This is after all not mere unconscious reacting. It is not fantasizing without
any content, like the phantasmagories of the sick and so on. In myth there

is an internal consistency, within it there is a particular "logic"—if by logic we mean a certain internally lawful order. Here this internally lawful order above all has an affective tonality—and this we already tried to sketch out; we tried to show how the antithesis of what accepts us—home, and then its opposite—is terribly important in myth. This peculiar element of *affective spatiality* is at home within myth everywhere. Just as in massive, intensive myth, engaging the life of man in the most elementary degree, so in derivative phenomena of myth, as were maintained with a certain degree of intensity through to the nineteenth century.

This affective tonality is connected to the fact that myth is something reconciling man with existence, which calls up from him the sense of *unity* and *confidence* in reality. The fundamental in myth is seated in this affective tonality, and perhaps just in this consists that *awakening*, that peculiar shift, which we naturally did not analyze in any depth and which would be necessary to take apart more thoroughly. I refer to the shift that I said could be characterized in contrast to the temporal stamp of all of experiencing. Myth is oriented to the *past* with its entire character, by the fact of its storytelling, and then the connection with tradition: no one ever created myth, myth is always givenness, myth always merely indicates some kind of original age. Affectivity in general itself alludes to this temporal dimension of our existence, which some label as discovering or *finding oneself*, that means the state in which we *already* are, and this *already* is again testimony to *the original past*.

With the arrival of *philosophy*, something like the crossing from this temporal dimension to somewhere else begins. From the dominance of the temporal dimension of the past is passage to a greater emphasis on what is *present*, to what is given here. With this naturally also comes this peculiar *sobering* connected with the shaking of feeling of trust in existence. That is why philosophy is dangerous in a peculiar way.

While as you know, in myth there are also horrors, there is a whole dimension there of "*Unheimlichkeit*," the opposite of what accepts us and with which we can be in agreement. But this dimension can be pacified somehow. It is not a fundamentally problematic dimension, just as myth is not problematic, because everything is *given within* it, everything in it is already accounted for and complete in its own way: there, answers are given before questions.

Whereas in this great transformation, which is the birth of philoso-

phy, in an immense transformation of the entire situation of our existence, ✗ ✗ ✗ ✗
all of a sudden *problematicity as such* surfaces, problematicity of ourselves,
problematicity of the world, impasse, the question, and looking for some
kind of answer. Looking for, which turns to us ourselves, because there is
not anyone anywhere except us and our comprehending of that which
shows itself in which we might find refuge. So much for the second.

There is still a third item I wanted to speak about—and it regards the   #3
care of the soul in its third aspect. In Plato, this third aspect is the relation
of the soul to it itself and to its *temporal* and *eternal* being. As we saw, in   1
Plato the care of the soul was developed in three dimensions: first in the
plan of the philosophical problematic, the problematic of *being* that is
in Plato is also the deepest and highest existent, of which all the rest is in
some way a picture and reflection. The second thing is then the existence of   2
man in the company of the community. The truthful man, the man-
philosopher, cannot be a philosopher just for himself, but rather has to
exist in society. And this society cannot be a freely chosen society, but
rather has to be a society of philosophical truth and philosophical authority
gained naturally by care of the soul, through work upon oneself in society,
in society with others, because in the end, no one will escape this situation.
And then there is that third thing, *the relation to one's own* temporal and   3
eternal *being*, to one's own body, to one's own bodily existence and to what
awaits us all—that is, to death.

First of all, we saw that the problem of the immortal soul is somehow
brought up again. It is no longer a soul that survives for the other, but
rather the soul that now lives on "for itself"—but how?—that is the question. Plato, as you know, always somehow tries to prove that the soul—
meaning the peculiar movement of our comprehending being and upon its
basis comprehension of existence around us, the existent source of all
movement and all life—is essentially *alive* and as a result cannot perish.
Understandably, these are all sophisms, as are the so-called proofs of immortality described in the *Phaedo* and elsewhere in Plato, for example, the
thought that there exists a symmetry of birth and extinction that would be
broken were not death balanced by rebirth somewhere in the world. In that
lies the thought of the projection of the soul into the universe as its essential
mover. Even all the other proofs are similarly short-winded.

If it is true that man is a being in whom takes place, in whom this entire essential and untransferable into anything merely existent (in the sense of given reality) process of manifesting is at home—that man is the domain of this amazing occurring, that the world shows itself, that reality not only is but also is manifest—if that is the case, then this peculiar moment, which we can rightly conjecture belongs to the fundamental elements, to the foundation of the world in itself and not only to the world of our subject—meaning an immense dignity of the human being, this also means that *man is much more* than all the actualities of the world, embedded much more deeply than the *material* world, material elements—which we conjecture to be indivisible and indestructible. Although, conversely we know that in a certain sense they degrade and are, as if they never were, heading to the always smaller, always diminishing, declining manner of being. Man *is* much more than all this. If the most essential element within man is the showing of existence, to which also belongs *being,* if man is the place of being, then this *unreality* in its core, this unreal and *to existence unreducible being,* is it not something having some essential *relation to the finitude* of our existence? Is it not something coinciding with the finitude of our life not only negatively, not such that it just disappears one fine day, but also *positively*?

Our life, to the point it lasts, is constantly in crisis after all, in deciding, in the yes-no, in a kind of equivocal twilight. As long as we live, we are clear about much, but never ever about the most essential, especially *for us* most essential. Our cognizing about whether we are within good or within evil, truth or untruth is never completed. The question is whether this existence in this alternative, in this indecisiveness, which is at the same time our existence insofar as free beings—and we are *free* because we always stand within these two alternatives, in the question of good-evil, truth-untruth—whether that circumstance, this freedom, takes place in this kind of being, as is man, in just such a way, which is finite and which knows about its finitude and which must reconcile itself with this finitude—whether this does not have an essential *meaning* that is not negative, but rather *positive.*

We already showed that the phenomenon—that existence manifests itself—is something that cannot be converted into existents themselves, into their reality and their internally real structures. It is something, then, which is essentially *not-real.* And what is death? Is not *death* something like the *reality of this not-reality*? As long as we live, we always live face to face with this most fundamental situation, whereas death is at the same time *the completion of our freedom*, completion in the sense that from the world of things we cross to *mere being*.

Let us remember just the mythical tales where Plato does not speculate in a fantastic manner about the survival of the soul. (In Plato, Socrates proves immortality in the *Phaedo* through the similarity of the soul to the ideas: he proves it by explaining that the essence of the soul is alive and that it thus never accepts into itself something like its opposite, and the very things like that: we know that this argument is short-winded.) But let us recall Plato's myths, let us remember that in these myths something like *freedom, choice* occurs everywhere. Plato's grand myths are all about life *after death or before natality*, about life before this life. The myths about prenatal existence of the soul are in fact even more important then those after death. Why? Because in prenatal existence takes place *choosing* of all of existence. There takes place the fundamental act of freedom, by which man becomes the being always living in the alternative of good and evil, truthful and untruthful. This alternative of good and evil, truthful and untruthful always presupposes clarity, presupposes *manifesting, being* after all. In these myths, in the peculiar atmosphere the *Phaedo* portrays for us, in an atmosphere where the philosopher is to complete his whole concern, care of the soul through that final and definitive way, this eternal combatant for the human soul expresses himself only approximately. In what consists the care of the soul, we know: a constant conversation of the soul with itself and with others. Conversation with others is always a conversation of the soul with itself at the same time, and care of the soul takes place in this conversation. Here is this last day, and there it is to come, we might say, to it itself. With what is it going to be concerned? The relation between *the soul, being, and freedom.* For this reason the *immortality* of the soul is talked about there. In this is then completed the whole cycle of the care of the soul.

In the end we could say the words of Heraclitus: "That which they do not expect nor hope for awaits human beings after death" (fr. B27). To expect and to hope means to expect and to hope within time, to expect and to hope in this world. This world is the world of things, it is the world of *realities*, whereas what awaits man in death is *mere being*—and it is not any kind of thing.

So that is it. Please, do not be angry if I spoke for so long. Now tell me your own comments.

Discussion

Q: I would like to ask something regarding the third part you spoke about now. What do you mean [in saying] that the material elements are headed toward declining being?

P: By this I mean the tendency to thermal extinction and the entropic tendency in nature. This is something about which, for example, ancient materialism does not know, and neither does the materialism of the beginning modern world up to the nineteenth century. This actual historical and that decadent historical tendency in nature is something that forced itself into human reason very late.

Is that so? Today, the not very popular, but still very noteworthy epistemologist Meyerson claimed that this has its essential reasons, that this tendency in nature is at odds with human thinking, with the fundamental law of human reason.[1] That human reason, not merely analytical reason but also explicative reason, the reason of natural science according to which reason is not merely legal, but rather explicative, which wants always the answer to the question "why?", not simply to the question "how is it?", how does it take place and according to which laws. Human reason anticipates from reality what is in harmony with its fundamental tendency to identity, whereas everything that is in opposition to this tendency has to be forced upon it.

Q: I would like to ask about something you spoke of last time, about faith. I want to know what is the relation between *faith* and *looking-in*.

P: That is a tough question. I will try to answer it a little, but I think that we will busy ourselves with this still more often. Philosophy has as its ideal complete responsibility, in thought as much as in practical life, meaning to regulate everything according to insight. That is the ideal. Ideals move life, but understandably insight insofar as an ideal already itself presupposes that we do not have full insight: and the question is whether it is realizable at all, whether for our life, for life clarity, so things manifest themselves to us, whether to this does not also belong fundamentally and principally the *concealment* of things. Because we see this after all: these things around us, which are manifest, these vulgar phenomena, what

1. E. Meyerson, *De l'explication dans les sciences* (Paris: Payot, 1921).

shows itself us from a thing—this presupposes *deeper phenomena*, and these are *originally concealed,* these must still be examined, these must be then brought in some way to light.

How do we really bring them to light? And do we get them to light fully and definitely? Is there not always going to be something here like an obscure margin, something which Heraclitus thought of when he said that φύσις κρύπτεσθαι φιλεῖ (nature is accustomed to hiding itself) (fr. B123)— this peculiar character of things, meaning the being of things, likes to conceal itself, that it is hidden? But in any case, were it not that the philosopher wants this clarity, then this entire situation of man would never get out of concealment. As a result, there exists a certain primacy of clarity and effort for clarity against its opposite from the moment that philosophy is philosophy. Philosophy wants clarity, and as far as possible a radical one, yet radical clarity leads it to see *limits* of this clarity and that man lives in this equivocacy, in this peculiar polarity.

Then what does the philosophical will to responsibility and the philosophical impetus from obscurity to light, to want to answer for this life face to face with this human situation mean? This is after all a decision that is not blind, yet it is not a decision without risk—in this there is something like a fundamental element of faith.

Plato is the philosopher who recommends and objects to faith. Of Plato, it is said he is the philosopher of radical clarity, that in him all obscurity finally disappears and that important is the sun which shines its rays into ever greater and greater darkness. But darkness is there; the cave does not cease to exist. Of course, Plato philosophizes less about that cave than about the sun and so on; ultimately, not very much can be said about it. Because there exists not only the primat of clarity but also the primat of logos that is connected with it, we should not know about clarity and unclarity were it not for logos. For that reason Plato is the philosopher who recommends faith.

But faith, as the Greek philosophers saw it, is the foundation of what we call faith in the Christian tradition, but is not *entirely congruent* with this. Because we will still talk about these things, I would like to reserve closer differentiation for later. Now I should just say this much: it is said that Christian dogmata is irrational, but it is peculiar after all. No other religion other than that which passed through Greek philosophy has dogmata. It is also peculiar that dogmata were not established merely by some kind of *sic volo, sic iubeo*, but that they were always prepared by a very circumspect discussion.

Q: At the end of the lecture before last, you generally evaluated Greek thinking and philosophizing and talked about it as thinking that is thought of more as the manifesting of this whole as manifesting of a specific existent, rather than as manifesting itself. In this you glimpsed a certain limit of this thinking.

But is not manifesting itself without the manifesting of a specific existent the first direct truthful perception that however lacks the self-responsible question? And is not manifesting without the assigned manifested existent philosophy half way there, that is, a mystical vision, and is it not the limit of Greek thinking referred by you rather the limit in the sense of faith that is the condition of the possibility of not-self sufficient extremes? That is, on the one hand, the manifesting existent without view upon the whole of manifesting and, on the other hand, the totality of manifesting that is never determined?

P: You will have to say that again.

Q: You give precedence to manifesting in itself, and in this, for example, that being—as you said—is in Plato always existent in the sense of the highest valid existence, and in that you see a certain *limit*. As you spoke, let us say about the immortality of the soul, you glimpsed precisely immortality in this manifesting—that you expressed very succinctly.

P: Look, you made a whole series of objections, can I for the moment hold on to what you just said now?

In what I see the *limit* of Greek philosophizing. The Greek philosophers from the oldest philosophers to the classics see a fundamental difference between the things around us and what things around us show to us. Plato, for example, sees expressly, so profoundly directly that things around us could never ever show themselves to us were it not for the ideas. Also were it not for some other things, but the ideas ultimately show them. That is the light in whose rays only then can any thing at all show itself. But this light, in whose rays things can only then show themselves is comprehended by these philosophers as a *hyperthing*. At the very least, it is always like that; this difference is weakened because manifesting, showing—into whose framework belongs being—is not radically distinguished from existence as such, from eternity.

Q: Is there not already a certain intent in that?

P: There certainly is, but intent—that is, perhaps, still not well said. These philosophers really did this not out of mere naïveté, rather that is their strength. For this reason their philosophy is so voluminous; that is why it is a teaching about the whole of the world and why it is sufficient unto itself. For example, no kind of science is necessary. All of antiquity did not need any kind of science. For philosophy this was *paradisus animae*.

Q: But the sciences were made possible by this.

P: Yes, that is true, but they were not around then. They did not exist.

Q: But, after all, in the Platonic academy itself, the fundamental debate occurred precisely between scientists and philosophers.

P: But these scientists were *also* philosophers. Greek mathematics was *also* philosophy. It was the teaching about realities, about objectivities that exist in their own way. When we teach elementary geometry in first and second grade, we still teach children about these realities, we teach them about Platonic bodies, and we teach them planimetric figures as if this existed. All this is something entirely different from science in our sense of the word. Our science is the *predicting of experience*, that is, experience anticipated and captured in certain general structures. Whereas, for example, Greek mathematics, which deserves the title of special science in antiquity, was concerned with certain objectivities and their perceiving, recognizing intelligible relations perceivable in these objects, graspable. About some kind of predicting of experience or something like that—that was not at all what it was about. And, for example, the sciences of observation—look, what is observation like in Aristotle and in those greatest? It is all so unsystematic, so inexhaustive, imprecise, but it is always directed to some deep, into depth-going relations capable of being *looked-in*. That is there. All this so-called ancient science is really *philosophy*, when philosophy is this looking-in; whereas our modern science is rendered complete, even there where it eventually philosophizes, by this *practical activity*. This is an activity that wants to prove itself in every moment and that is why it is this so-called *efficacious* knowing. That is the essential difference.

With this great difference undoubtedly is connected the role of philosophy in antiquity—and its role today. Philosophy today, in today's world, is nothing—for the moment. In this moment, when the world is still obsessed by the thought of seizing reality, as far as possible, the most intensive and, as far as possible, greatest extent, and to draw from it as much and as quickly as possible. At that moment philosophy has nothing to do. And you see, that this idea of knowing ultimately led even the historical situation of man to that kind of position where philosophy and the entire hitherto spiritual world, what we call care of the soul, stopped having any kind of rate of exchange. For this very reason in our first lesson I put emphasis on the presence of certain symptoms that this era is at an end. Because it ran off into an apparent infinite, into the inexhaustibility of means given to human disposal. Now all of a sudden the end is here and it was thrown out for nothing.

But the difference between antiquity and today is not superficial. There is also a further and deeper thing here, that is, that the situation of antique philosophy prevented philosophy from sharply posing the question of manifesting as something *fundamentally* distinct from existence itself, from existing things. Understandably, philosophy also has to constantly count on this other partner—science and technology and this whole modern, emancipated and enlightened world, this after all is not nothing: this is something that has an enormous significance and its own justification. But who is going to reflect upon this justification and its limits? After all, science is not going to reflect upon this! While it shows what reflection can do, that most fundamental reflection has to come from somewhere else. So much for your first point.

You of course told me that philosophy that remains in mere showing without existence, manifestation without anything that manifests itself is a kind of mysticism that cannot . . . ?

Q: No, I did not call it a mysticism at first, at first I called it something absolutely essential.

P: I did not understand you well, so excuse me.

Q: If this manifesting itself, without manifesting of a specific existent is not the first unmediated truthful intuiting that however lacks the self-responsible question.

P: Why would it lack the self-responsible question? Precisely here is that self-responsible question posed with a perhaps greater emphasis. Look, after all—so that I again repeat it—from what arose our questions?

[They arose] from reflection about Husserl's phenomenological reflection. Husserl's phenomenology—what was it? It was a repetition, a repeating of the modern question about the *subjectivity of the subject*. Man posed the question of the subjectivity of the subject because, in order that something manifests itself, it has to manifest itself to someone, so *manifest-*

ing is always *mediated* by some kind of *subjectivity*. But we saw that Husserl conceived his problem as the constitution of existence from the subject, which it captures in the original. And while following this philosophical program, we saw that something like the constitution of existence from the subject cannot be carried out. For subjective being captured in its original presupposes the act of "turning inward" that does not exist; as a result, this entire constitutive systematic does not exist.

But this does not mean that mediating of manifesting by the subject does not exist. Except that mediating by the subject shows itself to us precisely in the narrowest coincidence with things and directly in things showing themselves to us. Except that the subjective indications to things—for example, that here we have a cup in its original and then the surroundings and so on, which is always in radii of givenness, and finally crosses into deficient modes of givenness and indicates on and on—only these indications, references, and this whole system of indicators is subjectivity, is us. *We* give "signs" to ourselves in things. But from this kind of formal subjectivity I will never constitute presence, I will never constitute the world: it is the essential mediation so the world shows itself, but it is never material, from which the world could be constituted. This is also the reason why these two things are inseparable and why the manifesting of things even in their concrete form, if we try to capture it in this way, also shows us that the world "exists." That is pretty much my conception. This is not, after all, an uncritical approach to the problem of subjectivity, nor . . .

Q: I did not want to say that.

P: But you say "without question about self-responsibility" or "without self-responsible questions." This is not without self-responsible question, but rather together with it. You know? In this regard we do not lose from sight our point of departure.

Q: Yes, but I had in mind these consequences, what follows from this, when we constantly hold on to this. Of course, we actually do arrive at manifesting as such through a comprehensive self-responsible reflection, but this does not stop here. If we are constantly diligent and comprehensively are responsible, then this manifesting for that reason is always *manifesting of something*, it is always the specific, always is that νόησις νοήσεως (the intelligence of intelligence)[2] in that highest sense. In that I am thinking more about that result, when we constantly hold everything inside.

2. Aristotle, *Metaphysics*, XII, 9.

p: Except look, when we comprehend manifesting as an autonomous lawful ordering, that is not the lawful ordering of the constitution of the world, but rather the lawfulness of its showing, then νοήσις νοήσεως is a matter of *the absolute*, and not of finite manifesting with which we have something to do in concrete in our reflections.

q: If this is not an implicit indication that the idea always has to be an idea *of something*. It is just that I see in this a philosophically very refined orientation in those Greeks, that is in those principle historical figures, that in them actual manifesting was always the manifesting of existence.

p: Yes, it is true. This is the intention of their metaphysics. Of course, when we complete this intention, we get to where Hegel stands with his absolute reflection. Absolute reflection has terrifying difficulties; if I would expand upon this, then this would be another new problematic. Absolute reflection has in common with concrete reflection—with which we can occupy ourselves because we basically constantly are within it—that things show themselves to us through the *intercession of comprehending being* and not such that we would directly understand existence. But, in that lies the entire trick, that *through the intermediary of understanding of being*, and not that we should directly understand existence. It is not like that. In absolute reflection there is a terrible difficulty: the absolute is something, after all, that does not have any kind of limit, it is something never-ending in contrast to everything we, as finite beings, come into contact with, and as a result of this it is ungraspable. Νοήσις νοήσεως (the intelligence of intelligence)—that is a circle. But look, already in Aristotle it is said in Book 12 of the *Metaphysics*, which talks about νοήσις νοήσεως· αὐτὸν δὲ νοεῖ ὁ νοῦς κατὰ μετάληψιν τοῦ νοητοῦ (the intelligence of intelligence: the intelligence does understand itself because it partakes in the intelligible). Νοῦς (intelligence) understands it itself by that μεταλαμβάνει τοῦ νοητοῦ (partakes in the intelligible), by that it has a share, that it takes part, "identifies itself" through its being becomes indistinguishable with this known. Νοητὸς γὰρ γίγνεται τυγχάνων καὶ νοῶν, ὅστε ταὐτὸν νοῦς καὶ νοητόν (it becomes intelligible by touching and intellecting, so that intellect and intelligible are one). . . . The knowable it becomes, touching καὶ νοῶν (and by intellecting), that means so that the same is νοῦς (intellect), and that which is its object, the identity of both. Where there is identity, this becomes indistinguishable; there you do not find boundaries. When there are no boundaries, there is nothing to hang on to.

Q: But in it the dual is constantly spoken of.

P: Yes, it comes out from this duality, but then is said: νόητος γὰρ γίγνεται τυγχάνων καὶ νοῶν, ὥστε ταὐτὸν νοῦς καὶ νοητόν (it becomes intelligible by touching and intellecting, so that intellect and intelligible are one)!

Q: But the fundamental, it counts further; it is precisely that unity dividing it. That is the fundamental crisis.

P: Except that if it is to be dual, then we are in that finite reflection, and absolute reflection is again not going to be accessible to us. Dual in one—that is our reflection. Look at that terrible tension in the Aristotelian νόησις νοήσεως: on the one hand, there it is said, ταὐτόν νοῦς καὶ νοητόν (intellect and intelligible are one). Then suddenly Aristotle starts to ask: And what does νοῦς (intellect) know when it knows? Νοῦς cannot know something not worthy of it; it cannot know anything other than itself. Only itself. And then you have an account of that absolutely empty relation with itself in νόησις νοήσεως. So you have already there the problem of the *ungraspableness* of absolute reflection.

Q: Yes, here is the apparent priority of this manifesting. Of course, for example, I think that it is quite succinctly expressed also in Plato's *Seventh Letter* (341 c), that is the friction. . . . There it is, of course, distinguished in more than these two, but . . .

P: You are right.

Q: Whether for that reason Plato does not say, that only then, when we hold all these four things, when we constantly somehow rub them against each other, only then can we capture manifesting, whether this does not mean the inexpressible internal proof of the indispensability of this manifesting, so that the manifesting of the determinate—with the priority of this manifesting, will then be really indispensable. The manifesting is there right at the beginning.

P: Yes. You see, in the *Seventh Letter*—this is genuinely phenomenology, it is a reflection about manifesting, about what belongs to it that also to it belongs ὄνομα (name), and proof ὄνομα for λόγος (description), and this indicates εἴδωλον (image), and εἴδωλον indicates πρᾶγμα αὐτό (the thing itself). This is all true. Except that with the turn of a hand, from all these things become particular existents.

Q: Yes, of course without that πρᾶγμα αὐτό (the thing itself).

P: Instead of seeing *stages* of reflection about manifesting as such, he makes independent realities out of these individual stages. One reality is λόγος (description), the other is ὄνομα (name), the third εἴδωλον (image), and the fourth is that πρᾶγμα αὐτό (the thing itself), meaning that circle in itself. And through that, suddenly this manifesting is gone. He again approaches each of these individual elements separately, and he always has the same manner of givenness for them, meaning the spiritual eye opens—and it comes. This is, after all, the collapse of that reflection. In the beginning it began to play out so beautifully—and then all of a sudden it turns into this kind of mess.

Q: But I just do not see this mess there yet. Of course, actual manifesting is phenomenologically, philosophically primary; but this is not given to us, we have to thus get to it by reflection—but this is still not an argument. Then we come to the argument: all that is concrete is actually rendered possible by manifesting. But if this is not comprehensive developing, actual conceiving of all the results of that, that we have grasped manifesting, then manifesting is possible only such that it is the manifesting of things. Manifesting is of course prior, but it has to assert itself upon something, take effect.

P: Fine, but what comes up short in this case? That *the same* manifests itself in *various* ways—this does not come into play there. There each way of manifesting has its correlate.

Certainly, they are then conceived as various degrees of approximating to this last thing, that is the truth. But each of these degrees has its own ontological status, and through this all of manifesting is schematized in a way that itself is no longer drawn from the movement of manifesting.

Q: But I think that it is, and that it is a *determined* existent precisely because it is determined by this manifesting.

P: No, look: λόγος, ὄνομα (description, name), and so on, regard the *same* thing, and the problem is how does the same show itself in these various manners of givenness. And this problem is all of a sudden combined with that this *does not show itself the same*, but rather that each of these stages has its own correlate. As a result, the entire problem of autonomous manifesting movement stops being a problem, because these four stages—this is terribly rough, and at the same time we do not even ask what is the relation of these ὀνόματα to those λόγοι and what all this really means, how it develops. Here always appears that peculiar slide from the problem of *manifesting* to the problem of *existence*; instead of a completely autonomous problematic of manifesting, the problematic of a determined ladder of existents is introduced, and we somehow get closer to each of these individual stages *en bloc*.

So that is how it is—at least it seems to me. I do not see so far where this needs correction. Plato saw this fundamental difference, except he constantly interprets it, as if it were the difference between various degrees of existents and not a difference between stages and aspects of manifesting as such.

Q: If Plato speaks about these five matters, along with this πρᾶγμα αὐτό (the thing itself), does this not already express that he does not merely see these as degrees, but actually as stages even with this manifesting itself?

P: Yes, but that is why this πρᾶγμα αὐτό is the most problematic in this. This πρᾶγμα αὐτό is still once more all of this together, or better said, it is this *manifesting yet again*. This entire movement is then taken once more as the highest existent. In that lies precisely the terrible problematicity of this thing. The difference between being and existence—that is there, but being is taken as a more intensive, deeper, higher form of the existent.

Heidegger also maintains that there exist two manners of the being of the existent, that there is an essential difference between the being of some kind of existent like a cup or Mont Blanc, and the existent as is a colleague X.Y., because to the character of this kind of existent as is X.Y., to his being belongs a comprehension for being, a comprehension of the word "is"; he knows that things not only are, but that they also show themselves to him. Whereas Mont Blanc—it could not care less. That is the positive characteristic, meaning that to the being of existent, such as Mont Blanc, belongs an essential inability to be interested in something like that, or to be at all touched by something like the word, significance, the meaning "*to be*"— that means "*to show itself.*" And naturally, Heidegger maintains that the being characterized in its own being by *the relation to being*, has a different kind of being. This being in its own manner *is* more, its being is amplified, it is not only a mere fact, which the being itself does not touch. Rather it is something that in and of itself is touched by its own being. As a result, this being "carries" its own being. It is not only passively given to it, but in its own way is actively tied to it, and that means freely, in the function of author. Not such that man could make himself, but such that his own being always responds to it and carries it, and does not only accept it passively.

This difference is already there in Plato, of course not in that form, but there is a teaching about gradation there. That is the motif, which is still something else in regard to the question about which we have now spoken.

Q: Yes, by that I just wanted to say this much: whether the actual intention of the conception of manifesting in Plato, which is always the manifesting of the highest existent, is not the following: I always have to speak about manifesting as if it were the highest existent because in the opposite case, we would completely lose that manifesting from sight—if we constantly maintain it as a comprehensive, asking about itself question. It is always something to which these degrees basically belong, this always determines these degrees. I see something like that in this. Before in Heraclitus, there perhaps was rather manifesting that was not this existent, perhaps he already had experience with this, that certainly.

P: But when you now speak about the highest existent, then you speak about it from the point of view of the highest existent, or do you speak about it from our point of view?

Q: I am just trying to answer why manifesting is always the highest existent in Plato and in the Greek systematicians. And this difference— perhaps I am mistaken—was then clear to Plato and to those creators, that there actually is this manifesting here, and after that the existing, but even when manifesting is primary, things are always here already—that is why evidently it was the existing. That is how I explain it.

P: Could you now tell me: but you yourself said that Plato is the philosopher of faith, and in this sense I would agree with you, if we would take this as a certain *profession de foi*, then yes, but as a result of reflection— no.

Q: Certainly, but Plato was aware of this risk, which is in that, when these things are written about.

P: Fine, then we are in agreement, but we have to be aware that Plato's philosophy is then, after all, *not absolute reflection*, but rather only a certain philosophical faith in this sense.

Q: Yes, Plato's philosophy is evidently what he says of it: he speaks about it, but it cannot be said, it can only be comprehended—that is how I understand Plato.

P: Well, perhaps then.

Q: The second question ties into that, and is the problem of whether there are one or two pillars of European thinking. But you said that we will talk about this later, so perhaps there will not be any point to developing this now. That is just that faith.

P: So look, to that I should say only this much, so that we do not leave this completely unanswered. I said that this Greek column is in reality the only one, because the peculiar characteristic of European life lies in the primacy of *looking-in*. Just awhile ago, among other things, you conceded this in that second discussion. Were it not for that Greek element, if the second one, the Hebrew one only existed—then Europe would not be Europe. Only through the Hellenization of the Hebrew did the Hebrew also become what it then became in these contexts. Certainly, it then could be said: but why did Europe not remain Greek, why was that Hebrew element necessary? But perhaps there are certain *immanent* components in Greek thinking itself that required something like that. I now pointed to something similar a moment ago, when I spoke about that movement between the obscure and the clear. And apart from that, I always pointed to this in the history of the mythical framework of Platonic philosophy.

The myth of Socrates, the myth of the absolutely truthful man, it has so many eminent elements of the Christian myth, that it seems positively strange that they are so little emphasized. When the myth of the Antichrist is talked about, then it is usually sought, I do not know where, in Iranian religions—in the Persian dualism, and so on. But after all the motif that the Antichrist must be indistinguishable from Christ to the word and the letter is comprehensible only from Plato. It is at the beginning of the second book of the *Republic*: complete wickedness is in that, to be completely wicked, and at the same time to seem good; you will not find this element anywhere else. Or the element of divine anger—why is the entire world in evil? Because he who was sent so that people care for the soul, he *eo ipso*, just because he erected the ideal of an entirely responsible life, came into conflict, and for this very reason has to be destroyed. For this reason the whole world is in evil, and it even has this kind of historical-philosophical justification. It is connected to the entire Platonic conception of Greek myths as those of the world and as that by which Greek history dominates over the history of the oriental colossi. Certainly it does not contain everything, and something like Christian inwardness is only in embryonic form in Plato—for example, the element: freedom and its coincidence with finitude, mortality and care of the soul—that is the embryo of European inwardness—it all grew out from this.

Q: Just because I tried to show the indispensability of these *two* things in my own way (manifesting and the manifesting of existents), I would like to say something about the question of one or two pillars. Is not just this so sovereignly responsible Greek philosophy evidence of the inevitability of religion in Plato's definition as the noble lie, which maintains not-philosophy in orientation toward philosophy? And is not such necessary religion the ground from which philosophy grows and which constantly requires it as its ground, and to which it returns as to its picture, that is to the existing, for which it asks? And is not precisely Christianity this optimal religion, just this transformation of the Jewish by the Hellenization of the New Testament, that is the transformation of myth into religion?

[margin notes: completely ignores periodical process in Judaism / supersessionist]

P: Those are questions that it is sensible to ask. Of course you spoke a little about the necessary lie.

Q: I have in mind, as Plato says, how philosophers construct religious myths, such an ideology.

P: I think that is too sharply put—the lie. First of all we should have to agree on the conception of truth and lie. The conception of truth does not have as its opposite only lie, but rather a whole series of other contraries. It has as its contrary veiling, concealing. We would have to agree upon that by way of discussion.

Q: I mean lie in the way Plato meant it. Just in the meaning of concealing that most . . .

P: He does not say lie there, rather ψεῦδος, and ψεῦδος is not merely lie; ψεῦδος is also that which is not true.

Q: But I mean existing in contrast to manifesting.

P: I do not know whether we can get through in this direction. Perhaps in myths there are also specific elements of manifesting that cannot be substituted by anything else.

Q: Is that not an indication of manifesting?

P: In myth predominates, for example, the passive affective element, the German "*Befindlichkeit.*" But is this passive affective element eliminable from the manifestedness of human life? And then there is still another problem here . . .

Q: I did not mean by this just this passive element, myth, but rather religion, the active relation, that is orientation, directedness, just what Plato founded, religion, the transformation of myth.

P: I think that the transformation of myth into religion still keeps certain elements of myth, and this is such that from mere passivity it lifts this up into reflection, but at the same time shows that they are mythical elements we cannot do without. In this reflection goes further, but still in this there is the mythical element "*aufgehoben*" in the sense of conservation and . . .

Q: You twice mentioned that Europe in a certain sense has perished. Is not your mentioned perishing of Europe just such an externalness and emptiness, which, because it no longer has resurrecting, unspoiled inheritors, is now left to its own resources, it no longer has anyone on whom it can rely—that is, in the sense of myth—and it has no other option than going into itself and so finding itself.

P: Whether it has no other option? The grave situation of Europe lies of course in that it has disappeared as an elite great power, that it will never so become again, because its inheritors will not allow it. It could be what you say. But today's terrible situation lies in that it has stopped believing in itself, that it has completely accepted the standards and ways of life of its inheritors.

Q: But the inheritors have transformed themselves in their own way, here still counts what you mentioned in your first lecture, and in its own way also the myth of science, of course, in that science there is a tendency to gravity and reflection.

P: Yes, that is true. Here in this inconspicuous form, there is a certain possibility of resurrection, of course only rather potentially. We also have to realize that spirituality which comes out of reflection that is, so to speak, dissolved within the sciences is in an entirely different situation than the spirituality out of which all this arose. From this it is then understandable, when some contemporary philosophers say that philosophy now has to limit itself, and that it has to get used to being Cinderella, that philosophy is really at an end, and so on. These are defeatist formulae with which I should not agree, but which are in certain moments understandable. I resist this defeatism, as we spoke about this not long ago, of course the presupposition of each kind of that—not optimism, but just some kind of redressment, there is some concept of this repetition and . . .

Q: Is this concept not already indicated by the situation, that is, that Europe which is ruled by the myth of science, just as is the whole world, in which is the implicit internal impulse to the bindingness of internal self-reflection, this Europe does not have anything to rely upon. It thus has to rely upon itself. Then implicit internally binding reflection has to rely upon itself. What can arise from this? There is a certain possibility here that will lead to the maintaining of those four things necessary for friction (*Seventh Letter*), that is a kind of heading toward philosophy—this possibility is here I think, and I think that things are heading toward it.

P: I should say just this much: for the moment, we notice that Europe is terribly avoiding this reflection, that no one is taking care of this matter at all, that from the time that Husserl wrote his *Crisis*,[3] in actual fact no philosopher has reflected upon this problem of Europe and the heritage of Europe.

Q: These are philosophical attempts, of course I have in mind just this kind of necessity, which evidently has to be felt only by science itself.

P: Science itself has only gone so far in the meanwhile, that a certain realization has broken through in some scientists, that their science is in reality philosophy; that can be found in some contemporary physicists. But there are still a series of steps from that to reflection about origins.

Q: I see a tendency there taking place among scientists.

P: Yes, I was noting that something like this is possible, and you are noting that it is occurring to a significant degree. I do not have anything against that. Yet, it also has to be realized, for what you call this reflection, is for now only a matter of exceptions and culminations, and that the mass tendency—and science today is also a mass one—is the contrary.

Q: Yes. And a fourth question: once you lectured about myth and about that myth does not exist in our time, there exist only pseudomyths. And I just see the analogue of myth in art and in relying upon art. Art and especially the art of logos—literature—there are encompassed those two components of myth, art has its own Fausts, Raskolnikovs, Strangers, that is a kind of second pole of relying (upon science). Scientists, because they did not discover the original manifesting within science itself, thus rely, just like the vast majority of people, upon art. This is an experience, of being deeply moved. I see the task of philosophy first of all in its relation to science, second, in criticism of art.

P: That well defines the problem, but I think we must see that the desire to rely upon art is in the same situation as art itself.

3. E. Husserl, *Crisis of the European Sciences* (Chicago: Northwestern University Press, 1970).

I should like to think through this problem separately. There was a whole great tendency in the nineteenth century—because the mood of the end of certain spiritual tendencies is already old: away with religion, metaphysics. Masaryk, for example, used to say: I lived my metaphysics in poetry, in art. This domain was relied upon, but man must not forget that in this domain the same question had been posed for over one hundred and fifty years. Already Hegel spoke about that, that art in its proper form is at an end and that . . .

Q: That should indicate that art is actually the analogue of myth and not religion, and that now people nonetheless live in the impetus of a binding reflection, and so they have to pose this question.

P: Yes, but the way this question was posed, coincided with the fact that art was originally, as Hegel developed it, the religion of art, or better said, it was not religion in the sense of faith, but rather myth. But in the domain of art these questions are especially difficult. On the one hand, we see that art is, contemporarily and undoubtedly, in a no less profound crisis than, let us say, philosophy. When man remembers, it is not terribly long ago, the great American novel, where is it today? Great European music at the beginning of this century, creative arts, which were passing through an apparent renaissance—all that is gone!

Q: It is looking for a way out from myth . . .

P: It was a searching, but it is no longer today. Here the situation is particularly difficult. That is because in this domain a genuinely creative mythical force should be needed.

Q: Rather than the transformation of myth into religion . . .

P: Perhaps, such transformations, but in any case such forces that cannot be transformed into anything else, cannot spring from objective rationality, cannot also spring from some kind of mere philosophical reflection, but rather have to grow out of an authentic, imaginative sphere. There something is silent.

Q: You mentioned Masaryk: I suppose that we can find in him these four or five things, about which we are speaking here. Of him it is said, that he was not a philosopher but rather an eclectic, that he did not understand art, that he was a positivist . . .

P: I did not want to say that.

Q: I know you did not, but it is a kind of general tendency. And just for that reason I think that he did not say the most important things, following Plato's model.

P: Masaryk was not only interesting just by his relation to Plato; he was primarily interesting because of his relation to Comte. And Comte is a huge figure. Very few people realize this and Masaryk knew that. He was one of the few who read Comte carefully. Comte was the unconscious renewer of the Platonic idea of spiritual authority.

Q: And at the same time the birth of that tendency to positivism of science, even if so naively catholically expressed, there after all was that internal impetus to self-reflection.

P: But there is not just that, there are many other things. Comte had this strange conception of metaphysics—some time, when we are more fresh, we can spend the whole evening on Comte; he is an extremely interesting and important figure. In Comte there is an entire mythology: Masaryk knew this as well. He used to ridicule it a little bit, yet he did not as well. When Masaryk speaks of the rational religion, as he sometimes expresses himself—that we want the kind of religion that should not be in tension with human reason—then he does not think about any kind of eighteenth-century deism, as he is interpreted all the time. But rather he is thinking about Comte's conception of the "*politique positive*," where it is said that religion is the state of a completely inner human harmony and that religion, whereas it was once something fictitious, and then manifest, is now proven. And from what arises this proven religion? Not from some kind of superficial things. Comte's conception of religion arises from what could further be called empirical immortality. And it must be thought through philosophically. It is the thought that there exists something like the experience of living on. Everyone of us is familiar with this. Every one of us is constantly outliving himself, and outlives in himself others who coexist with him, and those who stopped coexisting with him. And this process is in reality our life and also our history. In this empirical surviving takes place something like the just process of elimination of what is private and insignificant in human life. As a result, a supraindividual human life is elaborated in this process. And it is the concretization of human life. All this is expressed in Comte in a very primitive manner, but if we brought these motifs back into the terrain we talked upon today, then they would show their power.

Comte defined metaphysics as the rule of abstraction. That is the era of the human spirit when humanity as a grand concretum retreats before certain fictitious concepts. For this reason he sees metaphysics in Protestantism, especially in the eighteenth century.

Q: In the French Revolution?

P: In the eighteenth century. In all these teachings that led to the breakdown of traditional society, in which still lived on certain organic elements, just in this negation. You see, this has nothing at all to do with the conception of metaphysics in the strong sense of the word and in the traditional historical sense. Comte himself in the *System de politique positive* even comes to that, that in a very naïve elementary way he postulates something like a general ontology. This only as a hint, so you see what kind of philosopher he was.

It is often said that Comte did not leave any space for philosophy. In actuality, he conquered for philosophy a completely new terrain. Reflection upon science, up to that point in philosophy, was occasional, desultory. No one before Comte reflected through science such that he should think through each of the fundamental disciplines (even if in the end this system of sciences, as Comte sketched out is far too naïve—it is comfortable, it is practical, and so in reality is still used) both systematically, into its methodical structure and into its history. No one before him had done this. Through this Comte created an epistemology. Through this he really created for philosophy a new domain of reflection. All of these are enormous philosophical deeds. And Masaryk was one of the few European philosophers who knew about Comte's greatness.

At the time when Masaryk got to Comte, in France Comte was counted as a dead dog; no one cared about him. They cared about Comte in England, John Stuart Mill was in correspondence with Brentano; and at one point, just when he was seventy, when Masaryk was studying in Vienna, [Brentano] came up with a strange and wonderful thought—as a strange bird in general—that with Comte's help it would be possible to overcome what he called "*Entmutigung auf dem Gebiet der Philosophie*" [discouragement in the field of philosophy]. His introductory lecture in Vienna had this title: *Über die Gründe der Entmutigung auf philosophischem Gebiet.*[4] And there he explained that the main reasons were the overly exaggerated German speculative philosophy, that it had disappointed and that it should be good to hold to Comte and his teaching about the gradual scientization of fields of knowledge, that it is now time for philosophy in the context of psychology, and so on.

4. F. Brentano, *Über die Gründe der Entmutigung auf philosophischem Gebiet* (Wien: Braumuller, 1874).

From this Masaryk likely took his inspiration. Several times I have asked our positivists and Masarykists how Masaryk came to Comte. There exists only one Czech book by the excellent expert on Masaryk and also Comte, František Fajfra, which is called *Masaryk and Comte*.[5] There you will find demonstrated that Masaryk's main thoughts are also those of Comte. Fajfra did not emphasize that the deeper background of the Comtian conception is in actuality an attempt at a renewal of the great European tradition from the spirit of modern methods. Here is something which deserves greater—naturally critical—attention.

Comte's positivism does not have almost anything in common with modern logical positivism other than the emphasis on science, and on that metaphysics is not supposed to be, and so on. But Comte's philosophy genuinely wants to be positive; it does not want to be such a negative philosophy as was Hume's and as is modern positivism or linguistic philosophy, where the task of philosophy consists in showing the impossibility of traditional philosophical questions and answers, in this negative task to clarify why it is impossible. Comte's philosophy is positive in an entirely different sense.

5. *Masaryk a Comte* (Kdyně: Nakl. Okresního sboru osvětověho ve Kdyni, 1925).

9

Discussion (Continuation)

There are several questions someone wrote down here. Of these the most important is: Why is the problem of being a part of, or moment of, the problem of showing? And why is the problem of showing more original, more fundamental, and profound than the problem of being?

This is really the question that goes to the root of things and that requires a closer explanation of how Heidegger remolded the whole concept of phenomenology, why in Heidegger the problem of phenomena and their analysis crossed into the problem of the meaning of being. This is the question requiring a very thorough analysis; actually it should require an account of Heidegger's entire philosophical point of departure and of the development of the problem. I think that this kind of work has not yet really been undertaken. There is Richardson's huge work, called *Through Phenomenology to Thought*,[1] showing how Heidegger overcame phenomenology—that is, the science of the showing itself of existents, the thinking of being—but as far as I can judge, the question of what is really the relation between being and phenomenon is not the leading theme there. So how are these things?

The common, traditional view of the problem of being was, of course, that being is something that characterizes things in their structure, that

1. W. J. Richardson, *Heidegger: Through Phenomenology to Thought* (Hague: M. Nijhoff, 1963), (Phaenomenologica 13).

being)s the *general structure of existence*, existents. The novelty Heidegger comes up with is in showing that already in ancient thinkers like Aristotle, being)s not conceived as a moment of existence, but rather it really treats a thing's *manner of showing itself.* When it is a matter of, for example, that circumstance, that a thing is characterized by shape: thing, οὐσία (being), what is called substance, being, is determined by it having boundaries that are in a certain sense delineated. This delineation, entering into limits, means after all, that it sketches out itself, separates itself, de-fines. Defining—what is this essentially? It is already encompassed in the word: *finis*, end, boundary, limit.

This means that it is a character of the thing itself. But what kind of character? The character of its *dis-covering itself,* its showing itself. Showing as such obviously is not closely thematized in ancient thinkers; what actually makes it possible is not shown. This is left *in suspenso*, but it is possible to see all of ancient ontology from this perspective. It is not as obvious as is assumed—because of the influence of the time-honored tradition reaching all the way to scholasticism—that this concerns pure objective structure.

Take for example the sentence: any kind of contact with things which are is only possible as long as these things are taken out of concealment, as long as they are uncovered, discovered, as long as they show themselves. And to showing, to the domain of this showing, belongs, for example, this sketching out of things, their entering into their shape, into their form, their stepping out of the continuity of the surroundings of all the rest, which of course also sketches itself out in a certain manner.

Uncoveredness does not appertain to the existent, existent things, only to our judgment, rather every testimony about existence is possible only then, when it is already somehow unveiled beforehand, when it has already beforehand showed itself. Uncoveredness, showing itself-ness, showing-ness, is then the feature of existence itself. And so Aristotle can say that *existing* and *unconcealed* are the same. This does not mean any kind of subjectification of existence, it does not mean that existence is something created by us. In fact, even this sketching out, unveiling is not something that *we* do with some act, as is judgment. Rather, it is something somehow taking place directly in these things. Existence is also thought of as something present, and that, as far as possible, *constantly* present. To this just belongs, that it has a certain form, which is not only the form in a given instance but also the figure that unfolds in time. For example, the figure of a plant, a flower, is not only the petals, the fruit, and so on, but also is that entire process, through which it develops from a seed up to flowering and then back to the seed. In this sense φύσις (nature) is, that means growing, φύω, at the same time showing.

But what does this mean? Φύσις is, after all, itself the foundation of existence, what makes existence existence. Φύσις is one of the fundamental definitions of being. That Heidegger sees being as this showing itself, in what is this rooted? In that showing is for him the *guiding thread* to comprehend what is being. This means that he could break through this secular tradition, that goes from scholasticism (for which being is something like the objective character of existence, which does not have anything in common with showing) because the guiding theme in his philosophizing is the theme of showing itself. And this means the theme of showing itself, which from the very beginnings of his philosophy is defining for him, is just that theme we spoke about, that *the* philosophical question is not the objective structure of things that the sciences, in the sense of abstract and concrete sciences, were interested in. Rather it is the fundamental fact that things show themselves, that they dis-cover themselves. It is a matter of showing that this theme is not only a modern theme.

In Husserl, the theme of showing coincides with modern philosophical subjectivity, with philosophy of the reflecting subject. Husserl's philosophy is the philosophy of the subject that reflects upon itself. Heidegger tries to show that showing, which Husserl locates in the tradition coming out of Descartes and leading through Kant to German idealism, is in reality only an offshoot of philosophical effort in general. Philosophy is always, even from the very beginning, really philosophy of showing itself, of the phenomenon. The problem of being then coincides with the problem of showing.

Heidegger's ontology is an ontology in that sense, and through this it fundamentally differs from ontology, let us say, in the scholastic sense of the word, from the tradition seeing ontology as the study of being in its internal structures in general, and above all not in those structures connected with the fact that existents show themselves.

When you take paragraphs in *Being and Time* that are dedicated to the concept of the phenomenon, the concept of logos and the preliminary concept of phenomenology, then there you will come across a certain peculiar surprise. In the paragraph dedicated to the concept of the phenomenon, Heidegger lays out something like this: <u>we have to distinguish between the phenomenon and the manifest</u>.

The phenomenon is—already in its etymological sense, according to what the words φαίνω (appear) and φαίνεσθαι (appearance) say—<u>something that shows itself by and in itself.</u> The phenomenon in this sense is, for example, this table, that glass, this room we are in; all this shows itself somehow in and by itself. What does "in itself" mean? This means: it is given unmediatedly, in that phenomenon there is in no way present what would mediate it for *us*. This phenomenon shows itself as something independent: this is a lamp, not any kind of picture or imagination of a lamp. This shows itself in and by itself. This means not in some kind of travesty, in costume, in some foreign surroundings, but rather *as itself.* That thing is not something in some core of mine, but rather it is just there where it is, in the world, among other things. The phenomenon in this sense is the same as τὸ ὄν (the existing thing, being), that is, τὰ φαινόμενα (the manifestation, appearance) are in this sense τὰ ὄντα (the beings). What manifests itself, what shows itself, are existents.

In contrast to this manifest (*Erscheinung*)—says Heidegger—<u>is something that does not have this character of manifesting by and in itself.</u> The phenomenon—that is, for example, the symptom of some kind of sickness. The symptom of a sickness can be redness of the cheeks. This redness of the cheeks shows itself by and in itself. But that it is a sickness is not shown unmediatedly, nor is it encompassed by that redness. There is just a certain causal relation here, which we still have to bring to light, which we still have to determine and analyze. Then it will be shown to us—always on the basis that something shows itself in and by itself—that it is an indication of something further. Thus <u>the manifest is in this sense something one step removed from the phenomenon.</u> Of course, it could happen that on the basis of certain theoretical reflections, this conception of the manifest is generalized in such a way that all phenomenon are interpreted as manifests. But the original approach to the manifest is through the phenomenon, and not to the phenomenon through the manifest.

All I now say does not fundamentally differ from Husserl's teaching; that is clear to you. Husserl also says that what we have before us here is the thing itself, and not some kind of reproduction. What thus gives itself to me as a self-givenness, as he says, as itself here, in this I have the thing, and not merely its picture.

So what is the problem in the teaching about manifesting? When we have unmediated access to things themselves, what is the philosophical problematic at stake? The problem is that the phenomenon that gives itself by and in itself is equivocal. Because it naturally gives me presence, but at the same time, it gives me more than this presence, it gives me *the thing*. And a thing does not fit, so to speak, into presence; a thing is something more. In reality it is shown that the phenomenon is a phenomenon, but the *phenomenon* of the existent is not the existent itself. While it pretends to be what is present here, it is merely pretense, and that has to be verified. How is it verified? By other phenomena of this kind. The phenomenon points to other phenomena, and during this pointing to, it may occur that the previous phenomenon, so to speak, explodes. With that is shown that the thing that showed itself as showing itself in and by itself was shown as something *else*; then it is. Thus, the phenomenon that shows itself so unmediatedly can give me a thing that shows itself as it is, but also as that which *it is not*. For this reason, Husserl distinguishes the teaching about phenomena and about the manifesting of existents from the teaching about the lawful ordering of things.

The teaching about the lawful ordering of things pertains to their empirical study and makes certain presuppositions about the existence of things, about their causal enchaining and so on, which have practical application but which in and of themselves are not philosophically clarified and justified.

The teaching about phenomena as such wants to get rid of all these presuppositions, by bracketing them off and holding on only to what shows itself. In what shows itself in this kind of unmediated manner ultimately has to be the key even to the comprehending of all ordering lawfulness and all originally accepted-on-faith theses, while phenomenology holds on only to what shows itself to me unmediatedly and in the original. I do not accept this on faith, rather I accept this on the basis of *opinion*. To transfer everything that occurs in our experience, finally, into this intuitive basis is the task of phenomenology.

But what is this intuitive basis? The intuitive basis is what is sensibly given to me. But if I would stay only with what is sensibly given to me, like this table, that tablecloth, and so on, I should stay with only mere pretenses that lead to other pretenses. Because that tablecloth merely *pretends* to be a tablecloth. What is in reality given is the present *aspect* of that tablecloth.

And if we interpreted this aspect in its entirely strict sense, perhaps we could not even call it a tablecloth. How does it prove to be a tablecloth? In such a way that the present tablecloth tells me: I will also be a tablecloth in the future, and also from that angle and from a distance and in a different light, and so on, I will be a tablecloth. It tells me all this, and this means that it leaves me to further and further experiences and in these further and further experiences it still remains the *same*.

If I should continue with these kinds of phenomena, I should never get any deeper, I should not get to anything other than pretenses. What do I need then? I need something that really gives itself to me in categorical definition. However, this can never be anything such as the tablecloth or the table, or the room, but rather what gives itself to me in definitive form— that is, *I myself* in my own past experience regarding the tablecloth and so on. While experience about myself also leaves me at the mercy of the future and the past and so on, but in every instance, what I can glean from myself, is not an aspect of something that lasts. Rather it is the *full-fledged existent*.

Of course, it is important that I see the existent before me, which gives itself to me in the original, that is *the tablecloth*, the *table*, and so on. This is not an image, a copy, and so on, rather it is the existent in its original. In the same way, I am in the original. Of course, my originality is of a different kind; it is an originality that is not given in some kinds of perspectives, but rather which gives itself *en bloc*. That my own experiencing of the tablecloth and everything else gives itself to me *en bloc*—this completely fades into the background with the original givenness of perspective things. What gives me things, what presents them to me, shows them—that is not at all given to me during this presentation of the given originally. It is here in some kind of manner, but it is not given—given are things. And the problem of phenomenology is: to render given what is not given, bring it to light, from the *latent* make *the patent*. How will we do this?

Husserl says: we have to take the *entire* experience about the tablecloth, about that carpet and so on, just as it is given, as Ariadne's thread, as Ariadne's thread the revelation of what gives itself. And how will the thing become Ariadne's thread? So that everything that is given has to have its own counterpart in something that gives itself. We have to go from the given to the giving, and the giving that is precisely us, but not in the sense of empirical reality, not we as a psychophysical thing. As a psychophysical

thing we are one of the things among the different objects of the world, whereas our profound I—that is, the I giving all this—both the things apart from us and also us as a thing among things.

Thus, it is shown that without us even being aware of it, in every phenomenon, in the immediate and in the equivocal, is encompassed something that originally is not a phenomenon but that can be made an unequivocal phenomenon; that is the current of this *giving experiencing*. This is, for example, the perceiving behind what is perceived. But perceiving is itself an extraordinarily rich and varied structure, encompassing within itself both the already immediate past and the remembering past and imagination and so on. And these subjective activities in their entire immense richness and meaning can be discovered just then when all that is unmediatedly given to me as existent, becomes Ariadne's thread for me in seeking and finding the giving in its effectuation, when the given shows itself to me as the *effectuation* of the giving.

So you see, the phenomenon is distinguished in two senses of the word here. The first, the unmediated and equivocal phenomenon—that is, not the phenomenon of phenomenology, it is only a phenomenon from which phenomenology "takes its élan." The phenomenon of phenomenology is originally hidden, latent. Only when I bring to light this hidden phenomenon, for the time being latent, do I then get the phenomenon of phenomenology.

For this reason, you see how immensely important is the idea of *correlation* which I expressed with the image of Ariadne's thread. Each of the equivocal phenomena is Ariadne's thread; it is correlative to the phenomenon in a profound sense. Every phenomenon in its profound sense has its objective correlate, and it is its effectuation. For example, that tablecloth, an object, is in actuality the effectuation of subjective activities, as is presentation, the synthesis of what was presented previously with what is presented in the present, the identification of the past with the present, and the immense number of other activities, which arise from what is passively given and cross into what we carry out with the participation of the conscious I. So, for example, judging is already always the accomplishment of the active I, whereas mere perceiving does not pretend for something like that, although in perceiving we already have the structure "something as something," that is, comprehending, the explanation of something as something. When, for example, I merely walk across the floor, then

already *eo ipso*, I interpret this floor in a certain manner, I account for it as solid ground, upon which . . . and so on. That is to say, I interpret experiences through other experiences, and so on.

As you see, in all this the guiding problem is still that of showing-itself. I have already more often than not critically commented on Husserl's theory here, which we repeated today with a certain kind of change, with the duality of this dual phenomenon, that is this critical commentary: What presupposes the difference of this dual phenomenon? And what does this second, originally latent, phenomenon mean? It means that there was something here that remained, so to speak, unnoticed, but is noticeable and graspable in its original. Seizable in its original by what? Turned with its gaze instead of outward, to things, in the opposite direction, that means *inward*. But do we really have something like this view turned inward and seizing in the original, something that was here already before? Does there exist something like this seizing itself in the original by an inward-turned gaze? Is the phenomenon of phenomenology really something like the mere turning of the eye from outward inward? These are all only meta-phors, especially that original seizing. Husserl appeals here to Descartes, to Descartes's *cogito sum*, to self-certain consciousness. But the self-certainty of consciousness only pertains to that, that *sum*, everything else, that origi-nal seizing of itself, is not encompassed in that *sum*—except under certain conditions. Only as long as it could be said that what I seize is the *sum* in the purity of its being—then perhaps we could talk about the phenomenon in the true sense of the word. But even otherwise, if we have here basically the pure being of its subject or its I, can it be said it is this subject or this I, this pure being of my I, from which as its effectuation follows something like an object, that it is the phenomenon in the other sense of the word?

Husserl's crossing from the equivocal phenomenon to the unequivo-cal is the crossing from *finite things* to the *in-finite* subject, that is to such a subject whose accomplishment are phenomena that, in reality, are the proper essence of things. Because after all this is a thing in its original, not in some kind of replica or some kind of secondariness.

But then the question is: Does the crossing from the equivocal phe-nomenon that shows the thing within it and by itself, so that it itself shows itself, to the deeper phenomenon, presuppose the crossing from the finite to the in-finite? Or is some kind of passage possible where this *salt mortale* (deadly leap) is not carried out, but where there still remains a difference

between the phenomenon in its common, vulgar sense and the phenomenological phenomenon, that is, the phenomenon originally concealed, which is only brought to light and shows itself by phenomenology?

Here Heidegger intervenes and asks: What is really the continuing experience of this present object here? This is nothing other than interpretation, the explication of what gives itself. And what is an explication? An explication is a certain *comprehending*. What do I have to understand when I have an existent before me? I have to understand this existent, what *to be* means. And that is why interpretation is interpretation in the light of being, I have to understand the being of a thing, when I want to take it as a thing, when that thing as a thing is to show itself to me. You see, the problem of showing is still the leading one. Only here is it a matter of the transition from the patent to the latent phenomenon. Now it is a matter of getting this comprehension of being in hand, which has to guide us and which only then makes the phenomenon the phenomenon, which only then causes that what shows itself to me here is actually a tablecloth, a table, a room, and so on. It is about this—that is, the transition from the patent to the latent phenomenon.

Of course, our thesis was: the problem of showing is deeper, more fundamental, more primary than the problem of being. Just because I can only get to the problem of being through the problem of showing, whereas if I depart from the problem of being in the abstract sense of the word, then my conception of being becomes an abstract concept, a completely formal label, not even a category, rather something above categories, that is to say, it no longer even has any kind of content. After all, categories are always determined by content, whereas something like being is merely transcendental, that means something that is even more general than categories. From this point of view, it becomes impossible for me to bring alive the problem of being in any way. It becomes a mere formal matter, and then succumbs to the criticism of logicians who will say: this is nothing but a word, a certain συνσημαντικόν, that is to say, something that has meaning only in connection with certain other terms, and its concrete meaning disappears entirely. For this reason, the problem of showing only then gives the problem of being its own meaning and its own depth. This is then "*der langen Rede kurzer Sinn*" (to make a long story short).

We could further say: showing certainly leads us to concretize the meaning of being. But the showing of a thing presupposes something like the characteristics of this showing, something, in which the thing shows itself, characteristics of givenness. Only in these characteristics of the given can something like a sense for being express itself; only in them can our sense for being offer "the sign of its path." These kinds of characteristics of givenness are, for example, just givenness in its original, unoriginal givenness, unoriginal accessibility, mere intuition, then unintuited givenness and all similar things. Of course, because in these characteristics something more profound expresses itself—precisely our sense for being. Only by that does it get a unified outline. But the study of characteristics of givenness and this entire apparatus, by which we comprehend what is our true situation and our relation to what is, the study of all these things is something primary that only then teaches us about being in the proper sense of the word and about its possibilities of expressing itself. Apart from this, it is shown that here not only existence shows itself to us but also quasi existence; existence shows itself *like that which is* and also *like that which is not.* Only then the possibility of something like the problem of truth shows itself here. Because truth, as Aristotle used to say, consists in that in our comprehending we synthetically grasp what is, in such a way that we put together what belongs together in the thing and separate what does not belong together.

All these things show that the study of manifesting is something that inseparably goes together with the study of being, but the study of manifesting has its own certain autonomy. The same goes for the problem of time. Heidegger very rightly and profoundly recognized that *time* is something that, unthematically and with a kind of instinctive necessity, was always taken as the horizon, in which only then existence determines itself, reveals and defines itself. But the horizon is something other than the thing itself that reveals itself within the horizon. Time is something without which being can never show itself to us, but being is not time and time is not being.

So that I might somewhat clarify what I want to say by this: Why is time the horizon of existence or why was it always taken so? Real existence is being within time. For ideal existence, such as, for example, a logical formulation, time does not have any sense. Eternity is, to the contrary, a domain of certain bounded realities characterized by a certain specific temporal structure. And it is clear that from the very beginning of metaphysics, just these differences were the center of attention. And in what way were these differences given? They were in reality temporal structures, but they were appealed to unsystematically and not consciously. In the history of metaphysics, time as such was never thematized as a horizon, in which only then existence in its being reveals itself.

But first still several comments about *Being and Time*. Why *Being and Time*?

In *Being and Time*, the fundamental conception is still very close to the Husserlian, although the leap from the finite to the infinite is rejected here. The transition from the equivocal phenomenon to the phenomenological phenomenon is in Heidegger the transition from the vulgar phenomenon—from the phenomenon with which Aristotle occupies himself, that is, from existence that shows itself in itself and by itself—to *what actually shows that phenomenon*. What is it, if it is not the absolute subject XXXY that as such is captured in absolute reflection, if that kind of absolute reflection does not exist? What could it be? It is what Heidegger calls: *Dasein*.

What is *Dasein*? The word *Dasein* is supposed to say it itself: "*Sein, das da ist*," that is, being that is *here*, that is, in a specific concrete form. It is *situated* being. And what is "situated being"?

Remember, as we said, in the Cartesian *cogito* nothing other than pure being is guaranteed. There is absolutely no guarantee for what Husserl thinks, that is the whole various stream of consciousness that is reflexively captured. Everything that is in *Dasein* and is graspable is only the modus of its being. And what characterizes the being of *Dasein*? Only that in contrast to everything else that is, *Dasein* has comprehension for its own being.

What does this mean, that it has comprehension for being? That it has sense that things are. This is shown in that things show itself to it: things do not show themselves to any other being. But that things show themselves to it, is rooted in that *Dasein is* differently than are things. How *is* it? Such that it is not indifferent to that it itself and things are, that they regard it. This further means that things and its own existence are not for it a mere fact. It is not that *Dasein* is, and then claims that over there, there are some kinds of things. If we were to understand it in this way, we should interpret the being of *Dasein* after the manner of the being of things, for which, that they are, does not touch it at all, is indifferent, and cannot relate to their being or to another. Things are characterized just in their very being by their lack of a relation to being. Whereas *Dasein* is characterized in its existence by relating to its own being and to the being of all other things through its comprehending being. This also means that we realize our own being, we do not carry our own being, we do not just have it somehow passively given, as things have them. We bring things into relation with being, that means that they are indifferent in regard to being, whereas man, that is *Dasein*, never is. Even then, when it apparently is indifferent this indifference is its own accomplishment, its own deed, its decision. This means that man has an entirely different manner of being than things. And this further means that there exist at the very least two fundamental modes of being. All this follows from, as you see, from the problem of showing.

There is an old teaching that there exist different ways, not forms or the content of being, but of being itself. In theology this is an old teaching. The being of divinity is completely different from the being of created things. In theological metaphysics the difference between the being of the creator and the being of the created is fundamental. This difference, for example, still plays a role perhaps in Kant's teaching about the thing in itself. The *intellectus archetypus*, which is god, is not left to the mercy of the passive opinion of things, but rather creates them by the fact that things think. This kind of relation to presence, to materialness, as you see, characterizes the being of divinity in an entirely different manner than the being of man and than is characterized by the being of created things. Created things are naturally dependent upon the *intellectus archetypus* in its existence, whereas the *intellectus archetypus* is not dependent upon anything. Except that in the created it no longer concerns different modes, but rather merely various content of being. When some kind of determinant, like a plant, mineral, animal, person, is conceived only as a certain categorical material thing, it can be more or less rich, more or less structured, but in the same mode of realization, in the same mode of existence. We are concerned with the mode of existence itself. Teaching about the different forms of existence, not only the content of given existence, is traditional. Except that traditional metaphysical teaching is theological-hypothetical, whereas, as you see, Heidegger tries to carry this too over to the ground of phenomena. He tries to draw from this an ontological teaching that is the beginning of ontology, from the phenomena themselves, from that, what shows itself, and what can be shown. How? Just as I have now demonstrated for you.

That *Dasein* always has comprehension for being—and that its being itself is characterized by comprehension, relation to being—that is an ontological characteristic differentiating it from the characteristics of being of the type "*nicht-Dasein*" (the word *Dasein* is hard to translate; I have once tried to translate it with the word "*pobyt*"[2] but in this "*pobyt*" this "*byt*" [be] has to be heard.) This feature of *Dasein* can also be expressed in that manner, that *Dasein* is ontological in its entire proper essence, then. It is characterized by comprehension for being, and by that it is not indifferent in regard to being, it constantly realizes being, carries it, it does not merely accept it passively. This also means that within it constantly lives what could be called ontological difference, that is to say, the difference between existence and being. *Dasein* is a specific existence, and in it difference is constantly occurring, meaning the transition from mere existence to being, to the comprehending of existence.

Here, in this place, only then—according to Heidegger—opens the possibility of answering the question what really is a phenomenon. The phenomenon in the proper sense of the word, is that something shows itself, is possibly only by that, that there exists existence, such as *Dasein*, in which takes place the process of ontological difference—that is to say, *transcensus, transition* the stepping from existence to being. And this transition also means that manifesting takes place in the domain of being, that means in something that *is not existent*, in a fundamentally not-existent domain. Only on the basis of something like that can things show themselves, manifest themselves.

Now what all belongs to this *transcensus* and to this entire structure of ontological difference? From this point of view, phenomenology becomes an ontological phenomenology, meaning the phenomenology of ontological difference. Is it possible that something manifest itself without, for example, showing itself in a determined tonal coloring? Mood is, after all, not something subjective, phenomenologically considered. Landscapes have mood, an interior has a mood, so does a person we encounter, and so on. But to what does mood in actuality point to? Disposition points to something we do not create, but rather into which we are, so to speak, placed. Mood points to that we are always already in some way seized by things, captivated. In German there is the word *Befindlichkeit, sich be-*

2. [literally "stay," where *byt* means "to be"],

finden, by which Heidegger characterizes disposition and which succinctly expresses just this *material* stamp of disposition. In disposition is manifested not perhaps what is called a certain emotional accent, something subjective, but rather the manner in which we are already always captivated, "the face" the world turns toward us. That we are captivated, that our world has already somehow caught us, that it has two aspects: on the one hand, this aspect of the world and, on the other, we ourselves as placed factically into the world. But this "factically placed" has a determined temporal character, the character of an "already," and with it the entire dispositional and emotional domain. That mood naturally places us into the world in a certain manner; through specific deeds it closes us off and through others opens us up. It has this characteristic of "opening-closing." This also means a temporal stamp for other deeds that are opened up or closed within it! In these features Heidegger then seeks the *more original* temporal characteristics than are those derived from merely objective time.

I said all this only so that I should try to show you how the phenomenon of ontological difference leads to further and further phenomenal structures and how these phenomenal structures are not merely juxtaposed, how they form a continuity where one cannot be simply pulled away from the other. Heidegger's phenomenological phenomena are not somehow rhapsodical, as they are for Husserl. Husserl always underlines singularity, whereas Heidegger sees a kind of grand structure of the whole. I will not demonstrate this now, that would lead us too far away, I only wanted to point to how the problem of showing in Heidegger leads to the problem of being and how only in the problem of showing, the problem of being in Heidegger gets going in a new way.

But with the passage of time, Heidegger realized that this manner of thematizing being is still too close to Husserl's subjectivism, and his further attempt was then an effort to get rid of this subjectivism, that being should still be only the achievement of the finite subject, this *Dasein.* He then tried to reformulate his doctrine so that, to the contrary, *Dasein* be characterized as rendered possible by something like being beginning and taking place within it, and this again out of showing. So that is it for the first question.

Q: I should like to return to the first question I posed to you, that I would like to make specific. It is a matter of whether manifesting without the gradation of that which exists, that is without a certain deduction of existence from manifesting and so corresponding of the existing through manifesting, whether this manifesting without this gradation does not betray its self-responsible demand, and whether it does not live in its own manner on credit, and is not the mere memory of manifesting, through such a never-ending progress and deficient mode.

P: You are asking this in regard to what was laid out today?

Q: As well, but I would rather qualify my last question.

P: What do you mean by this deficient mode? Whether manifesting, which . . .

Q: Whether manifesting that does not answer to its existent point of view . . .

P: Hold on, does not answer from its existent point of view. . . . This means manifesting, which does not answer to that existent?

Q: No, to the contrary, if we take manifesting from standpoint of existence . . .

P: So hold on, how can we take the point of view of manifesting from the point of view of existence?

Q: In such a way as, for example, Heidegger got to being through phenomenology.

P: No, not through existence. According to Heidegger, the point of view of manifesting is taken through being.

Q: Yes, but that obviously was not clear to Heidegger right away, that required a certain process and depth of elaboration, and thus had to begin with some unmediated phenomenon. In this way the philosopher gets to the standpoint of manifesting and now the problem is—of course, it is the path of the answering of this phenomenon—how he looks at phenomena, the existent from this standpoint. But I suppose that if from this standpoint that individual existent stops answering, then manifesting stops being manifesting.

P: Why should it stop?

Q: Because in its own way, in this way the moment of responsibility falls away, and I suppose that it is then a kind of maintaining of this manifesting on credit, recalling of it, and so it leads to a never-ending progress and deficient mode. I suppose that it is merely manifesting *as* manifesting, but not in its original.

P: This vulgar phenomenon is justified only then by that, that it is reduced to a phenomenological phenomenon and in this phenomenological phenomenon it is shown, *why* this vulgar phenomenon is equivocal, and why it cannot be any different. And yet, an appeal is made to such a phenomenon that in itself is not equivocal, because it encompasses the possibility of the vulgar phenomenon in its bifurcation within itself. What you say—that manifesting is really the mere memory of manifesting and not manifesting of the actual existence—might be applicable to Husserl's method. That is, for Husserl true existence is nothing other than the phenomenon; whereas for Heidegger the phenomenon is the phenomenon of existence, that is to say, the showing itself of existence, for which we have comprehension, the key, within the nonvulgar phenomenon. This fundamental difference then causes that in Heidegger it is no longer a matter of a mere memory of manifesting, but rather about manifesting in the strong sense of the word.

Q: I just assume that in Heidegger there is missing something like the Platonic descent back into the cave. That it is still a kind of most fundamental view from the point of view of manifesting upon existence, and this descent is never realized there; I mean in that sense, that this being cannot always be achieved, that it is already given once and for all—perhaps I am mistaken.

P: It is my fault that I did not get to this thing here. Heidegger's novelty is precisely in that—and it is a large error of any account that does not emphasize it—that being in its entire essence is in Heidegger an un-ended process—of course process is the wrong term—it is something that is dynamic in its entire essence. In Plato being is the great whole, which, for example in the dialogue *Parmenides*, actually unfolds in a kind of grand topography. In Heidegger it is such that being in its own essence is the surfacing of something hidden and coming into manifesting, into the manifest.

Q: I know that is what Heidegger says, but I suppose that in a certain sense this is merely a postulate, something like the difference between the pre-Socratics and Plato.

P: And what does this postulate sound like?

Q: Just as you said, that being is something dynamic, that constantly surfaces, that constantly is. And I see a kind of fundamental limit in that, that no actually honest submersion into the gradation of existence from the point of view of being, manifesting, is carried out, and I just think that this dynamism is not there in the original.

P: The difference between the vulgar and phenomenological phenomenon presupposes that the phenomenological phenomenon is originally *hidden* in its entire essence. As a result, this philosophical feat consists in capturing both the phenomenon and, above all, this *hiddenness itself*—that is to say, that mystery, which lies in that manifesting. Manifesting is not pure light, rather it in its entire essence is something equivocal. Not in the sense of equivocalness as is the equivocity of the vulgar phenomenon; the vulgar phenomenon is equivocal in *what* manifests itself within it; but here we are interested in the equivocity within the showing itself. Showing is *at the same time* showing and hiding. Perhaps it really is a large problem in Heidegger: that is if this deeper, philosophical phenomenon is also the phenomenon and hiddenness—then terribly essential differences vanish or at least *seem* to vanish. Here problems genuinely arise for the thinker. This cannot be ignored. But perhaps for this very reason it should be important above all to once again think through this structure, which I have tried to demonstrate here, from the point of view of primary showing. For that reason I still emphasize that we have to stick to the problem of showing as something upon which only then must be oriented the problem of being, and not to shoot the problem of being as from a revolver and eventually to do violence to the phenomenon.

Q: But to do that, it should be necessary to concretely describe individual phenomena, so that this should mean that we should, for example, have to invent a new language for the unmanifest. All our contemporary language is oriented to the evident forms of things. The object is really that arises through the objectification of the eye. Then we can talk about it—the objectification of the ear, and then vision and hearing as objectifying senses; that should mean to objectify touch as much as theoretical reason, to invent a language for tactile relations with the world. Here there is a paucity of words.

P: All the sensory domains are, in the end, represented in our language in some kind of way. But you are right, the ontology that Heidegger has in mind wants a language of an entirely new stamp. I should say that Heidegger's expansion of intentions and field of philosophical analyses up to this time does not sufficiently take care of that, that the primat of logos nonetheless still exists, the primat of ὄψις (vision) and light, because only from this point of view is it also possible to thematize this difference. I think that it is not really possible otherwise. This primat has to be ontologically formulated in some kind of way, it has to be manifested in some kind of way. In Heidegger it looks as if these things were equivalent.

Q: Except for one place: he only talks about this once, somehow in passing, in the seminar about Heraclitus, where he says, "And if we are to ask what is first—we have to say, light." Of course this is the only place I have found. But de facto, materially that equality is there, which is really a mythical matter. And it means the equivalence of truth and lie, truth and untruth, good and evil.

Q: Even this is somewhat shown in the requirements of the new language. For it does not depend so much on a new or old language, as much as on that, that language never is exactly what we are interested in, that it is rather constantly an indication and approximation, as Plato used to say.

P: Yes, but one interpreter[3] I think emphasized very precisely that in Heidegger the problem of *truth* in its proper sense of the word is lacking— but here we then cross from the question we originally posed to something else. But that presupposes laying out the problem of truth in Heidegger— we did not do that today. Of course, the problem of truth coincides with the spreading of the problematic of truth against tradition. In the traditional conception, truth is correct judgment, that is to say: the truthful is only what is expressed through declaration. In Heidegger it is not like this. In Heidegger, and as well already in Husserl, the truthful has a much wider field. The truthful or untruthful—or, better said, the concordant and discordant—can already be our behavior, because already our behavior has the structure of "something as something," already, for example, when I interpret this as a table, when I see this as a table, within it is something like truth, or if I am mistaken, eventually error.

Heidegger's conception, where he lays out truth as not-concealment, or better said, as unconcealment, of course coincides with the theory of the phenomenon, as I laid it out just now. Except Heidegger identifies the problem of *truth* already from *Being and Time* with the problem of *showing-itself* of things, whereas he neglects the surroundings, that something can show itself as it is, and also as it is not. The very problem of truth is not that things show themselves, that they become the phenomenon—

3. E. Tugendhat, *Der Warheitsbegriff bei Husserl und Heidegger* (Berlin: Walter de Gruyter, 1970).

that is a presupposition for the problem of truth. That the world shows itself is of course the most important, the most profound fact and problem *with which* philosophy operates, and *in which* it operates. But showing in and of itself is only the ground for the problem of truth, because truth is the showing-itself as things are. And the same counts for the phenomenon in the profound sense of the word. In Heidegger, the phenomenon in the profound sense of the word is the phenomenon of *being,* and it is seen entirely *outside* this problem. Then he can say such a horrible thing: "We lack not only every kind of measure which would allow us to estimate the completeness of one metaphysical epoch to another. There does not exist any kind of right to evaluate in this manner. Plato's thought is no more perfect than that of Parmenides. The philosophy of Hegel is no more perfect than that of Kant. . . . "[4]

More perfect—what does that mean? In what does philosophy pretend for perfection? In truthfulness, in the completeness of its capturing of what is being. For Heidegger, then, there does not exist any possibility of evaluating metaphysical philosophies, that is their conceptions of being, from the point of view of truth.

Q: That is in its own way, positivism.

P: It is hard to say positivism. It, after all, does not have this one-sidedness. Positivism denies sense at all to philosophies; but Heidegger does not do this, and at the same time he denies us entirely the possibility of evaluating philosophy from the point of view of truth.

Q: I suppose the analogy is in how positivism looks at the facts of the world—that we have to take them such as they are—and if someone interprets them, that is philosophizes, then this is metaphysics. That is the kind of view of philosophy it has.

P: That still should not be correct, because for Heidegger each of these philosophies, of course, has in its conception of being something unveiled and something concealed from being, and they are all equivalently placed in this, so the fact that Aristotle discusses with Plato is in reality wasted effort. It cannot be done. Just as Hegel debates with Kant, that is in reality an entirely useless thing. But that is horrible! And this is connected to the fact that the process of unveiling-concealing is seen by

4. M. Heidegger, "The End of Philosophy and the Task of Thinking," in *Basic Writings,* ed. David Farrell Krell (London: Routledge, 1993), 427–49.

him again just as unveiling in general, without the difference of concordance and nonconcordance, without what makes up truthfulness in the proper sense of the word.

Q: This denies our commonness and the commonness of the world in which we live. If we cannot carry on a dialogue for example with Plato, then we are, in actual fact, not in the same community with him, and his world is, in actual fact, different from ours.

P: This is also connected to that, because the conception of the world, as Heidegger formulated it—of course, he formulated it during the period of his subjectivism—is naturally the world as an existential one, and it is always *my* world. But naturally it is not possible to get out of subjectivism this way. These are all reasons why I consider the problem of being as Heidegger formulates it incomplete, and why I think the entire problematic—beginning with manifesting—which I think is an important, fruitful beginning, without which one cannot even move in philosophy—has to be thought through again, so that we avoid subjectivistic consequences. That, then is the grand thing of phenomenology.

"Each philosophical epoch has its own proper necessity."[5] What is an epoch, he describes here before this. "That a certain philosophy is, as it is, we have to simply acknowledge."[6] Why? Because it is not an affair of those philosophers, but rather it is the "*Geschick des Seins,*" it is being itself, which gives itself in this manner, and we cannot do anything but accept this giving. We are, so to speak, passively left to this giving itself of being in this indicated manner. "However, we do not have any right to give one philosophy precedence before another, as is possible in regard to various *Weltanschauungen.*"[7] Philosophy is not a vision of the world, philosophy does not occupy itself with existents as a vision of the world, it does not give a picture of any kind of reality, rather philosophy occupies itself with the fact that things show themselves—that is, with being—which only then renders them accessible for us.

Q: Do you think we could then try to elaborate certain measures for perfection through an exhaustive working through of manifesting?

P: Yes, what is placed before us here in this kind of way, are after all,

5. Ibid.
6. Ibid.
7. Ibid.

as you rightly say, decadent consequences. This entire article about the end of philosophy is defeatist. How, for example, does the entire problem of philosophy, as it is indicated from the classical epoch look from this point of view? What do Socrates and Plato want? To live in truth—that is their own definition of philosophy. Now we have gotten there, where the sophists were.

These questions are, of course, complicated by the fact that already encompassed in the very beginning of phenomenology is something from philosophy's modern situation. Husserl's phenomenology itself after all encompasses within itself, or better said, overcomes, but encompasses (*aufgehoben*) the positivistic concept, that philosophy is not a discipline of content, that the real subject of philosophy is not the structure of things— that is the subject of science, and science has analyzed the whole region of existent things—rather, it is the phenomenon as such, that means manifesting, showing of things. So that we already have to take this into account, we also have to evaluate Heidegger, after all, from this point of view. Phenomenological philosophy, from the very beginning, battles with positivism and occasionally certain results of this manifest themselves, that this battle is not complete—for example, in Heidegger's final defeatism.

Q: There is also a question here about Ingarden: the work of art in phenomenological aesthetics, especially in the literary work of Ingarden, is conceived as (1) phenomenon, and (2) intentional object. As an *intentional object* it does not have a real being, because it depends upon the intention that created it and upon the intention that maintains it. Its existence is then *not-real*. Then there is the question whether it is not-real also because it is conceived as a *phenomenon*. In the case that this aesthetics did not give itself only the name of phenomenology, but consequentially wanted to apply the findings of philosophy to the domain of art—which after all is nothing but, as Heidegger says, one of the manners in which truth occurs—then this should mean that the work of art should be conceived as a phenomenon in the proper sense of the word, as one of the phenomena of being, in which is also manifested that not-real side of the universe. From that it should follow that the work is also something *not-real*. Does this connection exist here—that is, between the not-reality of the existence of intentional objects and the not-reality of works such as the phenomenon?

P: It is like this. The work of art as an intentional object is only Ingarden's concern. In Heidegger, for example, the work of art is not an intentional object, not at all. So this duo does not go together. Of course, the work of art is a phenomenon in Heidegger, it is a phenomenon of being, it is in fact the eminent manner how *being*, not existence shows itself, but it is not any kind of intentional object, because an intentional object is a certain existence, not being, it is a certain reality maintained by the subject in existence. According to Ingarden—for those who do not know the matter—the world, things, and so on, have a real existence, whereas judgments, and also, above all, the objects of fantasy and then for example artistic objects, have *intentional* existence. The real object is real because it exists, so to speak, independently from any kind of subject. The intentional object is not subjective in the sense that it should be composed of experiences—how, for example, the life of man is made up of experiences. The life of man is a series of experiences. The work of art is not a series of experiences, but it is possible only on the basis of human experiences. Human experiences maintain it in reality. For example, painting is not anything other than a picture, painting is the underlay of the picture, painting is in a certain manner a worked-out intuitive complex. And that I see in a certain manner and necessarily interpret the specific structure of the painting—that is a picture. This interpretation has a certain structure, a whole row of layers, and in the ordered building up of this interpretation lies the work of the artist. What Husserl says, that it is the essence of presentness in general, according to Ingarden only applies to the work of art. And Ingarden is interested in this entire problem because he might show how Husserl's general thesis that all objectivity is subjectively constituted is not truthful, because there is a fundamental difference between an intentional objectivity, such as is the work of art, and real objectivity that is not constituted in this kind of manner. This conception of the work of art as an intentional object is specific to Ingarden. About the deeper connections, as we have spoken about today—that is, that intention and interpretation in general stand upon a much deeper foundation, that is on the foundation of *comprehending of being* and so on—understandably, nothing is said about this here. And Heidegger himself then tried to interpret the work of art entirely differently. How?—that is another question that would take us terribly far today. But if you are interested in that, then we can talk about that sometime over an entire evening.

One thing that strikes me is that you all only have questions about phenomenology, and Heidegger, and so on, but that no question came regarding Europe, what were my most particular theses; that European reality is anchored in two great turning points, in the care of the soul that summarizes all of antiquity, and what all is connected with this. I hoped that you would help me further develop this through critical questioning. So I tried to give a certain account of the history of philosophy, and in vain I am trying to raise some objections, and in this way at least to give some life to this. That is why the problematic with which we have occupied ourselves today is connected with this—I have no doubt about that. But I should be also interested in your eventual objections regarding the historical material I have presented here. I have the impression, you see, that precisely a great deal in our actual life and our world is clarified through this historical perspective, and that for this reason we should really concern ourselves with this. It is also indicative of our current situation that no one hardly concerns themselves with this today, and that in the daily present, this is directly ran away from. Europe in its political sense is always talked about, but at the same time, the question of what it really is, and what it grows out of, is neglected. You hear about the integration of Europe: but is it possible to integrate something regarding some kind of geographical or purely political concept? This is a concept lying upon *spiritual* foundations. Only then is seen what kind of question it is. This is all that is at stake.

10

The Transformation of the Ontological Project
in Aristotle—The Return to the Cave

Last time we started with an explanation of philosophical reflection about European history. The thesis I tried to develop regarded the tight connection between the origin of Europe and the resume of Greek life, which Plato offered in ancient philosophy through his founding of life in philosophy as the care of the soul. We then tried to show how the principle of the care of the soul was developed in Plato in *three* directions:

1. As the general philosophical teaching that brings the soul into connection with the structure of being.
2. As the teaching about the life of the philosopher in the community and in history, that is, as the teaching about the state, in which the care of the soul is both possible and is the center of all state life and also the axis of historical occurrence.
3. As the teaching about the soul as the principle of individual life that is exposed to the fundamental experience and test of individual human existence, that is, death and the question of its meaning.

I have already indicated several times why I think this concept, elaborated by Plato in classical Greek philosophy, is the fundamental theme of European history. Already Plato himself—and I think that in this Plato is not only the creator of a fiction but also he seizes reality within it—he sees the theme of the care of the soul as the reprise of everything essential in

Greek life. This is the *restitutio in integrum* of the Greek community in its essence and in its historical mission. This historical mission showed itself in strong guise in the great equalization between the Greek world and the East in the Persian wars, when Plato's community played the deciding role. However, Plato stands essentially at the end of the history of the Greek polis; he philosophizes already after its catastrophe. His philosophy after the catastrophe is to reconcile itself with the concrete situation and eventually to open further perspectives. While it is certain that this further perspective is not the sketching out of the future history of Europe, it is still certain that without the perspectives opened by Plato, the future history of Europe should have an entirely different form, and that these future histories took advantage of and were formed in a peculiar way—we will still talk about this—by what Plato opened.

Before we cross to this next history, I would like to formulate the objection that ought to lead us a little further, the objection that, at first glance, is merely an objection, but which surfaces for everyone. For Plato is not the only figure who attempted something like a resume of Greek life. The second, no less great and no less noteworthy philosopher, Aristotle, after all does not philosophize about something like the care of the soul, and the questions we tried to raise only play an episodic role in his thought. It is true that Aristotle's philosophy is in large measure the transformation of Plato's philosophy, yet it is a *peculiar* transformation. Our task in this connection will be to look at Aristotle's significance for the spiritual birth of Europe and for later history, and to reflect upon this. Today's lesson, then, I dedicate to the subject Aristotle and three fields in which Plato formulated the theme of the care of the soul. These are:

1. the birth of a *systematic ontology*;
2. *the teaching about the state* where philosophers will be able to exist, and where philosophers will have to rule; and
3. the teaching about the *individual fate of the soul*.

Perhaps someone could still object that these fields are unsystematically sketched out, that we do not see clearly why the theme of the care of the soul should be exhausted just by these three domains. This is one possible objection. For us, I think it is sufficient if we realize that these three are indispensable, essential moments, without which the later spiritual history of Europe is not even conceivable and that they have a constant internal link between them, which is the essence of the soul—its ontological essence and its possibilities.

Let us take the first domain—the most important: the care of the soul and an ontological systematic. We notice that Aristotle led to the destruction of Platonic ontology and also the construction of a different concept. It goes without saying that concepts such as ontology and so on are our modern terms. Plato, of course, speaks about *The Sophist*, the γιγαντομαχία περί τῆς οὐσίας (the battle of gods and giants about reality), about the colossal fight of philosophers over existence. Actually, he tries to build a consistent teaching about the various ways of being that do not stand on the same level, but rather which are in a particular hierarchical relation. Even if the Platonic dialogue reflects this concept only to a certain degree, at the same time there are other attempts to reconstruct Plato's own school teaching, that teaching which Plato, as far-sighted as he was, never wrote down, because he considered that kind of writing inappropriate for philosophy, equivocal, not grasping philosophy as such, throwing philosophy as such into the situation in which it is today, that is to say, into the situation of *quot capita, tot sensus*—into a situation where the heart of the matter is not pursued, but rather where tangential questions are debated about and where irrelevant considerations cause the proper thread to be lost, which lies in that: not only to discuss but also to see. The most important Platonic teaching is that in philosophy the technique of thinking is insufficient. You know that Plato created what is called dialectic and that logic really owes its birth to Plato. But according to Plato, this *is not philosophy*. According to Plato, philosophy begins where something begins to be seen, where meaningful speech leads us to the thing itself, which we must see, catch sight of—but not with these very eyes, because to catch sight of with these very eyes, while extraordinarily important for philosophy, is only one of the manners of catching sight of. There exist *two* ways of catching sight of, which is why all talk about philosophy is equivocal. That is why speech is insufficient in philosophy. In what sense then is it possible to speak of something like ontology in Plato? Above all, in the sense that in Plato it genuinely is explicitly formulated; it is necessary to ask about the meaning of the verb *to be*. This is in the dialogue *The Sophist*. You know that in *Being and Time* this passage is cited as the motto of the entire work: "It is clear, that you," says the Eleatic host there, "have known for a long time, what you really want to say, whenever you say the word "existent"; while we also used to think this, but now we have come into a quandary."[1]

There is also a peculiarity in the Platonic manner of thinking in the way that Plato answers the question, what the word "to be" means exactly, because he sees the problem of *being* as a problem of truth, as the problem of what is *truthful*, veritable. And this "veritably"—what does this mean?

In explanations of Platonic teaching, the dual world is usually spoken of: on the one hand are the ideas; on the other hand is that which is around us. How does Plato come to such an insane, mad idea that does not fit into any sensible person's head, that apart from what we commonly called existent—these things around us—there exists something else, something completely different, incommensurable with this and that only can answer for us the question of the meaning of "to be"? How Plato develops this problematic is essentially the *second birth* of philosophy. This is one of the most exciting things in the history of thinking; to be is not an obvious thing; it presupposes some kind of *measure*, and measure is something essentially different from the measured. This is something each measure encompasses within itself. We can measure things only because they are imprecise and measures are precise. As a result, measures are something essentially different from what is measured by them. This is one of the themes that can lead us to comprehend what Plato thought.

But why does Plato consider these measures—which are, after all, from our daily point of view evidently totally our own work, our fictions— as the highest, truest existence? You know how Husserl, for example, explains the problem of measuring as an idealization on the basis of certain privileged forms occurring in our experience.[2] What does idealization mean? The creating of certain fictitious approaches to the limit in experience that allows for precision and points toward it. But idealization in this sense means the creation of something that does not exist. But why does Plato turn this whole matter around and claim that on the basis of what we measure, that something is or something is not, and that it is something more and something less—that this is most of all? Where does this come from? Is it in Plato simply some kind of transparent slip of thought, or what

---

1. *The Sophist,* 244a.

2. E. Husserl, "Science of Reality and Idealisation: The Mathematization of Nature," in *The Crisis of the European Sciences,* 67.

is it? None of us has the intellectual courage to go after Plato in these things, but none of us, by contrast, dares to qualify Plato as a thinker of phantasms. Great thinkers are the announcers of not only truth but also errors, but in the sphere of *singular* truth and error. Only behind these singular truths or, better said, these rightnesses and wrongnesses, is that genuine truth, that genuine clarity that is at stake here. One thing that can clarify to a certain degree what Plato thinks is the circumstance; the measure of what is, and what measures how things show themselves, has to be in its own way more truthful, clearer than what is measured. This greater truthfulness lies above all else in that this idea—measuring—is identical with itself; it is constant. The constancy of ideas consists in their identity. The idea is conceived so that we can always come back to it. In fact, so long as we do not see it so we can go back to it at any time, we do not see it clearly.

εἶδος ε

In addition to the fundamental thought—that what is around us is in its own being measured by something not on the same level as things that are measured—is Plato's great systematical thought that *mathematics is the model* according to which something like a systematic of measurements and the measured can be developed. Why?

I have already laid this out once for you, so we will not repeat it today. I will just mention it again *pro memoria*. When, under the influence of Plato, geometry is only being created, mathematics is above all geometry of plane figures. And, you know that in the *Republic* Plato himself maintains that all has to be as systematically developed as had been developed in the geometry of spatial representations and other disciplines that follow the same model. For Plato, mathematics is above all geometry. And its essential problems, as you know, are connected to its dimensionality, with the dimensionality of its object. Mathematics occupies itself with something without dimension—numbers. Numbers are in the Greek conception units, and units are points; the point is still in later mathematicians defined as μονάς θέσιν ἔχουσα (a monad having position), as a unity having space. Then there are forms having one dimension—lines. Then there is the surface, and then there is something like the body in its mathematical sense.

The fundamental thought is that the progression from μονάς, from units in the sense of numbers, to lines, from that to the surface and from that to bodies—is the model according to which we can comprehend how the individual orders of life belong together. From our modern point of view it should look like this: the body is something more than a surface, a surface is more than a line, a line is more than a point. But in Plato—for mathematical reasons—it is the other way around. In this dimensionality the higher signifies the beginning; and the beginning is what, once I strike it out, carries away with it all the rest that relies upon it. If we strike out the point, then we strike out lines. When we strike out lines, we strike out surfaces. When we strike out surfaces, we strike out bodies. And even more important is that number is more comprehensible than the line, the line is more comprehensible than a spatial form. If we have a square and within it a diagonal, then that diagonal immediately raises the problem of irrational quantities, which according to Plato does not arise when I am considering only lines. That is one of the reasons why Plato maintains that there exists something like the atomic line, for which Aristotle criticized him very much.

The progression from the number to the line, to the surface, to the body—is a progression always to *another form of comprehensibility*. Where, for example, irrational quantities arise, I can mathematically comprehend something like the relation between the diagonal and the side, but this comprehension shows me this cannot be so simply, so transparently solved as, for example, arithmetic problems. That is to say, mathematics points to the *difference in comprehensibility*, to the difference in *the revealedness* of things, in the revealedness of these various dimensions of mathematical existents. And so the difference in the manner of being of a line, a spatial or bodily form—occurring just where, for example, the problem of irrationality poses itself in a spatial form, that is not posed elsewhere, in the more fundamental and higher—this shows *the different manners of being*. And because mathematics is *the model for being in general*, it points to the great manifoldedness and gradation of being. This is the peculiar meaning of mathematics for philosophy—for ontology, if we want to call it that—in Plato.

How does this Platonic existent look according to this analogy? How does the hierarchy of being look then?

In the highest place, in the mathematical world where there stand points, that is, numbers, there are *first principles*, and the first, most fundamental principle is the One. Everything that is, has to be one. Why? In order that something can *show itself* there has to be something that can be captured, identified in and of itself (in our modern terms). Everything that is has to be one; that is the first precondition for something to be called existent. It could then also be said that the teaching about the One is something higher than the teaching about existence, and that for certain reasons I will not develop here. There are those who maintain that ontology is subordinated to henology in Plato. But besides this One there also has to be something that is the exact opposite of the One, that is the principle of all *multiplicity*, something that multiplies what is one, either by repeating it or by dividing it. Plato calls this second principle, the *indefinite dyad* just because it doubles—for each kind of multiplication is originally a doubling, every kind of multiplying can always be transformed into doubling. Just as the One is always determined, so the dyad is essentially indefinite. There, then stand the first principles.

Beneath them stands their result. *Numbers* are the result of the mutual penetrating of the One and the multiplying principle. But other numbers other than those we work with in mathematics, in arithmetics. Plato calls them ἀσύμβλητοι (incomparable, not of the same kind), because they are not numbers one counts with. Rather they are *models* of all numbers and are always unique. There are ten of them and they are the *ideas.* Ideas are numbers. Why are ideas numbers? Because in these first models of this unified multiplicity we have before us the *archetypes of all dimensionality.* There we have that, from which arises, mathematically taken, something like the surface and like the body. The primeval examples of this forming of existence are here, in the first unifying of the One with multiplicity.

Let us take something like the tetrad, the simplest solid, in it are encompassed the "four." We cannot think about this simplest of all bodies other than by first thinking about "four."

Plato's effort is to think up the genesis of these first prototypes of all diversity, all that has form. And at the same time, you see these two principles: one of them signifies *form*; the second has the significance of something only multiplying itself, that only weakens, as it were this unity, that somehow waters it down, that in a certain sense is the opponent of this first unity. And the element having the initiative in this mutual tension is that unity, because even numbers as types are types of unity. Unity of course encompasses variety. But only when variety is unified do we have something like a number before us, for type is something determined, something that has a certain form. What is important here is: *form,* that is, idea. The ideas are *archetypical forms,* the primeval forms of everything.

Εἶδος

And then comes something analogical in existence to line and sur- Ⓘ face. Lines are analogical to ideas that already encompass within themselves something analogical to irrational relations. Such ideas exist, and Plato tries to show that the mathematical analogy can make us understand the mutual relations of ideas among themselves, that is, the mutual interaction of ideas. Then comes something analogical to surface—the soul.

The soul stands at the center of all existence. Everything we have spoken about thus far—principles, ideas as numbers, ideas as linear relations—all this belongs to the realm of the invisible—and the soul as well belongs there, except that it stands *at the boundary* of the visible and the invisible.

The soul has that peculiar privilege, that with it existence comes into movement. The soul vouches for the movement of everything that exists. Naturally, the soul under consideration is the soul not of the individual, but rather the soul of the world. That is what introduces movement, not into the individual body, but rather into the body of the world, and which presupposes before it the entire hierarchy of preceding existence. And the soul is what takes into itself this hierarchy of existence. This taking hold has a certain concrete form, it is *understanding* existence. The soul introduces itself into movement through understanding. How can this be comprehended? The soul after all thinks. Thinking is formulated in judgments. Judgment means to say something else about something. And this "else" cannot remain foreign with regard to the first. We depart from some kind of subject, we give a predicate, but then we have to join this, we have to return to the subject. To come to another term and then to return—this is something like movement, in fact, a circular movement.

Beneath the soul are visible things. Everything that is in the soul, ⒾⓋ everything that it comprehends—that is, as long as it comprehends—are, understandably, relations. And the soul is also the domain of mathematical numbers and formations, which differ from ideas and from numbers and from what is analogical to surfaces and so on, in the domain of being. Mathematical conceptions have numerous exemplars in contrast to ideas-numbers. The dyad is a never-ending multiplicity, any kind of natural number has a never-ending number of exemplars. On the basis that every number is a type of an infinite number of exemplars, arithmetical operations can be performed. And only on this basis can concrete mathematics be performed. All this exists only on the basis that the soul thinks.

Under this sphere of the soul, then, exists a bodily world characterized by movement, constant change, and insufficient identity. The visible world, although it is so appealing to us, suddenly shows itself when we measure it with measures we have gotten used to in the world of the intelligible, as something immensely vague, ungraspable, as something living in constant change of features, none of which is precise, graspable, precisely measurable, none of which can be identified and defined in the proper sense of the word. For this reason this world is of such an order of being, it is inferior to the preceding one.

Only when we clearly realize all this, this colossal Platonic system, do we understand the significance of Aristotle's stepping out against Plato. When we read Aristotle's writings, it seems we constantly hear the echo of Plato's teachings. In Aristotle the only science is that of the universal; just like Plato, Aristotle constantly speaks about εἶδος, about the shape of what is essential in each thing, about the form; Aristotle in his theory of movement borrows from Plato the conception of the form that permutates upon a common substrate, in fact, he borrows from Plato the concept of materials and form; so that it seems to us that Aristotle is a Platonist of his own kind. Only when we realize that Aristotle rejected this fundamental model of the manner of being that served as a systematic guiding thread for Plato do we see what happened when Aristotle came upon the stage.

For Aristotle, mathematics is not a model, according to which various manners of being could be developed. But how can Aristotle dare such an impertinent revolution against his own teacher? What leads him to this? That could justly be marked by the words of the Eleatic citizen in *The Sophist* dialogue, where during discussion about the conception of not-existence, the Eleatic host tells his assistant: now we have to carry out the murder of the father Parmenides. Aristotle committed something like that.

What we are now speaking about may be a very interesting story for someone, but the proper living impulse behind this whole ontology is naturally Plato's care of the soul. Because the soul, as you know, is that which moves by itself, within it constantly lives the impulse to get to existence either through thinking, to unity with it itself, or through irrationality to fall into not-existence. We live in this dimension of the soul. And I have tried to show you that this is the most distinctive dimension of Plato's philosophy, that Plato's philosophy is not proven through any kind of external demonstration, but rather is the praxis of this soul bringing itself into movement by itself. And from this springs the fact that it is the distinctive experience leading to the *seeing* of that existence there, on that other side, and that not-existence here. This leads to that measuring. The soul either is constantly in revolt, measuring itself against that unity of existence, or . . . What in fact does the care of the soul mean? It means to want to be in unity with one's own self. Man, originally and always, is not in this unity with himself; this is incredible work, the work of a whole life. Behind this stands that impulse to unite. And where does it head? Plato's ontology speaks about this.

Aristotle does not have this experience. In Aristotle begins the *return to the cave*. The Platonic cave—that is, care of the soul aiming for unity, identity, and during this it uses measures orienting it within existence. With the help of measures that differ from the measured, one gets from one level of being to another.

For Aristotle all of philosophy is within the Platonic cave. You know that Plato himself forces the philosopher to return to the cave. Philosophers must return to the cave out of duty, even if they do not want to, because something like human life, that is, life where care of the soul is possible, is only realizable under these conditions. For that reason they have to return to the cave; it is their duty, and should they resist, force must be used against them.

Aristotle returns to the cave, but without violence. He carries out such a paradoxical philosophical movement. While he sees the difference between the measure and what is measured, he sees the difference between existence and that which forms its being, but he tries to join this being with this existence so that existence does not double itself. This profound, paradoxical, and not facile thought is the distinctive essence of Aristotle's philosophy. But seen by Plato, it is as if it were an impoverishment of his ontological concept. A great impoverishment because it is as if the entire invisible had collapsed. Any independent ideas do not exist any longer. As was later said: separate ideas. The ideas are, but here, the idea of man is in that particular man. There exists a measure telling us whether something is or something is not. While this measure is and is not distinct from individual things in its own manner. So that we may measure existents with being, Aristotle claims, it is not necessary to develop the transcendental features of certain existents, which have as their function to reveal, to show things as they are; and this means that I must have the capacity to understand, to see, to comprehend, *that* something is and *what* it is. In this peculiar character of certain existents, in that it was encompassed. The Platonic thought, which was criticized and abandoned here, was nonetheless fruitful. It is an essential presupposition for what occurred in Aristotle.

The possibility discovered by Aristotle is an ingenious insight. It may be that in certain things Plato sees deeper than Aristotle, but Aristotle sees a certain possibility Plato does not see. And this on the basis of the problematic Socrates and Plato developed, that is, on the basis of the problem of the measure. How according to what will I decide whether something is good? That is the problem of the measure, the problem of agreement with itself in the process of measuring, which is our vigilant and conscious life at all. This is that Socratic-Platonic problem. For it, Aristotle has his own distinct solution.

o - holy et c...

It is rather comprehensible that in the question of the principles of existence Aristotle builds upon Plato. We have already said that he borrowed from Plato the antithesis of matter and form. In Plato, material formed here, in our world, is in essence space filled with chaotic movement.[3] What is in movement here is hard to say. Plato wants to indicate by this, that this receptacle is the precondition for the bounding of geometrical formations. Recall that the Platonic elements differ from one another by the various shapes of their fundamental forms: one attributes the cube to the world, fire to the tetrahedron, and so on. And this means that Plato's matter is in reality geometrically formulated space, which presupposes some kind of receptacle. It presupposes just this unformed space, devoid yet of any boundedness.

In Aristotle, similarly, there is this duality of material and form, but it has a slightly different significance. To begin with, Aristotle does not see matter and form in this kind of incredible hierarchy of manners of being in which each consequent one depends upon the previous, but rather he strives to see each thing in its internal distinctive stamp and he glimpses it first there where a thing reveals itself in its true form. And the unveiling of a thing in its true form is its own distinct movement—from the concealment of its own distinct form, from its not revealing itself, to its full presence and development and then again back into absence. Aristotle sees things in this context. The showing itself of *being*: in him, that is the showing itself of

3. *Timaeus*, 52e.

things. A thing shows itself by what it is. And showing is movement because it is necessary to comprehend things in their movement. It is possible to comprehend things in movement.

In Plato it should be possible to comprehend things in movement only up to a certain point. It also could be said that, for example, the movement from first principles, the formation of ideas, the formation of the soul with the help of the ideas, the forming of the cosmos with the help of the soul and in the cosmos then the forming of individual elements and things composed out of elements—that is movement. But it is an *ontogenetic* movement. It is not the movement of things before our eyes. And Aristotle is concerned about movement where things are before us here, where things show themselves and unveil themselves to us. He wants to comprehend this movement.

According to Plato this movement can be comprehended ontologically. But this movement is the subject of mythology: because the present world cannot be the subject of knowing, it can be the subject of mere opinion.

But Aristotle wants science, knowledge, comprehension of just these things in movement. He is then forced to develop an entirely different ontological concept. Aristotle's ontological concept understandably will not be mathematical; mathematics will not serve as the guiding thread to allow Aristotle to develop a hierarchy of the manners of being. Nonetheless, even in him there is something like the difference between higher and lower being. Some things *are* more than others. Against this many positivistic spirits of the nineteenth century raged, and many rage to this day: such an insane conception, that something could be more than something else— for being, after all, is a mere word! But for the ancient thinkers this is a serious problem. The gods are *more* than we. And in Plato, the ideas were more than things, they had more being within themselves, they were more present, they were filled with being and there was nothing negative within them. But in Aristotle for example, the gods are more than people, but they are not any kind of archetypes. Aristotle's gods are individual existents. That is one of the most important moments, important in the highest degree, for the future spiritual history of Europe. From this invisible existence (you know that in Book VI of the *Republic*, where there is that great comparison between the domain of existence and the line, he divides first of all the line into the visible and invisible part), in Aristotle only the deities remained, because the soul, all except for one of its parts, is indissolubly joined with the body.

The divine beings are invisible existents, which for a peculiar reason must be labeled as incorporeal. This reason is not as it was in Plato, that the gods were the measure of existence or goodness; rather, they are the source of movement for everything else that is.

Let us try, taking Plato as our point of departure, to characterize the ontological principles in Aristotle. In Plato we have the antithesis between the active principle, which is the One, and the second principle, which is the undetermined (the δυάς, duality). The first is the form, the second matter; form and matter are active: form unifies, material multiplies, divides, causes multiplicity. Both of them *are effective*. In its own way form is a unity, the same as the Good. Because after all, form, boundedness, is good. The opposite is indeterminacy, dissolution, negative infinite. Into this principle it is necessary to project everything that causes chaos in our life: passion, license, and all that which wants to grow or repeat itself infinitely, without having any precise limit and without having any reason for this. Our life moves between these two principles: at one end is the good and at the other evil, and both are active.

In Aristotle material stopped being active, material is mere possibility, only the essential substrate for its forming. As a result, the entire Platonic conception of the movement of the soul between the poles of good and evil cannot be applied here at all. Of course, now we cannot go through all of Aristotle's ontology and cosmology. It is necessary to realize that Aristotle's ontology is oriented to things, to individual existents, and like the Platonic, is an ontology of the perceptive mind. It is an ontology that also—like the Platonic—wants to explain not only that things are but also that they show themselves, that they manifest themselves. But this manifesting, this showing, is the showing of present things for the contemplative point of view. In the contemplative point of view is, of course, emphasized an entirely different aspect than in Plato—the aspect of the point of view, with these eyes and with all other bodily organs. It is the point of view of the being placed into the cosmos, into that cave, almost by everything that it actually is.

But what causes such a being as man to be able to reconcile himself with this world in its entirety, that he sees it as a whole, comprehends and understands it, analyzes it? Nothing else other than, like all things, even man is a being of movement. The natural movement of the human being is that kind of movement leading not only to that—that we are a form for others—but that within ourselves, in this movement of our life, we reveal other things and us ourselves. <u>Our own life is movement</u>. The movement of the shoot is from the grain of wheat to the mature plant, which flowers, is fertilized, and creates new grains. Then this movement is repeated. This movement is of its own sort the revealing of what is hidden in the germ. The movement of the human being—qua human—lies in the human capability to comprehend the movement of all other beings, that he can take them into himself and give them, in his own mind, in his own proper existence, a certain place. He, so to speak, fills himself with them. For that reason, Aristotle says that the <u>distinctive character of our being, that is our</u> ψυχή, <u>our soul, are in their own way, things.</u> It is the *place of things*, not in the material sense, but rather such, that in it things show themselves to be that which they are. The soul is εἴδος εἴδων, the form of all forms and the place of all forms.[5]

  It could almost be said, in an analogy of a modern philosopher, that the movement of the human being is directed toward obtaining clarity about it itself. It cannot obtain clarity in itself other than when it obtains clarity about all other things surrounding it—the *privilegium* of the human being lies in that in its movement it internally relates to itself, whereas other things are indifferent with regard to themselves. This is the peculiarity of the human being and for this reason it could be said that the human being *is* more than others. Other things reveal themselves, but such, that this revealing is hidden to themselves and foreign, and it is only because man, the human ψυχή (soul), discovers them, do they then come to true discovery, to true showing themselves. Only then do they show themselves in the strong sense of the word. The human ψυχή has this power within it. The movement of our life is also this helping of all other things to be. We are the ones who come to them in this. The grand strength of the human being rests in this, in that is the strength of the soul, its substantial privilege. We are *more* than anything else, and all other things have their being within us, in ψυχή. By no means does this mean subjectivization. Things *are* there, outside us, but they are less. What I have just

4. Aristotle, *On The Soul,* 431b21.
5. Ibid., 432a2.

indicated is naturally not here all in one stroke. Something like the unveiling of the cosmos occurs gradually, and so it is a movement. It is a movement both within individuals and in history. Something like the unveiling of the cosmos first in myth and then in philosophy. This is, after all, a great historical movement.

In this way, Aristotle completely reformulated Plato's ontological concept; it is something entirely different. In connection with this, Aristotle's practical teaching will also be different then, just as his teaching about the individual fate of the soul.

11

The Movement of the Care of the Soul in Plato and Aristotle—
Thematization of Action in Aristotle—Human Freedom and
Its Problematicity—*Nicomachean Ethics*—Discussion

Last time I told you that we want to look at Aristotle regarding those
aspects that answer to our analysis of Plato's teaching. We tried to grasp it
from its center, which we took to be Plato's care of the soul. Something
analogical can also be carried out in Aristotle. Why do we emphasize in
both thinkers just the care of the soul, when this term is only Platonic and
nothing like it is directly spoken of in Aristotle? I suppose that in both
these grand thinkers there is—as we would say with a modern term—an
effort for the *good life* as the ground upon which their entire philosophy is
to unfold. We should not imagine that Plato and Aristotle are professors,
that they are philosophers in some professional meaning of the word, as is
known from the newer age, when the philosopher sociologically cannot
exist except as a professor, or at least society has gotten used to seeing the
philosopher in this guise. And you know also that the greatest philosophers
of the modern age—the Kants, the Hegels, and so on—are professors in
actual fact. Whereas the grand philosophers of the ancient world are first of
all thinkers of *human praxis*. When, for example, Aristotle says that philosophy, at least the kind he lays out in the *Nicomachean Ethics*, is not concerned with knowing what is, nor about knowing what are moral values so
they should be theoretically analyzed, but rather that we philosophize in
order to become *good people*: this is the peculiar feature. No modern philosopher is going to step out before the audience with the pretense of
turning them into good people—everyone would laugh. But for the clas-

sical philosophers—Socrates, Plato, Aristotle—this theme of seeking the good, the true (if we use the term not long ago used in philosophy, which today is no longer modern), the authentic manner of life, is the most proper ground upon which moves their philosophy. Socrates, Plato, Aristotle—even Aristotle, this we have to realize! And that, even though it is said of Aristotle that he is the creator of the theoretical conceiving of philosophy, the conception of philosophy as pure θεωρία (theoria), pure intuiting. We will only understand Aristotle's θεωρία as coming from this concern, care, will toward the good life, and not otherwise. What is regularly called ethics or morality in Aristotle does not follow from his theory. This is incomprehensible from a purely theoretical conception of ethics; that it should be an analysis of a certain domain of reality, which should be called moral acting and moral values. This is inconceivable for Aristotle. To the contrary, as we will see, what he calls the theoretical life, the perceptive life, the life in view of the entire features of the universe, entire features of reality, existence, on existence in the whole, follows from care for *the good life.* And if that is the case, then it is necessary to thoroughly notice that fundamental theme in all these thinkers, particularly in Aristotle, because there it is especially neglected. We see Aristotle understood by modern philosophers precisely in the modern manner, that is, "theoretically"; first, as the great scholar and professor, when in reality he is the continuator of the path of philosophical movement, founded by Socrates and reflected in Plato, movement, which we gave the name concern, care of the soul. In Plato, it is the specific *vertical movement,* vertical in the sense that it heads from that place where, so to speak, we originally, usually, and first of all are—in the lowlands of existence—to its peaks, to that from which springs existence and from which it develops, to the principles in Plato's sense. The possibility of this movement shows itself to us in that, in the sphere of logos, in the sphere of meaningful speech, the decadent manner of existence announces itself in its decadence as in-coherence, whereas care for the soul takes place in logos, makes the person whole. It makes him close to the principles in that sense; he who withstands the examination of the care of the soul is concentrated within himself. He is not in contradiction; he is unified in his entire perceiving of life; and just in this way he gets to the proximity of the unifying measure, which measures all actualities here around us. This unifying measure is just the idea. For this reason, the movement the soul performs in the concern, care of the soul for itself, is that distinctive experience, the ontological experience if you like, that there exists something like the idea.

In his own way, Aristotle is the continuator of Plato's work. In a certain sense, he also cares for the soul. In him there is also care for the soul both personal and in connection with the community, also in him, as we will hear right away, care for the good personal life goes hand in hand with care about the good life of the community. In all this there is formal agreement. But Plato's care of the soul in reality cares first of all so that he who performs this movement we have spoken about, gets from what is multiple, dissolute, and contingent to what is eternal, perpetual, and unified, that he gets from the measured to the measure. As a result, he is concerned with evaluating, with comprehending what is good, as if it were obvious that by understanding what is good, I already carry out that further important deed, that is to say, *acting* in the sense of the good. Aristotle is the first philosopher in the entire tradition who thematizes *action,* the acting of man. This moment, the analysis of human action in Aristotle, which he does not see something as exterior, but rather as determinant, which takes place within the soul, which takes place in the sense of the good life and has an influence on life in its whole—this acting actually concretely—is the experience leading Aristotle to bend into the *horizontal* that vertical movement that the Platonic philosopher carried out. It is *the same* life experience, again it is care of the soul, that leads him to what is ordinarily considered as a mere theoretical difference between Plato and Aristotle. Aristotle's philosophical metamorphosis, the change of the entire concept of philosophy, even in the relation to what is in the end, in the relation to the state, the community, even in the relation of the soul to itself, is rooted in this transformed experience, in the movement of life, which is the business upon which philosophy reflects, which is the most characteristic business of philosophy. If you like, it is the existential experience upon which philosophy leans. But how can something like action lead to a change in the direction of this reflected movement?

Notice that the metaphor of movement, that philosophy reflects a certain movement, is not used by chance. Perhaps it is something more than a metaphor. That Plato speaks about the soul rising and falling is not accidental. This entire experience cannot be expressed at all except with the help of such a metaphor, and so it is in Aristotle. When you look at modern philosophers concerned with the question of that most fundamentally reflected experience of the philosopher, then you will again and again see that one speaks in metaphors of movement. These metaphors are not mere metaphors, but perhaps they are the most fundamental experience of movement man is capable of at all.

Why then bend it into the horizontal? Before we take Aristotle's text, we will τύπῳ (in a summary fashion, succinctly), as Aristotle says, generally, express it in a few words. The activity of philosophy, as Plato sees it, regards what is eternal and necessary. However, human activity regards what does not have to be. That is the essential difference. But this is still not enough. Cognizance can, after all, regard contingent things; it will naturally be cognizance in the not-proper sense of the word. It will not be ἐπιστήμη (knowledge), rather it will be δόξα (opinion), that is, it will not be knowing at all really. But we can then say: things exist in the world, which as known things are known in their common, and that means necessary and eternal, essence. Φύσις, nature, is changeable; φύσις is in constant movement. The elements are in movement, the stars are in movement, plants, animals are in movement, histories are in movement, but φύσις itself is recognizable because its *principles*, its foundations, what forms its essential skeleton, is *constant* and *eternal*. But even the principles of human action are not eternal! Human action is characterized by action being led by principles, which *are not* eternal, which are *contingent*, which are in change in the same individual and also in various individuals and eventually also in the carried-over sense of the word, let us say in the adult person and also in the person-child. What then is the principle of action? The principle of action is that which action seeks. What realizes action is what concerns it. We can say: in a certain sense we are all concerned with the same. In a certain sense, we are all concerned with—and this is just what Plato said—the good. Man is characterizable in that he goes after the good. Right away there is the paradox, that going after the good, we appear to others and often to ourselves as those who strive for evil. What is good for one is evil for the other. How is this possible? The Platonic idea that the good, what one seeks, the ultimate goal of human activity as such, in the final instance, the idea, *the idea of the good*, should mean that all goals must participate in the Good, must be in some way unequivocally good, something like, as all white things express the one and the same by participating in Whiteness. Is this so in human action? Is this so in what human action seeks?

It is easy to say that we all want to be happy and that human action ultimately pursues this. Saying we want to be happy means that our acting is somehow concerned with our manner of being, that our acting is also a comprehending of its own kind, comprehending oneself, comprehending what in the end we are and want, except that in acting we realize something that *is not yet*. Just these principles—what we seek and in what sense we realize what is not yet—in themselves do not have anything eternal, unified, or, at least, there is not univocity of the sort that is in nature, which is always unchangeable, always the same. A stone always falls in the same way; fire always heads upward in the same way; the stars always revolve in the same way. But human action, the realization of what man seeks, does not have this character. In other words: man is *free*. For the first time in history, through these distinctions, Aristotle reaches for the freedom of man.

Of course, even in its own way, in Plato there is the problem of freedom. Why? Because in the care of the soul, in the Socratic ἐξέτασις (close scrutiny), in self-examination, and through self-examination in the creating of one's own unified essence, man freely makes himself what he is. He either makes himself solid, in himself unified, a solidly existent philosopher, the soul fixed and disciplined, or he makes himself unruleable, undisciplined, unbounded, a decadent existence, which is the victim of the negative infinite, license. Why negative infinite? Because desires, pleasures, and pains can grow forever, they always demand more and more, and by this they distance man from possible form, they deprive him of a solid shape. Man thus has the possibility either to give himself this solid life-form, or to let himself fall into unformedness, into unshapedness. In this sense, Plato also sees the problem of freedom: this is the work of each soul within itself, this is its own proper work. Aristotle sees this entire problem in another way as well. Aristotle does not see it merely in the problem of the measure with which man measures himself, but rather in the problem of actual action, where man has to decide and to realize decision. If man realizes what does not yet exist through his action, and if he realizes it according to principles that themselves are not solid just because they regard something that does not yet exist, how then will it be with the problem of the good? How will it be with the Platonic idea? During human action, which as you see, is also comprehension of its own kind, is comprehending of something, of its own kind, that is of it itself, then the Platonic idea will not help us at all. For the Platonic idea regards what is always, *what already is*, but we need principles for the realization of something that *is not yet*, that does not exist. I think this is the main and essential reason why Aristotle gives up the Platonic ideas, why Aristotle does not go in Plato's direction.

To give a concrete shape to Aristotelian reflecting, to what I have so roughly told you here, let us read an appropriate section regarding the good life and what is good for man from the first book of the *Nicomachean Ethics.* Right away you will see that the problem, as it is posed from the start, is the same one as in Plato's *Republic* at the beginning of Book II, where Adeimantus and Glaucon express their dissatisfaction with how Socrates disposed of Thrasymachus in the first book. They want Socrates to praise justice, that is, the good life, as Socrates sees it, not from the point of view of mere consequences, results following in justice's wake, but rather from the point of view of how justice acts within us, what justice is within our soul. And we know that when Plato's brothers present these objections to him, Socrates says: you do not want a small thing from me, you want me to show you how justice acts within the soul, but how show, how demonstrate the acting of the good within the soul when the soul belongs among the invisible things? The next thought is: between the community and the soul is something like a similarity in the geometric sense. So, if I demonstrate something like the activity of justice in the community, through this I will allow for a more subtle reflection about the activity of justice within the soul. So that you see, the care of the soul is what is common between Plato's *Republic* and the situation into which Aristotle leads us here.

Each practical ability and each scientific conversation and just like that every kind of acting and every kind of choice heads after some kind of good. That is the general opinion. For that reason it is right to determine good as the goal, after which everything goes. With that however, there is a difference between a goal and a goal: once the goal is pure activity, a second time it is what overcomes this activity and is its result, that is a deed. Where those goals overcoming activity itself are, there of course, the result is more valuable than mere activity. However, because there are many forms of acting, practical ability and knowing, from this follows also a whole row of goals. The goal of medicine is health, the goal of shipbuilding is a ship, the goal of the strategist's art is victory, the goal of economics is wealth, or let us say prosperity. (1094a1–10)

And then here he speaks about the mutual supraordination and subordination of these arts and crafts, but we will leave that out.

You see, it begins with the multiplicity of the goals of human acting, and *the goal* is the proper definition of the good. Why is there talk here about various forms of activity and various forms of achieving? Somewhere activity itself has within it something like a goal, somewhere it creates a deed, some of these activities are subordinate to another, that is, a certain activity does not occur for itself, but rather for something further; it is merely a means. A means is always subordinate to a goal, through this is created a whole hierarchy of goals and so on. Of course, this does not say there should exist only one hierarchy, one entire orienting, rather it merely shows there is something like subordination and supraordination. But then the problem arises: Is there one subordination, one supraordination and subordination of all else, or do more of these kinds of hierarchies exist?

Does knowing good, that is the goal, have some kind of weight for how we lead life, or not? Is there an actual importance to knowing about the subordination and supraordination of these goals? If this is so, then we must to try to capture at least in outline the problem of the highest good and examine, first of all, in which domains of seeing or practical skills, τέχναι [practical skills], we can find something like this. Immediately, here, the answer is raised: this problem, the question about the ultimate goal, belongs to the realm of craft, which is in its own and sovereign sense, the highest, and as this kind of ability must be considered the art of statecraft, the art of ruling the community. (1094a22–28)

This book is called *The Ethics* and it expressly places itself into the province of examining the state, the community.

Statecraft is what determines which forms of practical abilities undoubtedly must be represented in a certain community, further what kinds of skill, and to what extent, the ordinary citizen must perform. We see that even the most popular skills are subordinate to statecraft. For example, the art of war, the art of economics and butchery. Because statecraft then uses all other practical skills as its means, and also legislatively determines what we are to do and what we are to leave, then the goal of statecraft encompasses within itself the goal of all other skills and its goal is then for all people the highest good. But if the goal for the individual and the community is the same, then it is also more clearly shown in the community. (1094a28)

You see this is the same thing that Plato shows in the first books of the *Republic*, this great similarity, great parallel between the state and the soul.

And where we achieve this goal, even there, where we ensure this goal. Certainly it is not meager when the individual achieves something like this just for himself. But it is more beautiful and more noble when entire communities and entire nations come to something like this. (1094b7–10)

So that is the introduction, situated where Plato located the concrete form of his care of the soul. In this beginning, right away we see that Aristotle's examination of acting, his examination of human life in regard to the good, is in line with the Platonic care of the soul. Now I will leave out the rest of the first chapter and cross over to the second. There, Aristotle starts again and says: "If then, every cognizing and every decision aims after a certain good" (1095a14–15). Why does he say every cognizing and every decision? Because our cognizing is also an activity and our cognizance also has a certain goal. What do we follow by cognizance? Certainly it is not only something contingent, undoubtedly we cognize methodically and purposefully, cognizance is an achievement, for it, it is not enough to open one's eyes, it is directed activity. And such directed activity has to naturally have its goal, which obviously is connected with our own character, with our ψυχή (soul), with what we are in our own essence.

So just as cognizance, so also decision heads after some goal, wants to satisfy something within us, is rooted in a certain kind of self-comprehension, in the comprehension of what, in the proper sense of the word, we want, and what we want, in a certain sense, who we really are. "If then every kind of cognizing and every kind of decision goes after a certain good, let us begin again from the beginning of the question: What is the goal of the art of statecraft and what is the highest state possible to achieve through acting?" (1095a14–17). Here, all of a sudden only acting is spoken about, cognizance is subsumed under activity. Also cognizance is activity of its own kind. "In its naming all people are in agreement. They say, that the highest good, the highest state, is called happiness. So say simple people and so also say refined spirits, with which a good life and good acting should somehow be identified with being happy" (1095a17).

What Aristotle alludes to is the very peculiarity of the Greek language, for which εὐπράττειν, that is, "to do good" also means "to be happy." When someone is doing well, then Greek says εὐπράττειν (to do well) about this, and the wish of all good is εὐπράττειν (that is, literally "to do good," even though naturally, it is not perceived thus).

So, all say it the same way, but what is the fundamental nature of happiness? The Greek word is εὐδαιμονία (happiness). Many translate it as "bliss," but this is utterly false, because with the word bliss we imagine the blissful state of that other world or of beings singularly perfect. But what Aristotle is concerned with here, is the exact opposite; he is concerned with emphasizing that everyone, even the most vulgar, use the same expression. It is terribly important that just in these principal things there is disagreement among people. Disagreement between the manifold and the one, and the same in various periods of life and perhaps even otherwise, but this is just that important thing we spoke about at the beginning, that the principles of human acting are changeable and differing. This neutral word "happiness," about which Kant, as you know, said that it is not any kind of concept; it is something terribly indeterminate, it cannot be defined in any way, perhaps cannot be enclosed within conceptual limits at all. And you see, Aristotle takes his point of departure directly from this:

What is the essence of happiness—we are uncertain about this, and most people's answer sounds different than the answer of the thinker. Most imagine something that can be seen, for example, prosperity, honor, and, above all, pleasure. Everyone something different. Sometimes he changes his opinion; when he gets sick, then for him happiness is health, when he is poor, then wealth; and the ignorant, they terribly admire [and through this is understood that they consider as happy] those who perform something noble. (1095a20)

And when it sounds very good and looks as if it were beyond their comprehension, they consider such people to be happy.

But some thought that besides these many tangible good things there exists also some independently existing good that is also the cause that all other good things are good. If we should examine all the nuances of this theory, we should not get anywhere. Let us limit ourselves only to those most widespread and those of a certain scientific character. (1095a26)

Here follows an excursus showing that this regards Plato. Surprisingly, Aristotle still does not start with a critique of Plato's teaching, he only cites both the many, οἱ πολλοί, examples of unhappiness in life, and changes in human fate, and then introduces the teachings of philosophers to show the variety of principles according to which people direct their decisions, that is to say, realize what still is not, to show the variety and instability and such direct confusion in these most fundamental things.

Of course, it is not that this changeability and multiplicity of principles should go on forever, for after all there are only certain fundamental forms; certain laws of order exist even in the domain of what man considers as happiness. There are fundamental types of opinions about happiness. When Aristotle analyzes these fundamental types, he relies on Plato again, he relies on that place in the *Republic* we have already spoken about: the dividing of the fundamental functions within the state, in the community, that in Plato is parallel to our fundamental functions of life, to the function of our ψυχή (soul). You know that in Plato there are the rulers-philosophers, then there are guardians, and then craftsmen. To these three functions correspond three various ways of life and to these three, differing ways of life correspond three different fundamental functions and powers of the soul. The philosophers and lawgivers are those who use above all the capacity of comprehending, which rules in Plato's ideal community, and to this corresponds life in the pure domain of the spirit. The function of the guardians corresponds to life in the domain of honor and political risk. The life of the craftsmen moves about in the domain of appetite. These are also three fundamental functions of the individual soul, the individual person.

Aristotle builds upon this Platonic three-part division, but in a peculiar manner. He demonstrates three various fundamental types of ways of conducting life and he reverses their order. Most people—especially unrefined natures—desire pleasure and so, says Aristotle, they opt for a life of pleasure-seeking. There are three fundamental forms of life the aforementioned life of pleasure; life in the service of the community; and life dedicated to philosophy. Similarly, the characteristic of each of these ways of life: Οἱ πολλοί, the multitude, the mass, reveals its unfree way of perceiving, because they seek a beast's way of life. Although we can say it is really in life where man does not distinguish himself from the animal or, in a certain sense, even falls beneath the animal, because man can never be purely only animal in animal innocence—"to a certain degree, these unrefined characters have an argument for themselves" (1095b21). Even people of high standings often have similar passions as Sardanapolus. So much for the life of pleasure that Aristotle calls βίος ἀπολαυστικός (to live a life of pleasures, to live a pleasurable life).

Then comes the life of those desiring honor, the life of those who dedicate themselves to the service of the community. Aristotle says that even this goal is, to a certain degree, external, because honor is more in those who accord it than in those to whom it is accorded. "Nonetheless it is clear that these people, who have a sense for honor, look to obtain it from those, who actually have moral insight and who themselves are in turn honored on the basis of their excellence" (1095b27–30).

I will not read this entire passage because in it there is much requiring deeper explanation. For our purpose, the following characteristic is sufficient: the life of honor and risk, which keeps itself at a distance from the life of pleasure, is no longer a life giving itself up immediately to life's temptations; it is not a passive life, it is an active life.

This moment is important: Aristotle is concerned—we do not yet see into this—that life, which considers itself happy, would be happy, in the sense that it does not place us at the mercy of something external. Of course, the pleasure-seeking life takes place through external things, to a large degree in what can be had very easily, that everyone has within reach. In this case, the argument against the pleasure-seeking life is not that, just as the life of honor, it should go after something difficult to obtain, which demands great effort, but rather that in this domain man is on par with cattle.

And then comes the third form of life, which Aristotle characterizes ③ rather briefly. He says that "the third form of life is dedicated to philosophy" and that this "will be expanded upon later" (1096a4–5).

Happiness—I said—is something in which takes places comprehension of oneself. When it gives itself a goal, our life returns, in a certain sense, to itself; its activity is oriented to itself; it comprehends itself. We must take the characteristics of these three forms of life from this point of view. The question is: In the case of this βίος ἀπολαυστικός, the pleasure-seeking life, is the core of the proper self itself actually somehow crippled? Is the core handicapped in the case of the life in honor and risk? This is what this is about. With this thought we must approach interpretation of Aristotle's words, which you all know from textbooks where you have heard them one hundred times, and which nevertheless encompass something more than what usually stands in these textbooks. For, each of these ways of ✗✗✗✗ life concerns the realization of what is still not yet realized. In each of these orientations, our life gives itself a certain shape from fundamental possibilities among which we can choose. That is precisely characteristic for a free being. This positive principle of freedom is hidden in the contingency of principles of human action. And what belongs to human freedom? That man can find or not find himself in the choice of his life and in the realization of what follows from that choice, that he can, so to say, seize or miss himself, that he can seize his—what? In this we see the problematicity of freedom, the problematicity of the being which is free, the problematicity which no one and nothing can take away from man. Plato takes this problematicity away from man. For Plato, what is good is already here. The Good is written into the very last essence of things; the good is its first principle, from which entire existence follows and upon which entire existence hangs. To focus upon it and to direct one's attention to it means to constantly measure oneself with an absolute measure. The absolute measure says what is good. But human life is more problematic, and Aristotle sees it as such, as far more problematic. That is the new fundamental experience with which Aristotle goes to the problem of the care of the soul. What the soul is, is learned only now.

Deciding itself is a certain comprehension. Deciding itself is of its kind—hard to say cognizing, because we know something that already is. Here we have something more like comprehending, understanding, which at the same time forms what still is not, and which forms—or misses—the human ψυχή (soul) as human, as its own. . . . In this is the thought: Why, for example, is the life of honor insufficient. Despite its high value, the life of honor is a life in tension, in risk, in activity that distances itself from all easy immediacy, which the life of pleasure-seeking singularly claims for itself. In the Greek community, to live the life of the guardians, to live the life of political people, meant this: to risk one's life at every moment, so in domestic conflicts, as in conflicts the community could not avoid. You have to imagine that the community, constituted like the Greek state, could not exist otherwise than by a constant maximal exertion of all the strengths of all the citizens. With enormous world-historical tasks, such a small community—the Greek communities were all small—could not exist otherwise than with this kind of exertion. Aristotle says that political life, political science, political teaching, is the highest, because it decides what people in the whole, everyone together, is permitted and is not permitted, how their life goals are to be harmonized and so on. Only political teaching, only the teaching of the statesman can decide this. And yet, for Aristotle, life for the community is not the highest. In that, we see something remained there from Plato, something essential. It is no longer the philosopher-ruler; here, there is a statesman. But this statesman naturally also has to take into account the philosophical life, he cannot ignore it: this remains from Plato.

But why is life for the community, the life of the brave and the risky, not the highest? Here it is said: "Τιμη (honor) is more in those who honor than in those who are honored" (1095b24). What is said by this? There is something much more essential here, by this risk and exertion we are much closer to the center of the human ψυχή, than in immediacy, in passivity, in lowering into that βίος ἀπολαυστικός. There one lives in the fascination of the immediate states of life, and hidden by it is all else demanding the highest human exertion and effort, which man can only create from what does not yet exist: brave deeds, great political things, and so on. But this is still not the most fundamental of which man, from all beings around him, is capable.

According to Aristotle the most fundamental, the most central center is still only the philosophical life. Of course, he does not pretend like Plato that philosophers should rule over others. For Aristotle, the life of the reasonable political, politically living person is almost on the same level as the life of the philosopher. But the life of the philosopher is divine—it is not entirely only human. Why? Because what the philosopher occupies himself with is divine.

If we said that the political life is the highest, then we should make man the highest in the world, the highest that is, but this is not possible. There are other, far more perfect, higher things in the world: the gods. And what do the gods do? Just that, which belongs to the gods. And the gods are eternal, blissful—here the word blissfulness belongs—the gods are εὐδαίμονες (happy), in the strong sense of the word. Why? Because in their activity, in their life, there is nothing disturbing, nothing that should indicate some kind of peak and some valley, some possibility to find oneself or miss oneself. Just what distinguishes man from other finite living earthly beings, freedom, is still only something deficient with regard to the life of the gods. The contingency encompassed within it, the possibility to miss oneself is a defect: god cannot miss himself. In himself, god is still divine. This means that god lacks freedom. That is why the gods are always the same. The example of the gods is always before our eyes. The divine life shows us the stars: these are the gods, or let us say, the bodies of the gods. For in themselves, the gods can do only what is divine, permanent, eternal. Of course, what does "to do" mean here? Their life has to be activity, but one that is always at its goal. It is not an activity like the human one, which is not at its goal just because man lives in the direction of the principles that he himself still has to find, in which he himself still has to constitute himself. This, the gods do not have to do. Such a hint of divine life exists within the human. On the basis of this intimation we also comprehend what divine life means. It is the life of constant spiritual discernment.

Aristotle tries to express succinctly this thought about the divine several times. It is most densely expressed in one of the chapters of Book XII of the *Metaphysics*. There, it is said, that to the divine belongs life ζωή (1072b26), and we already know what that word means: for ways of human life, Aristotle uses the term βίος that is, "style of life," whereas ζωή (living, being alive) is not a mere style, but rather that substance upon which this style lies, what is formed by this style in man. Thus god has ζωή, not βίος. And to god belongs ζωή, which has such a character, takes such a course, διαγωγή (a passing of life, a way or course of life), as is granted to us only in an insignificant measure. "And if divine life consists in what is granted us only seldom" that is, to touch the most essential, the fundamental in the universe, if its life consists in constant contact with the principal content of the universe, with what is the being of all existents in the universe, "then it is amazing. And if this divine way is still something higher, than it is even more amazing. And it is just like this" [ἔχει δὲ ὧδε] (1072b26). It is raised further above what we are capable of for a short period. We are capable of it insofar as we philosophize, when we, so to speak, open ourselves to the entire plan of the universe for which our mind is capable. In our way, we are capable of such contact. We understand the entirety of all things, not in details and not in all things individually, but somehow we understand; we know that we are on earth, we know that the world is in a certain way an ordered whole—all this we know and on this basis we can penetrate further, we can penetrate into greater depths. This is something belonging internally and essentially to our being. Because something like this belongs internally and essentially to us—and only to us, only to this kind of animal, no other animal has this, no other is in the world, no other has comprehension for the whole—for that very reason, where we understand ourselves in our core, this cannot be lacking. For this reason human happiness in its essential sense cannot lack this aspect of openness of man to his own most proper core.

Only then, after laying out the three ways of life, Aristotle turns to the critique of Plato. First of all, he mentioned the philosophical life—I explicated this here more than was necessary—and in this he touches upon what he has in common with Plato. For what man does when he philosophizes and touches the divine regards that which is and which is eternal. That is Plato's discovery. But we must take the specifically human in this equivocal sense: on the one hand, the core of man is somewhere in proximity to that which is eternal; on the other hand, man is something of his own, which in its own way holds itself besides the divine in a kind of amazing autonomy, because man is the "finite creator," man is the finite being which does that, which does not yet exist, and which does this according to principles that are not eternal, which it itself still has to constitute. In this lies the strength and originality of life; in it, and not before, man forms himself and discovers himself. This self-creating and self-discovering is one and the same thing. There does exist something like a moral truth, but it does not extend to something that already is. In the moral world we are "creators," but this does not mean that we create truth according to our fancy, absolutely not. Moral truth is the humanly most specific, most difficult. It is also the deepest and most difficult problem of that book.

Before that there was still a short remark about the goods, which are not goods in themselves, as is pleasure, honor, and fame, and the philosophically divine contemplation. Such an instrumental value is, for example, wealth; these are only values instrumental for other things.

Now, Aristotle focuses upon the critique of Plato.

It will be instructive to look at the highest good, as long as it is considered as the universal essence, universal substance, and to analyze what is intended by this universal essence. Of course, it is an awkward task, because our friends introduced the ideas. And still, undoubtedly it is better, yes even necessary, if truth is to be saved, to get rid of even what has grown close to our heart, particularly since we are philosophers. Both are dear to us, and still it is ὅσιον, a sacred duty, προτιμᾶν τήν ἀλήθειαν, to give precedence to the truth. (1096a10–15)

Such pathos-filled words are seldom found in Aristotle's works. We should not imagine that the tension between Plato and Aristotle was something hostile, petty; yet, we should also not imagine that it was small, or consider it trivial. As you see, it concerns a completely different concept of philosophical style, although it remained in the closest conversation with its predecessor. You see how Aristotle still works with the material with which Plato furnishes him. And you see that this fundamental parting of ways is genuinely indispensable. We should not imagine that Aristotle's secession from the Academy was connected merely with this philosophical separation. Aristotle was certainly in the Academy for a long time even after the separation. Even those people who did not share the Platonic teaching about the ideas were fully rightful members in the Academy. But naturally, when he conceived all of philosophy, as it were, along these new lines, it became important for Aristotle also to be autonomous as a researcher.

So now to those critiques: "The founders of this teaching do not erect any common ideas of things that speak about *before* and *after*. For this reason they also did not maintain that there should exist ideas of numbers" (1096a17). (That is to say, which should encompass, have numbers under them. There does not exist the idea of number. This is different from the idea that ideas are numbers. According to Plato, the ten most fundamental ideas are numbers, but this does not mean there should exist an idea of a number. I will explain all this later.) "And yet the good is encompassed in the categories of being, in quality and relation, but what it is in itself, that is being, is by nature anterior to the relation. Relation is something like a tangential offshoot or *accidens* of existence. As a result, there cannot exist the common idea of something like the good" (1096a19).

So that seems terribly enigmatic, we have to say that we do not understand even a word. So what does the poet want to say?

This argument is fundamental, essential, and to a certain degree connected to what we have already spoken about. I will repeat it one more time: the founders of the teaching about the ideas never dared to say there exist ideas where there is something like the first, second, third, and so on, where there is "before" and "after." We should not take this "before" and "after" here in its temporal sense. Aristotle's example for this is the substance, the property, the relation, the place. Where there exists something like "the earlier" and "the later," there the Platonists did not introduce ideas. For this reason, Aristotle says, there is no idea of number. Why? In the case of numbers, we are left only with certain hypotheses. The fact is something like the idea of numbers did not exist for the Platonists. We can then limit ourselves here to mathematical numbers. How is it for mathematical numbers? What do they have in common? What is universal in them? That, from which mathematical numbers are created, that is, units. Mathematical numbers are nothing other than units synthesized in certain ways. This means that here the common is not above numbers, but rather is within them. The unit is prior to the dyad and so on. The dyad is nothing other than two units and so on. The Platonists, of course, ask about the origin of something such as the dyad, triad, and so on, but a number in common to all numbers does not exist.

Aristotle then applies this and says that there exists something in common and that is not idea. Why do we need the idea when we explain the common in a different way than as idea? We have something like this, although in a much deeper form, in the following example. There we see this critique in a far more energetic form. The Platonic ideas are genera. The Platonic idea is that which is in common first to individual cases, then what is common to these individual types, and then what is common to the types of types, and so on, all the way to the highest family, genus. But, Aristotle says we have ten categories when we take those highest genera. (The highest genera are categories; they are substance, quality, quantity, and so on.) Categories are still content determinants. We know that if we are going to abstract from singular determinants such as, let us say, a living, or not-living substance, and so on, these are already high abstractions. If we are to abstract further, in the end, we get to the substance, and substance is something different from let us say quality or relation. Quality still remains a certain content determinant, common to visual, acoustical qualities, and so on.

But does the problem of generality end with this? Let us say, that the idea could be something like *genus* and *genus maximum*, that is to say, the most common. But does the problem of generality end with this? It does not end, because we can still say about all these genera: *it is*. All this is: substance is, quality is, and so on. However, if both substance and quality and so forth equally *is*, then there is something more general than genus. This determining "*is*" is more general than genus. But then genus does not resolve the problem of generality. And if it is insufficient for the problem of the generality—then what do we need it for?

Why is it said here that when we have substance, quality, relation, we have something similar to one, two, three, something before and something after? What is the analogy here, what is in common here?

So that there would be quality, there first must be substance. Substance is first, then comes quality. Only then can I quantify, whether this quantity extends directly to substance, or if it relates to quality. In each case, quantity can relate as much to substance as to quality, that is, it presupposes both substance and quality prior to it. Thus, we have something here like the order of numbers, something first, second, and so on. Aristotle further says: "The Good is also something like this, because we say good about things, about qualities, about relations; the good affirms itself in the same manners of generality as existence" (1096a23). The good belongs among universals, which stand above categories, which step beyond *summa genera* in their universality. They step beyond—the scholastics call this *transcendere*; thus, such predicates were called *transcendentals*. You see how the problem of transcendentals coincides with the very character of the discussion between Plato and Aristotle. Some of the most substantial arguments against Platonism, against the existence of ideas, are drawn from this domain of the transcendental.

Of course, it will be interesting to observe how this is related to the bold hypothesis we posited at the beginning of today's lesson, that the good life is the distinctive ground of this philosophy. Is the criticism of Platonism the result of the criticism of the ideas, or does the criticism of the ideas result from Aristotle seeing the practical domain, the domain of human life, *other* than Plato?

In that man is a substance that creates something that is not here, contingent things, and that it creates them freely and in this forms and comes to know itself—in this is the foundation of that bending into the horizontal. The movement of human existence upon which Aristotle reflects is different; it is a movement, which, although it goes from the low ground of the βίος ἀπολαυστικός (to live a life of pleasures) upward all the way to the βίος θεωρητικός (contemplative life), bends itself again back to earth and to realization, to acting, and that means, to the very individual and contingent things. In the multifariousness of the good, that the good, the goal man seeks, is not a necessary, eternal idea already here, but rather something dispersed in various conceptions of what is happiness—in that is the universality that can never be encompassed in the idea. From this new, different movement of life follows a different philosophy, different ontology, and naturally even a different politics.

Why are we concerning ourselves with these things in such detail? From the very beginning our task was to reflect upon what, in our opinion, created history. History is the history of Europe; there does not exist any other. Everything else is *analysis* of an entirely different level, not the continuation of a certain unitary task, capable of universalization. We ask: What is at the source of European history? What is at the birth of Europe? And our hypothesis is the thought in which is resumed all European reflexive effort hitherto, that is, the thought of the care of the soul.

The thought of the care of the soul has its first formulation in the Platonic teaching. Then comes the other. For this reason it interests us. When you consider how Aristotle's thinking is that against which the European tradition leaned and from which it nourished itself for one thousand years, then you see what this signifies.

Of course, you can say that these are all just ideologists' illusions. In reality, certain lawfully ordered economic processes took place here; philosophers only squawk along in feeble accompaniment.

Nonetheless, I think it cannot be denied that history is concerned with human actions. And human actions take the form of motivated activity, whether motivated economically or otherwise. This is a matter of comprehensible acting. Perhaps it is not fully comprehensible, or it runs away from comprehending itself, avoids it, and so on, but these are all ways of comprehension. What is at stake and what was at stake for philosophers from the very beginning—and this we are trying to comprehend—is to analyze the very ground upon which human acting unfolds as the acting of a being that understands itself—even if in deficient modes.

From Aristotle's critique of the ideas we analyzed only one point. Aristotle has a whole series of points here, but because the hour has advanced, and I think you have also had enough, it will be better to leave the rest for next time. I should still like to hear from you if you have any questions—I likely did not always express myself clearly enough.

Q: Is it really possible to say that the influence of Aristotle's thought lasted in Europe for one thousand years? If you count the influence of Aristotle during the Middle Ages, then from the moment he was allowed at the Sorbonne to the moment when the Renaissance overcame him—this is around two hundred to two hundred and fifty years, maximum. Of course, by this is obviously only meant mere Aristotelianism as an already ideologized teaching, a mandatory university teaching, and you did not mean it like that. Of course, all that is prior in the Middle Ages more likely draws from the well of Platonism by way of Augustine.

P: Yes, it is true that the direct influence, reception of Aristotle does not occur until the thirteenth century, but by Platonism is understood neo-Platonism in the early Middle Ages—and neo-Platonism draws from the well of Aristotle as much as from Plato. This is one thing.

The second thing: Aristotle is the foundation of all late antiquity; all Hellenistic philosophy is unthinkable without Aristotle. The philosophy of those Poseidonius and Panaitius and so forth, that means Cicero and that whole tradition—there Aristotle constantly comes and goes. Not only what Aristotle expressly thinks, but rather what this atmosphere adds here.

But it does not end with this. Aristotle lives in his opponents, he lives in those who overcome him. The battle against Aristotle and his overcoming is still again the life of Aristotle after death. And we cannot forget that when his life ends in natural science, the life of his political teaching, his poetics, and all those profound things and, for example, also ethics still endures—of course, in a form undergoing transformations of Christian ethos and Christian internalizing. But we must realize what we owe to Aristotle in our thought about the free being and practical reason today. We must realize that Aristotle is not merely φύσις (nature), in the sense of the fundamental conception of natural science, that it is not only Aristotle's physics determining his influence. Certainly, the thought φύσις—this we will still further show—determines even Aristotle's ethical thought. This is one of the immensely delicate points in the entire conception of human freedom, as it is developed in Aristotle.

But Aristotle is not just solving; Aristotle is first of all problematics. The scholastic conception of Aristotle is to the actual, historical Aristotle as we grope for him beneath historical sediments, as are the ancient elements of a gothic cathedral to the elements of the ancient peristile. The scholastical conception is a conceptual systematic where the problematic was extinguished. But this was not possible otherwise. The Middle Ages, which were not oriented historically in the sense that modern philology and philologically oriented history understand historicism, always comprehended interpretation systematically, and that means that from Aristotle's work, from that entirety of documents, which are only the sediment of Aristotle's thought—these are not any kind of completed writings, these are not completed works, they are in part the bases for lectures, which were always continually added to, and where those works are complete, there they are again ordered according to certain external viewpoints as required by the school. From this, in its interpretations the Middle Ages necessarily made systematic wholes, and of course, whoever wants to understand, whoever wants to force a certain systematic into something, he will always never pull it off. Many medieval commentaries are admirable. Sometimes it is a patient and honest work with conceptions, of which only some are Aristotelian, and very often it concerns conceptions reinterpreted or shifted in some other way. So that, as I say, the historical Aristotle, as we see him today, as contemporary philological teaching sees him, is entirely elsewhere.

Of course, philological teaching itself will be insufficient to open Aristotle for us in the philosophical sense of the word, because during all methods of analyzing the material, keys are unconsciously used that in turn must be criticized in all sorts of ways. For example, the interpretation of Aristotle as evolving—that Aristotle develops from a Platonist into an empirical scholar who can already serve as the archetype for Alexandrian scholarship—this key, which served as the guiding thread for Jaeger's book about Aristotle, which at one time was considered as the crystallization of modern understanding of Aristotle—this interpretation is itself led by a positivistic schema about the evolution of human thought, that it goes from speculation through abstraction to positive facts. This excellent philologist, who deserves immense credit for [our understanding] of the modern Aristotle, succumbed to such a common evolutionary schema. We have to keep a critical distance to all this.

Q: Since you already mentioned it, is Λ *Metaphysics* still considered the young work of Aristotle, or has this already been abandoned?

P: As far as I know, the Λ was never considered the work of Aristotle's youth. Lambda has markers from the later period, which is concerned with astronomical things. Further, it encompasses the part that is the extract from the *Physics*, and thus presupposes the *Physics* (in its core, *Physics* is likely from the Academy) and then there is the theology there. Λ is originally a completely independent work, and in the form that we have it today, it is certainly a *late* work of Aristotle.

Q: Last time you said that Aristotle's philosophy is de facto the return to the cave and that in this it is really not Platonic. To stick to the matter, I would like to keep to the opposite, to the Platonic elements in that return to the cave.

P: Now I do not understand this. Today I tried to explain in what consists Aristotle's return to the cave; that everything is in the cave. That cave is much richer than Plato imagined. It is exaggerated to say that everything is in the cave, because Aristotle also knows the divine, and this is in part outside the cave. Of course, the problem of the divine is in Aristotle so terribly complicated. But the return to the cave—that is not a Platonic move. Plato returns the philosopher to the cave because, while he would like to dedicate himself to this divine life, on his conscious he has the good life of all, the good life of the community. Aristotle does not return to the cave for this reason—this is not a forced return. Now, no one forces the philosopher to go there out of care for the community; rather, he has to return to the cave as the philosopher, not as a citizen.

Q: Even though the philosophical life concerns divine things?

P: Yes, even though and because.

Q: If the reason for this return is not in Plato also objectively onto-logical—so that we dedicate ourselves to the highest—we have to hold all these four things in mind, and also to maintain that graduatedness, and only through this can we . . .

P: Yes, but during this entire graduatedness this philosophical move-ment is directed vertically from low to high. But not in Aristotle.

Q: For that reason I suppose even in Aristotle the presupposition is movement upward.

P: Yes, undoubtedly, except that Aristotle judges this upward move-ment, as is carried out by the Platonic care of the soul, to be only a part of the concrete movement about which the philosopher has to reflect, of that concrete movement of existence, which is free and forms something con-tingent and for the moment still absent. In this "that it still is not" time is audible; not so for ancient peoples, for them in this only the negative is audible, that it is not eternal.

Q: To this point my question is: you said that Plato takes freedom away from man just by that vertical orientation to that which is already here, which is eternal. Is that orientation itself also indispensable, or does man in Plato have the possibility to not chose, to just not turn himself to the eternal?

P: Of course.

Q: So he is not unfree?

P: No. That is why I said that Plato already also has the problem of freedom. Man is always within two fundamental possibilities; he will go either upward or downward.

Either he will concentrate and become one—as is said in the *Gorgias*, where Socrates says that he should rather undergo everything else rather than contradict himself, so that he should not be one, or being one, contra-dict himself. In this there is that movement: to concentrate, to become an actual unity. But when I become an actual unity, then this means I can defend each of my λόγος, my opinion, my fundamental view any time—and it will remain standing. This λόγος remains standing, it does not flee, it does not change in discussion about what is the goal for me, what is the good for me, and so on. That testing, ἐξέτασις (close scrutiny), takes place over this, and it shows whether the soul has taken shape, or whether it is dissolute.

Dissolution is that second movement; there man gives himself to the mercy of "the negative infinite." Every kind of pleasure, delight, and so on always wants more and more and there is no boundary anywhere. This is shown in the *Gorgias* in the character of Callicles. He is the man who tells Socrates: you poor thing, if you are going to go about things as you are going about things, then any kind of bum is going to be able to spit all over you and in the end drag you before a court and you are going to end up . . . and so on. And Socrates shows him in this discussion that he is actually not a real politician, but that he is the tyrannical person, undisciplined, not ruling over himself, dissolute, that his life looks like the net of the Danaides; there is just that negative infinity, that constant taking on, and always fleeing.

This is the antithesis of two kinds of lives, the problem of that βίος (life), which already is in Plato. Each of these βίοι (lives) is the work of freedom, in each of them I do that which I in the end am. In the case of concentration, there I actually am something solid, there *I am* more than in the second case.

Q: And should it not be possible eventually to say from the Platonic point of view that this good we create in the Aristotelian conception springs just from estrangement, ignorance of that true good?

P: Aristotle also never maintains that the good, as is pleasure or exclusive ambition or even service to the community, should be on the same level as that which is highest. He only maintains that it is not yet discovered, that it was not discovered before man was here; that man finds and feels out this good with the movement of his life. *That* is his position. I still would like to say: we cannot appeal to any idea. The idea is to be the measure *we* need in order to know what is good. The entire Platonic problematic stems from our needing some kind of life measure, which should be analogical to the measures of geometry, which are the condition for measuring things that are not geometrical here. Geometrical forms with constantly increasing accuracy to determine the shapes of things that are here around us. Geometrical forms are precise, like every kind of measure, but that which is measured by the measure is not precise. We need something analogical for our own acting.

And Aristotle says: that is true, we need something analogical, but the idea does not give us this; this is our own most specific task.

Q: Of course in a framework that is already really Platonic. It is the task that was in Plato, that is to say, from the point of view of just those possibilities of deciding for either effort or dissolution. De facto, it is determined by the idea.

P: It is dependent upon this movement underlying the idea, but not upon the idea. Aristotle does not reject this movement, but he interprets this Platonic movement only as a part of that movement.

Q: From the viewpoint of man's position, it is just natural that he has to interpret it in such a way. Of course, from the viewpoint of that framework within which man always is, from the viewpoint of those possibilities, this Platonic demarcation is also determinant for Aristotle, even if Aristotle so polemicizes and actually finds much that is new, and even if Aristotle himself should evidently not objectively recognize this.

P: We can say that historically it is as you say, but philosophically this question is *sub lite* (under accusation).

Q: But I think that it is not only historical.

P: In any case, Aristotle sees something Plato did not see. In Aristotle, the whole problematic of human action is seen for the first time ever in the history of thought! The most important thing about this is: Aristotle sees that human action is not blind causality. This is the modern way of conceiving it. Aristotle knows that when we act, this acting is a question of truth. But what is truth in Aristotle, just as in Plato and in those ancients? In them, truth is not—as it is for us—a pronouncement. A pronouncement is just one kind of what the Greeks call ἀληθεύειν (to speak the truth). Aristotle says about ἀπόφανσις (a declaration, a statement) that it is λόγος, that is, meaningful speech, ἐν ᾧ ἀληθεύειν καὶ ψεύδεσθαι, that is to say, speech, to which belongs the quality of truth-seeing or schematizing (or as we should say it). This truth-seeing ἀληθεύειν (to speak truth, to be right)—what does this mean? When I say for example: "X is present, he is here among us," then when I say this before all of you, then it will obviously only take on meaning when it answers, let us say, a certain doubt. Or someone telephones me here and I tell him, "Mr. X is among us." Mr. Y who calls, does not see this, he only knows, that Mr. X left for here; I add something else to what he knows, I unveil this situation here. This means ἀληθεύειν, that means the uncovering of something that is covered from a certain point of view, or emphasizing in a certain context what is uncovered.

But what is uncovered by something like moral insight? It is comprehending oneself, it is the unveiling of that which I am. And this is my most proper work, no one can take this from me and lighten it. And this uncovering is not taken care of by merely looking at myself, but rather by my acting in such a way that I create something which is not yet here. This is Aristotle's thought—therefore, action is a way of truth!

Q: Of course, in the context of the Platonic possibilities of those two.

P: That is not of interest.

Q: Not for Aristotle.

P: Or at all, for us, because this is not in Plato.

Q: In Plato there is also the possibility that everyone can do what they consider appropriate with their own life.

P: Yes, but only in the framework of that which already is.

Q: Yes, but everyone has to really discover this again in themselves.

P: Yes, but in reality it is not human action, only the measuring of human action; that is the fundamental difference.

Q: I do not want to deny that; it is just that Aristotle's point of view is different, it is the point of view of action.

P: Yes, if you like, it is still consistent with Plato; we are always trying to show how the care of the soul is immensely important and common to them. Aristotle does not talk about it; this term does not exist in him, it is in Plato. But it is built upon, and what is the most essential at stake, that is the clarifying of that internal truth, cannot be understood factically without it. I do not know if there should be a more appropriate term for it.

Of course, in Aristotle there are also many other things, and above all, it is complicated by Aristotle's teaching about φύσις (nature). This is also a matter requiring closer explanation. What I am now laying out for you are not very orthodox matters. I am trying to show, or see it from that viewpoint, how the existential movement is in both these two cases the source of philosophizing—of a different style and that these are not philosopher-theorists in the modern sense, that is to say, scholars, who have accumulated a mass of knowledge and ideas, rather that they are people, who, so to speak, are held by the throat by the fundamental question πῶς βιοτεύον (How to live? What should be our conduct in life?). This direct life necessity to somehow reconcile oneself to the fundamental distress of life—that we do not know how to act and that we have to, and that no one will take this responsibility from us and that we cannot take it away from ourselves, to lighten it. These people philosophize from this position. For that reason, resemblance between our professorial "academic" philosophizing and the philosophizing of those of the Academy are superficial.

Q: If I understand you well, then the difference on this point between Plato and Aristotle lies in that in Plato this movement is already in the framework or on the basis of the given, of that which already is; whereas in Aristotle it is the creative discovering of something that really is not yet, through which we somehow find ourselves. Where then, in Aristotle, is the measure of common right?

P: You see, that is just the problem.

Q: And is it not somehow solved in Plato?

P: Well it is, but badly—says Aristotle; if we are going to solve it in this way, then we are going to pull ourselves up by our own bootstraps. *That* is the critique of Platonism.

Plato's teaching rests upon the experience of the movement of the soul, that the soul is τὸ αὐτὸ ἑαυτὸ κινοῦν (the mover of itself), that which brings itself into movement by itself. And the movement it performs is ἐξέτασις (close scrutiny), examining oneself, and in that it either becomes something that has form and a higher being, or if it cannot reconcile itself with this, then it declines. That is the experience that grows out of reflection upon Socrates. And from that arose the teaching about the ideas; that is their foundation. And for this reason, to Aristotle's critique also belongs the thought, that the movement, as the Platonic Socrates portrays it, is incomplete, insufficient, that it does not lead all the way to actual acting, which is characteristic for man and which distinguishes him from all other beings.

Q: But could it be said that it is not worked out in all its aspects, but that nonetheless it facilitates Aristotle's work?

P: Yes, that could be said. Then we always return to the same thing. That Aristotle is not possible without Plato is clear. In every regard. There is not one of Aristotle's conceptions that is not somehow derived from Plato. Here, for example, the whole posing of the question: on one side, the eternal; on the other side, what is subject to change—changing with or without eternal principles. Within this is placed man. These distinctions are Platonic, but suddenly here Aristotle sees something Plato did not see.

Q: I see that Aristotle actually elaborated in tremendous depth the possibilities of each individual human decision.

P: But no! Not only elaborated, this is not the elaborating of something Plato developed. This is immediate vision. It is like, when a chess partner guesses what the other is intending and immediately derives from this the exact opposite.

Q: I know that Aristotle says it is entirely otherwise, but . . .

P: No, this is hopefully a fact, this does not exist in Plato.

Q: It does not exist, Plato was oriented to . . .

P: But what Aristotle does is not elaboration, rather it is an entirely different concept, because all of a sudden, Plato, the teaching about the ideas, is on the scrap heap. I am not saying that it cannot be used for anything, but I mean this: from the point of view of the problem Aristotle sees, it is not good for anything. All of a sudden, this is an entirely different philosophical terrain before us.

Q: I should like to ask about something you said earlier in passing, and although it was not the first time you said it, it is still not entirely clear. How do we convince ourselves there really is no other history than the history of Europe?

P: It goes without saying that there are entirely different civilizations and that they understandably have their past and their recorded past. China, for example, has ancient annals. But each of these civilizations is a world in and for itself; to understand Chinese civilization, you have to penetrate into its distinctive principles, but once you get into them, you remain enclosed inside them. What is characteristic of Europe as Europe is that its distinctive principle is: generality.

I think Husserl might be right when he says that in all other civilizations there is myth, that means a tradition with which a human being has to identify with his life, essence, tradition, custom; that they have this peculiar stamp that you must immerse yourself in them, step into the continuity of their tradition. Not so in Europe. Everyone understands European civilization, because the principle of European civilization is— roughly spoken—two times two is four. From that arises a singular continuity and the possibility of generalization. For that reason, European civilization became universal, while those others, should they be generalized would signify the swallowing up of all others by a particular tradition, but not by the principle of insight into the nature of things. As its foundation, European civilization has insight into the nature of things, while all others have tradition as their foundation. Of course, all this must be taken with a grain of salt. In our civilization this counts only a fortiori, or *a parte portiori*, not absolutely. The Christian tradition or the tradition of classical literature, and so on—these are all traditions. Nonetheless, the most characteristic thing about European civilization is this *insight*, from it follows the possibility of generalization, the possibility of consequences as science, technology, and so on. That also means a particular, peculiar way of penetrating beyond the original sphere and thus, as well the continuity of certain problems. That all human problems are defined from the perspective of *insight*, that they can then logically develop, all this underlies the distinctive form of European history.

I do not say there are not problems in this, but this is the reason why from the European perspective it is possible to assess other civilizations, but it is not possible to assess Europe from the point of view of all these other civilizations.

Q: Yes, I think I understand that. But I still just think that history is not so simply identical with that openness or generality.

P: History, no.

Q: Yet, it does not seem to me that these other worlds somehow stand still, that they constantly draw only from myth and constantly repeat themselves.

P: Yes, you are absolutely right, I did not intend it like that. I did not want to say that man is not a historical being and that every civilization is not in its own manner historical and that it does not evolve in its own way. That is certain. But history as a specific continuum, phrased in the way we have become used to: antiquity, Middle Ages, and so forth, this is specifically European and we project it onto those other civilizations. We use this European standard for them and we cannot do otherwise. For this reason, and in this sense, we say that history is the history of Europe.

However, usually people do not realize—and eventually even those other nations do not realize—that Europe "forced upon them" its own schema and its own conception of history. They relatively passively accepted it, but it is a certain spiritual violence. In these civilizations, there does not exist originally, spontaneously, something as history in the sense I have now spoken about.

I am trying to debate with you here this crazy, roundabout thesis of mine that European history, which culminated in these universals—for European civilization arose through the means of modern technology and science into a world civilization, a planetary one—cannot be understood except from this point of reference that we call the care of the soul. For this reason I maintain that history in this understanding—not history as the substantial history of man in every civilization and every tradition formed by some peoples somewhere—this is the history of Europe.

Q: Do you then think that history, as the comprehending of the dynamic of being is precisely that which is European, that it is as if we were forcing our comprehension of this dynamic even upon all the rest?

P: "Dynamic of being"—that is too demanding. I should say that we force upon all the other nations the historical consequence of that, that our tradition is the tradition of insight, and not the tradition of pure traditionalism or something comprehended only by the fact that we live with and assimilate it. I think this is a marked difference. European civilization is abstract. For this reason, European history could generalize itself in such a way.

This preeminence is very delicate. Man is constantly problematic. Take, for example, the books of Lévi-Strauss; there you will find an underlying skepticism about this modern hyperrationality, expressed in the following terms: What if man had not gone any further than the latter stone age? Was not that the acme of humanity, a norm when man was able to remain in a state placing him in an elevated and spiritual place in nature, where he was not threatened by these horrible ends to which civilization is now heading? All sorts of nostalgia, which in European life always surface with periodical urgency—which we call Renaissance or romanticism—they are all related to the sentiment that something is not quite right with this peculiar abstract civilization, that somewhere, it has a deep "wound." And you know, today this problem is not any less urgent than it has always been, indeed, it is more urgent now, it takes on a form that can then be articulated precisely in this abstract form. And you see, this urgency presses down upon us even in our concrete daily life.

Cultural Memory in the Present

J. Hillis Miller / Manuel Asensi, *Black Holes / J. Hillis Miller; or, Boustrophedonic Reading*

Miryam Sas, *Fault Lines: Cultural Memory and Japanese Surrealism*

Peter Schwenger, *Fantasm and Fiction: On Textual Envisioning*

Didier Maleuvre, *Museum Memories: History, Technology, Art*

Jacques Derrida, *Monolingualism of the Other; or, The Prosthesis of Origin*

Andrew Baruch Wachtel, *Making a Nation, Breaking a Nation: Literature and Cultural Politics in Yugoslavia*

Niklas Luhmann, *Love as Passion: The Codification of Intimacy*

Nieke Bal, ed., *The Practice of Cultural Analysis: Exposing Interdisciplinary Interpretation*

Jacques Derrida and Gianni Vattimo, eds., *Religion*